Praise for Constance Malloy and
Tornado Dreams

"At her core, Constance is a teacher. One you run to for safety, and one who guides you with her thoughtful wisdom. In *Tornado Dreams,* she shows us how we can learn from her experiences so that we may find the very best within ourselves."

- Gina Gral

". . . A courageous account of weathering family storms. A must read!"

- Nancy Bauer-King, author of *Madness to Ministry:*
A Woman's Journey From Psych Unit to Pulpit

"'*Tornado Dreams,*' Constance Malloy writes in the Prologue, 'is for all the women and men, young and old, who need to know getting help can and does work.' This honest and beautifully written book does much more than reveal the author's years of trauma and confusion as a member of a largely dysfunctional family. Through her description of the subsequent help she received from professional therapy, Malloy tells a remarkable and intriguing story of how she learned that the proper help can heal many wounds. The themes explored in *Tornado Dreams* are universal, and we can learn much about ourselves from this author's inspiring journey of resilience. Love and forgiveness can endure, even in the aftermath of years of trauma."

- Myles Hopper, author of *My Father's Shadow*

Tornado Dreams

A Memoir

Constance Malloy

Ten|16
PRESS

www.ten16press.com - Waukesha, WI

For information, please contact:

Ten❘16
PRESS

www.ten16press.com
Waukesha, WI

Cover design by Laura Leach
Author photo by Nancy Rubly

The author has made every effort to ensure that the information within this book was accurate at the time of publication. The author does not assume and hereby disclaims any liability to any party for any loss, damage, or disruption caused by errors or omissions, whether such errors or omissions result from accident, negligence, or any other cause.

This book is dedicated
to my daughter,
so that she may understand,
and
to my husband
because he already does.

Table of Contents

Prologue

We never know when or how life will displace us. What trauma will befall us. In the autumn of 1987, I would have traded my identity (in fact, something akin to the witness protection program sounded quite inviting) in order to escape the reality forced upon me. Fully aware of the ripple I was in my father's pond, I wished with gut-wrenching desperation these events had never happened to me. Now, however, in the autumn of 2017, I am grateful, optimistic, and filled with compassion. I am not the person I am today without the circumstances of my young life.

It didn't begin in the fall of 1987, though. My life began on June 11, 1966, in southeastern Iowa. And, what I once viewed as the defining moment of my life has instead proven to be the culmination of bad things getting worse. In fact, by the time the fall of 1987 arrived, I had been functioning in a constant state of terror. In the parlance of our times, and as stated by my therapist, I suffered from PTSD. By the age of twenty-one, I had endured a series of traumatic events.

This is not to say I experienced a childhood devoid of familial good times. Indeed, a more than reasonable amount of fun and laughter infused my childhood. But sadly, the good times, which offered me a semblance of normalcy, were generally overwhelmed by the tension and trauma my father brought to our lives.

I think one of the more interesting aspects of being part of a family is considering what comes before us. What is the complexion of our family before we are born? For instance, I now know my father worked out of town, staying overnight on several occasions, and sometimes for days in a row, until I was one year old. So, my earliest childhood involved my family acclimating to having my father home all week, which now I can say doesn't seem to have gone well.

Tornado Dreams, I want to make clear, is my story. It is the story of my relationship with my parents (primarily my father), and how that relationship shaped me and impacted my adult relationships. It is not my siblings' story. My siblings are seven, nine, and eleven years older, and therefore, while they experienced the same major events I did, many of the events I describe in Part I of *Tornado Dreams* happened after my oldest brother and sister were adults living on their own. Most importantly, they have been affected by these events differently than I have. They have different personalities, and in the case of Sam, who was born with a double recessive gene disease, his ability to ascertain the consequences of these events on his life is limited.

It is my first priority to show only compassion to my entire family throughout this book. I am so saddened by the events of our lives, and to know that anyone should be made to endure what we have (and I know many people have endured much worse) is heartbreaking. Growing up in the absence of love (in our case from our father) can, and often does, leave one incapable of identifying, pursuing, trusting, and accepting supportive, healthy people into one's life. And, the manner in which my siblings have reconciled the events of our lives is their story to tell, not mine.

That being said, I have changed the name of my hometown as well as the names of every person (with the exception of some of my childhood neighbors) in my life except for my husband. I have also excluded any narrative regarding Sam's disease in order to focus solely on my relationship with my parents. And while, yes, Sam's disease and Sam's development impacted many things about my life as well, in truth, it is another story for another day.

I started teaching dance at the age of 19 in a local studio in Ames, Iowa while attending Iowa State University. I taught for the following twenty-three years. In that twenty-three years I taught hundreds of students, and from 1991 until 2011, for many students, I was their first and only dance instructor. This allowed me to come to know many students and their families well.

One evening in 2002, after opening my own studio, I was teaching my advanced class. I had taught all of these students, who attended various high schools in the greater Milwaukee area, for at least six years. Three of the students who attended the same school were discussing a controversial dress code policy that was making local headlines. I listened as the girls defended their right to dress however they wanted: camisoles that were low cut, pants that exposed their bottoms when they bent over, and stiletto pumps. Britney Spears was the style maven of the day.

Eventually, I engaged in a discussion with them. I asked questions. I wanted them to think about why adults might not be so keen on them dressing this way, and to think about the distractions this way of dressing might create in the classroom. I wanted them to think about the message their attire and behavior might send to others, particularly boys. I then told them why, from a dancer's point of view, it was bad for their bodies to walk around on cement all day in excessively high heels.

Then, one of the girls challenged me. She was quick to state that I was jealous because I obviously had not been as comfortable with my body when I was her age as she was with hers. Knowing there is no greater teacher than experience, I asked the girls to stand up and face the mirror. Then, I asked them to perform a simple jazz walk (knowing this would mimic their behavior at school) towards the mirror while looking themselves in the eyes.

None of them could do this.

This demonstration stood as proof to them, without me saying anything, that they were not comfortable with their bodies in the way they believed they were. When asked to look at themselves, and watch the attitude they affected while walking down the halls of school and while interacting with boys, they immediately became teenage girls: giggling, blushing, and nervously fidgeting. When made to watch themselves, and be accountable for their behavior, they were incapable of doing so with any seriousness or maturity.

"Miss Connie, you're one of the smartest people I know," one of my students, a senior, said.

I understood she wasn't referring to my book smarts, and so I decided to sit my students down. I explained to them that I had many things happen to me in my life, and while I had always been more thoughtful than a lot of people I knew, it was my parents' divorce, and my resulting therapy that had really challenged me and informed so much of who I had become.

Fast forward two years later.

That senior mentioned above, now a sophomore in college, walked into my studio one night late in the spring as I was ending my last class. Emily came in all smiles. It was wonderful to see her again, and she looked particularly well.

After some hugs and surface-level exchanges, she told me a story.

Paraphrased, her story went like this: she had attended a college in Ohio where bulimia was a trend on the campus, she began partaking in this trend until she reached a place where she felt she was out of control and losing herself.

"So, you know what Miss Connie?" she said.

"What?" I returned, full of curiosity for where her story was going.

"I said to myself that if Miss Connie can get help, so can I," and she smiled at me.

She continued explaining that she had received counseling on campus, and in the end had decided to transfer to a school back in Wisconsin. "Now," she told me, "my life is so much better."

I stood staring at this young person's face. She glowed. She had fought a battle and won. She had so dramatically altered the course of her life. And, I couldn't help but wonder if had I not divulged my story that night with her class, would she have had the courage to seek help?

"I've always respected you," she said.

"And I believed, if you didn't feel embarrassed about getting help, then, well, I didn't need to either."

I gave Emily the biggest hug. I was proud of her, and I was overwhelmed by this unexpected shared gift between the two of us.

My life changed her life, and by virtue of sharing her story, her life changed mine.

And, I believe, it changed her life dramatically because she, like me, got help so young. (Of course, seeking help at any age is hugely beneficial and life-changing.) She was, at an early age, able to stop the trail of misguided, dysfunctional, self-sabotaging decision making, and to begin making thoughtful, functional, self-aware decisions that led her to a healthier life. In other words, the mess behind her wasn't so big due to years of accrued ill-fated decisions that she couldn't overcome it.

It doesn't take much imagination to roll Emily's story forward: she gets no help, continues her bulimia, begins lying to cover it up, and inevitably finds herself in dysfunctional relationships wondering why things never work out for her. As time marches forward, her disease and its manifestations become too overwhelming to conquer. But Emily stopped that future from becoming her reality. She got help, and did so before the work necessary to change had become too vast a chasm to cross.

Tornado Dreams is for all the women and men, young and old, who need to know getting help can and does work. Please believe you are worth a better life; you deserve a better life; and, a better life is waiting for you, if you are willing to go get it. And, whatever your demons may be, let my story stand as a testimony that facing them is not nearly as daunting as the prospect of living with them unconsciously every day of your life, granting them ownership of your fate.

Open your heart to love, and you might find that it comes to you from the most unsuspecting place.

Constance Malloy
August 2018

PART I

DESTRUCTION

"Fear is the main source of superstition, and one of the main sources of cruelty."

– Bertrand Russell

"Fearlessness requires attention and receptivity – it takes focus to stand in the still eye of a tornado and not be swept away by it."

– Susan Piver

"I never throw the first punch."

– My father

"There is no living thing that is not afraid when it faces
danger. The true courage is in facing danger when
you are afraid."

– L. Frank Baum

I've never actually been in a tornado.

However, one early summer day when I was eight the sky
turned green and menacing. I remember making several trips
to the basement in order to secure the safety of my twenty or
so stuffed animals. As I passed the landing window on my final
run, the sun, once again surrounded by blue sky, caught my
attention. One look out the window let me know the threat of
a tornado had passed. I sighed, turned, and went into reverse,
returning everyone safely to my bed.

I first experienced a tornado riding along with Dorothy, as
a cow and the Wicked Witch flew past her window.

I loved Dorothy.

I loved *The Wizard of Oz*.

Fran, my older sister, took advantage of this fact in a good-
natured way. When I was six, my sister spent many Saturday
nights at our paternal grandmother's. Oddly, every Saturday
night she did so, Dorothy called me. We would chat and
chat. I asked about the well-being of Toto. I wanted to know
everything about her week. Had she seen any Munchkins? Was
the Wicked Witch still chasing her? How were the Lion, the
Scarecrow, and the Tin Man doing?

After hanging up, I rushed to my mother, who eagerly listened to my retelling of our conversation. Her smile, wide and knowing, radiated love and amusement.

Before falling asleep, I reviewed my conversation with Dorothy thoroughly in an attempt to retain every detail. Fran, who was seventeen at the time, made my day when she came home on Sundays and asked, "Did Dorothy call last night?"

It did take me some time to put two and two together. Why was it that Dorothy only called when Fran was gone? I have to admit I played along for a while, even after I figured it out. It was simply too fun.

But my real attraction to *The Wizard of Oz* was the transport of Dorothy into an entirely different world where someone sinister chased her. I had someone sinister chasing me in my world. Dorothy had three companions who recognized and acknowledged this sinister person, and they wanted to escape as much as she did. I had three older siblings, but they did not acknowledge the sinister entity in our house, at least not verbally to me. So, as far as I knew, we weren't *all* trying to escape. And, Dorothy had someone benign and beautiful who protected her and gave her a way out. Just a simple three clicks of the heels, and the recognition that there was no place like home. My mother was benign and beautiful, but she stopped short of protecting me, didn't offer me a way out, and naively thought there was no place like our home.

Bow Echo I

Associated with squall lines or convective thunderstorms, bow echoes
are capable of producing straight-line winds as strong as some tornadoes.
Creating a linear but bent-outward radar echo in the shape of an archer's
bow, these storms have a life span of three to six hours and are moved by
the wind inside them, which tends to push outward
until eventually dying out.

I asked for a doctor's kit for my fifth birthday. I didn't get it. It was the only thing I really wanted.

"This Sunday after church," my father says, two weeks after my birthday, "I'll take you over to Southside Drug, and I'll get you a doctor's kit."

I don't know what to think about this. I'm not accustomed to going anywhere by myself with my father, so the idea of doing so is strange. And, I can't remember a time when he has offered to get me something I want for what appears to be no reason at all except showing me kindness. It makes me feel both awkward and excited.

On Saturday night my mom puts pin curls in my hair. Cute hair is a must for my outing. This, my mom assures me, will be accomplished by sleeping with a clean pair of underwear on my head.

"Best way to keep the bobby pins in place," my mother insists.

I don't like it, but it's worth it. After putting on my favorite dress, the underwear comes off, my mother takes out all the pins, and my usually straight hair falls into a mess of bouncy curls. I love it.

Unable to sit still in church, I unconsciously tap my knee on Sam's leg during the service.

"Stay off me, Connie Sue," he whispers, and pushes my leg away.

"And stop fidgeting," Joe, who is on my other side, chimes in.

Older brothers. Who needs them?

I squeeze my legs together in an attempt to control my excitement.

Afterwards, at Sunday school, a friend gives me a big blue bubble gum ball. I can't resist. I pop it in my mouth.

I'm all happiness when I find my family in the crowd at the church's coffee hour following Sunday school.

I smile up at my father knowing we are soon to be on our way to purchase my doctor's kit.

He takes one look at me and scowls, "What's all over your mouth?"

There is nothing discreet in his tone. Everyone in earshot turns and looks at me. They all smile warmly and chuckle in a way I have come to understand people do when they think something is cute.

"What is that, Connie Sue?" my mother asks.

Face to face, I smell her tea-breath as she studies my mouth.

"I don't know."

"You're all blue," she says.

"Oh, Lisa gave me a piece of blue gum." I position the gum

in the middle of my tongue, open my mouth, and proudly display it.

"Well, that's it. We're not getting your doctor's kit now," my father says.

I close my mouth. I almost swallow my gum. I'm awash in disappointment and confusion.

"Why not?" my mother asks, just as I think the question. She presses against my shoulder and stands.

"I'm not taking her looking like that."

"Why not? It's just a little food coloring. It'll probably be faded by the time you drop us off at home."

"I don't care. I'm not taking her out in public looking like that."

We all leave church. I notice people looking at my father in disbelief, and looking at me with compassion.

As soon as the sun hits my face, I start crying.

My day is ruined.

Midway through the week, he says, "How about we try again this Sunday, Connie Sue?"

Still hurt, I tell myself that I don't want the doctor's kit anymore, but after a moment or two, I let my desire override my hurt; and, I think, this time I won't chew gum or eat anything. This time I won't spoil it.

"Okay," I say.

"That's my girl," he says, and rubs my back. My back curves and arches away from his hand. There is something not right in his touch.

Second Sunday, like the first Sunday: pin curls, underwear on head, favorite dress.

Second Sunday, not like the first Sunday: no gum.

After church we leave my family at home. I crawl into the front seat, and off we go to Southside Drug.

I know right where the toys are. In fact, I know Southside Drug well. My mother does their bookkeeping. I often find myself browsing while she is going over the accounts with the owner.

I start in the toys' direction, but my dad grabs my shoulder and says, "Let's go sit at the counter first."

"No. That's okay. I just want to get the doctor's kit."

He moves me towards the counter. "But you can have a milkshake," he says. Somehow he makes me think of the slipperiness of the oil I touched on our driveway last week.

"But it's almost lunch. Mom wouldn't let me have one right now."

"Well," reproach in his tone, "she's not here, and I'm telling you, you can have a milkshake."

He starts walking me towards the counter. It's clear I'm getting a milkshake, but I have no idea why. He forces me down onto a stool, pats my shoulder, and says, "That's my girl."

A waitress walks towards us, "Hi Bob," she says.

By her familiar tone, it is obvious she knows him. Odd, because I've never met her, and, to my knowledge, my dad is seldom at Southside Drug.

"Oh, you must be Connie Sue," she says. Her smile is not right: too friendly.

My father has talked to this person about me.

Agitated, I half slide off my stool and bump up against his arm. I immediately right myself, afraid he might ask me what's wrong.

She puts her hands on the counter and leans down. I can see her rabbit ears (a funny expression for breasts Joe used to say when he was little) pushed together behind her laced bodice, "What would you like dear? I'll make you anything you want."

Dear? Yuck! Why is she calling me dear?'

"A chocolate shake, please."

"Anything for you Bob?"

"No thanks, Nancy," he says with a goofy grin on his face. He reminds me of Joe when Linda, his not-necessarily-a-girlfriend-friend, comes over.

After the machine has sufficiently mixed my shake, she pours a milky mass of chocolate from a large cold silver cup into a smaller glass one. It looks so good. I can't help but smile in anticipation.

"What a perfect shake," my dad says as she places it in front of me.

Nancy takes a straw from her apron pocket and hands it to me. Her smile is still, well . . . too gooey.

I'm super excit . . ." I begin to say, but my dad stops me mid-sentence.

"Just drink your shake, Connie Sue. I'm going to talk to Nancy."

Nancy tilts her head in my direction. Her smile has changed. Something in it, and in her eyes, lets me know she has tolerated me long enough, and now I'm just an annoyance.

My father, with that same stupid grin on his face, halfway unzips his pale yellow jacket. He pulls out the brown tri-fold portfolio of my picture proofs.

Surprised, I gulp too fast and cough.

What's he doing with those?

"Look, Nancy," he says. "We had Anderson's take these pictures of Connie Sue." He opens the tri-fold displaying the six pictures of me in the dress I am currently wearing.

I drink my shake, one long continuous draw, to keep from saying out loud, "Who is she? I don't like her. I don't want her seeing my pictures."

Brain freeze hits me quick and hard. I'm distracted until it passes.

"She starts kindergarten this year. So we thought it was a good time to have some professional photos taken."

He presses down its edges so she can have a good look, and asks, "Which one do you like best?"

Why is he showing her these? Why is he asking for her opinion? What are we doing here? Who is she to him?

This is all wrong.

And then it hits me, right between the eyes. This never had anything to do with getting my doctor's kit. He didn't want to bring me with my blue-stained mouth because he's showing me off.

Nauseous, I push my shake away.

I watch my father act towards Nancy in a way I never see him act towards my mother. He tries to make her laugh, which she does at every stupid thing he says. He compliments her on everything, including her choice of favorite picture. He looks ridiculous. When Joe does this, we say he's flirting. What is it, I wonder, when a dad is doing it?

"Can we get my doctor's kit now," I ask. I need to put an end to this.

"You can go get it. I'm going to stay here and talk to Nancy."

"Sure, honey. It's okay. We're right here. We'll be able to see you," she says. She gives me that gooey, gross smile again.

First dear, and now honey. Yuck! And why is she talking to me like she's my mom? God, please make her shut up.

I go in search of my doctor's kit.

Finally, on my third insistence, my father says good-bye to Nancy, pays for my doctor's kit, and we leave.

Lunch is long over by the time we get home.

"What took you so long?" my mother asks.

"Oh, Connie Sue wanted a shake, so I let her have one." It's clear by the slant of his brow he expects me to agree.

"That's nice. What flavor did you get?" she asks.

"Chocolate," I say, distracted by a corner of my portfolio exposed above his jacket zipper. My mom doesn't know he took it. I'm certain of this fact.

He realizes I've seen it. He narrows his already small beady eyes at me.

"Keep your mouth shut, Connie Sue," his unspoken directive comes through loud and clear. He pretends to have an itch, and tucks the corner away.

After lunch, I take a few temperatures, listen to a few heartbeats, and never play with the doctor's kit again.

EF-0

According to the Enhanced Fujita Scale, which was implemented in 2007
as an update to the original Fujita Scale introduced by Tetsuya Theodore
Fujita in 1971, an EF-0 tornado is considered to be light in its destructive
power with winds ranging from 65 to 85 miles per hour. A tornado of
this scale has the potential to take the surface off some roofs, break tree
branches, and push over trees with shallow root systems.

I am six years old.

My mother and I are on the landing of our stairs.

Ten steps stretch out below us. I have on my favorite pink
nightgown, and I'm holding my most prized possession: a
signed Harlem Globetrotters' beach ball.

About two months ago, the Harlem Globetrotters came to
Forked River, Iowa (a big deal in and of itself), and my family
went to see them. Packed into this ball are three things of
significance. One, my father was relaxed that day, seemed not
to be bothered by any of us, and didn't appear preoccupied or
act as if he wanted to be somewhere else. Two, it was one of
the best family outings ever. And, three, I was allowed to get
this ball. I don't often get things when it isn't Christmas or my
birthday. These three things combined made the whole event
rare and memorable.

Back to the landing.

My mom and I are turning to start up the last bit of stairs

when my father, shirtless and in jeans, calls from behind me, "Hey, Connie Sue. Toss me your ball."

I turn around to see him rubbing his hairy chest. He smiles at me.

"No, Daddy. I'd rather not."

"Ah, c'mon, Babe."

"No, Daddy. I'm afraid it will pop."

The paint on our walls is textured with sand, and I have watched too many balloons fall victim to my brothers' teasing and the walls' grainy surface.

"Nothing's going to happen to it. C'mon. Toss me the ball," agitation registers in his voice.

"Bob, she needs to get to bed," my mom says from behind me.

"C'mon. Just toss me the ball. I'll throw it right back to you."

My brothers and sister are sitting on the sofa watching TV. I can see them through the banisters. Does anyone else think this is a bad idea? My siblings seem to disappear into the TV. I can tell by their blank expressions they know this isn't going to end well.

"Okay," I relent. "But please give it right back."

"I will," he smiles again.

For the first time in my life, I *know* my father is lying to me, and I *know* he is messing with me. I now understand what I've seen in him when he has been this way with one of my siblings or my mother.

But I am six, and so I toss him the ball.

He throws it back short of my reach. It bounces down the stairs. I timidly laugh. He throws it back again. I stretch to catch it, but miss. I relax some. I want to believe he's just having fun with me. However, the tense, stifled energy in the room exposes that we all know differently.

Then, he banks it off the wall.

My heart races.

"Daddy, please don't do that again. You'll pop the ball."

"I'm not going to pop the ball," he says. Anger is in his voice. Why is he angry?

He does it again.

Now I can hear my heart pounding fast and hard: a frantic drumbeat inside my head. I'm scared. I know I'm about to broach dangerous territory. I'm going to stand up to him.

"Daddy, please stop doing that to my ball. It-will-pop!" I say this with confidence. All the while my heart races faster. I feel little beads of sweat on my neck under my thick dark hair. I sense the tension mounting in my siblings.

"Hey, hey, we're the Monkees," cuts through the tension for a brief moment. My siblings look like statues.

"Bob, just give her the ball. You're scaring her," my mother tries. I love her for it.

"I'm not going to pop her goddamn ball," he yells, and launches it, hard, into the wall.

I'm out of my head. "STOP!" I scream.

The world falls silent around me. No one moves.

"Get her up to her room right now," he says, and throws my ball behind him.

I run up the stairs, terror nipping at my heels.

I run into my room, and dive into my bed.

"Bob, what are you going to do?" my mom asks. She tries to demand, but she just doesn't have it in her.

"I'm going to spank her! That's what I'm going to do. None of my goddamn kids talk to me that way!"

He grabs me, and begins to beat me. I make no mistake. I've been spanked before, and it was honestly earned. Now, I am being beaten.

He stops.

We lock eyes, and in one strange moment I am no longer six.

I grow larger than the room, and I feel ancient. I look for a moment at my mother. She stands stone-cold locked in fear. If I touch her, she will crumble.

I don't blame her.

I don't resent her.

I suddenly know them both in a way no six-year-old should be able to.

I look back at my father, straight and steadfast in his eyes. Telepathically, I say, "Now I know who you are. You can't fool me anymore. You set me up, just so you could do this. You've been exposed, and now I know you."

He hears me.

He hears every word.

And he understands. I can tell by the widening of his small, half-moon eyes. He blinks, flinches really, because he is momentarily shaken.

In an equally strange moment as before, I am six again.

I feel abject fear.

Now, for the correction: he puts me in my place.

He leans over me, points his thick, stubby index finger in my face, and says, "You'll be sorry if you ever talk to me like that again!"

He beats me until my bladder gives way, and urine drenches my pretty pink nightgown, my bed, and me.

With cold dismissiveness, he gets up. Without looking at my mother, he says, "Clean her up," as he leaves the room.

I have my first tornado dream shortly after this incident.

I return home from playing at a friend's, and sit down on our front steps. Sitting high atop our hill, I can see for quite a distance to the southwest, especially since the city cut down the huge elm tree in front of our house. I still mourn the loss of the tire swing my dad hung from a large branch just days before we were given notice they were going to fell the tree in order to widen the street. They felled the tree, took away my tire swing, but never widened the street.

Our neighborhood, which is normally quiet anyway, seems preternaturally so. As a mass of dark clouds moves from the river valley towards our house, a strange green hue fills the air. My maternal grandfather's words disrupt the quiet, "If the clouds start to roll, you've got yourself a tornado."

I squint, doubting my eyes. As the clouds indeed begin to roll, a long tail extending from their base reaches towards the ground. Its path is unmistakable: it's on a collision course with our house.

Fear paralyzes me. Through sheer will, I force myself to stand. The wind sweeps my hair over my eyes. Frantic, I brush my hair back to see the tornado gaining ground. Finding my legs, I fly up the stairs onto the porch.

I run into the house screaming, "A tornado's coming!"

I can find no one.

I look up when I hear my mother ask, "What's the matter?"

My mother, dressed in red shorts and a white halter, rounds the landing and comes downstairs. I can't help but notice how perfectly her shorts and lipstick match. "I look absolutely pale without lipstick," I hear her refrain in my head. It's the only makeup she wears. She does resemble Rita Hayworth. It's a comparison I've often heard.

The screen door blows open.

"We have to get to the basement. There's a tornado coming. Where's everybody else?"

"We're the only ones home, Connie Sue. Calm down. There's no tornado coming."

"But there is. Just look out the door," I gesture, my hand frantic and trembling, for her to look.

"I'm not looking out the door, Connie Sue. I know a tornado is not coming."

I'm stunned by both her calm and her refusal.

"But it is. Just look, and you'll know," I run to the door.

Hysteria overtakes me: the tornado, a predator on track for our house, is now only blocks away. A large branch rips down the side of our neighbor's tree. It lands with a deafening crack in the street. The house shudders in response.

"Mom," I yell above the roar of the wind, "we have to get to the basement, now!"

I turn. She's nowhere to be found. Where did she go?

The dream dissipates, ending before it resolves.

Gustnado I

Often confused with an actual tornado, gustnadoes are short-lived
vortexes generally formed by powerful downdrafts, but do not
connect to the base of a thunderstorm like tornadoes do.
They last only seconds or maybe minutes.

It's a few months after the Harlem Globetrotters beach ball
incident. I'm sitting on the landing staring out the window at
the brown peak of our neighbor's roof and the 'pregnant sky'
(as my maternal grandmother likes to say), hoping to spy the
first flakes of a predicted late-season snowstorm.

I am quite content.

I chew with much satisfaction my fifth and final piece of
Dentyne gum. (My final piece because that's all that came in
the pack.) Chewing Dentyne is all about that initial burst of
cinnamon that almost burns my tongue. Once the initial burst
fades, I spit out that piece, and with much anticipation, pop
in the next. It has taken less then ten minutes to arrive at this
moment: chewing on the final piece humming to myself in a
Winnie-The-Pooh-blustery-kind-of-day way when I hear Fran
in her once-again-someone-has-wronged-me way yell, "Who
took my gum?"

I abruptly stop chewing.

I spit the last piece into its wrapper. I scoop up the other
four wads, quietly run up to the bathroom, throw them all

away, and return to the landing in time to hear my father ask in his hoping-someone's-in-trouble-so-I-can-yell way, "What's the problem?"

"Someone took my gum," Fran insists.

"Did you look in all the bags?" my mother asks.

"There's only two bags, and they're right here. My gum isn't in either."

My sister's tone suggests that something worse than losing a pack of gum has happened. It has, "Who broke my Beatles White Album?" written all over it.

"Well, it was just a pack of gum, we can get another," my mother says.

My sister cannot abide my mother's nonchalant attitude.

"Can't I have anything in this house! All I wanted was a pack of gum!"

"Maybe they forgot to pack it," my mother says, in an obvious attempt to diffuse what is brewing.

"I put it in the bag, so I know it was in there."

"Who took her gum," my father demands.

I pull my knees up to my chin, and begin to rock back and forth. The landing is my safe haven when things get tense. Even though it waned for a while after the Harlem Globetrotters ball incident, I often lounge on its large square under the window, watching the weather or reading a book.

"Sam, get in here," my father barks.

I stop rocking.

I stop breathing.

Sam gets up from the sofa. I hear him shuffle into the kitchen.

"What?" he asks.

"Did you take Fran's gum?" My father's tone is unsettling. He hasn't been this way for a while, so I'm caught off guard, and frightened.

"What gum?" Sam asks.

"My pack of Dentyne that was in one of the grocery bags," Fran says in disgust.

"No," Sam says clearly confused. "I have no idea what you're talking about."

"Goddamn it Sam," always the swearing with him, "I know you're lying."

"But I'm not. I didn't take her gum."

I can't see my dad, but I know his face is getting red, and his eyes, mean. It doesn't matter whether Sam took the gum or not. My father doesn't care. He's looking for any reason to get mad and punish someone. The vitriol in his voice is completely without merit. It always sounds full of hate, which is strange to me. Why would a parent hate his children? Sure, all kids frustrate their parents, but this is something different. It feels sinister. And, what disturbs me most, from my perch on the landing, is that I can tell my father is feeding off it.

The unjustified accusations followed by Sam's understandable defense continue. I'm stunned at how unwilling my father and sister are to believe him. Granted, Sam is known to tell white lies from time to time, but that doesn't mean he's lying now. And it's obvious he has no idea that gum even entered the house.

It hits me, however, that if I say nothing, they will believe Sam did it, no matter how hard he protests. It also hits me that, of course, he's telling the truth. Not just because I know I chewed the gum, but because Sam always gets goofy when he's caught in a lie.

He's not being goofy now.

It's clear Sam is scared. That should be their clue he's not lying.

A wave of nausea washes over me as I also realize that he will be unjustly punished if I don't speak up. Realizing I'll be punished if I speak up causes terror to swirl inside me like a dust devil on a dry plowed field.

I am dizzy.

My internal conflict lasts a short time once I realize I will never be able to look at Sam again if I let him take the fall.

I gather my strength. I stand up and go down to the dining room. I stop just before the threshold of the kitchen. My dad and Joe are sitting at the table, Fran and my mother are standing on the far side of it facing me, and Sam, with his back to me, is standing directly in front of me.

"Goddammit Sam, this is your last chance to tell the truth," my father slams his fist on the table. He stands up, and nearly topples his chair when he pushes it back from his knees.

He yells, each word emphasized by that thick, stubby index finger of his, while pointing at Sam, "Did! You! Take! Her! Gum!"

He fists his hand, and bangs the table again.

My dad's anger churns inside him. His behavior, his boiling complexion, and his fisted hands are all a disproportionate reaction to the circumstance.

His energy is adversarial and predatory.

He is ready, willing, and wanting to strike.

Fear permeates the room, except perhaps for Fran this time around. She seems to want someone to pay for the disappearance of her gum. I can't really blame her. As the oldest, she feels everything gets taken from her.

Standing in the dining room, the smallest among them, I know if I don't speak right now, something bad will happen to Sam. Even though I know something bad is going to happen to me if I do speak, my conscience won't allow me to lie and let Sam take the blame.

Once again, Fran lets us all know, "I can't have anything in this house!"

I swallow hard.

My father is wound tight, ready to spin out of control. Fran is mad. My mother and Joe are stunned statues. And Sam's eyes dart from person to person begging to be believed.

"Come on Sam, we're going outside," my father approaches him.

"Bob!" my mother reacts. Dread possesses her.

I take a deep breath. It's now or never.

"Dad," I interrupt him just as he grabs Sam's shoulder.

"Be quiet, Connie Sue. Go back upstairs. This doesn't concern you."

"But it does," I say. I feel close to heaving. I can't breathe. I want to cry.

"No, it doesn't goddammit. Get upstairs."

"But I'm the one who took her gum."

I immediately start crying. I have no idea what is going to happen to me.

"Stop lying for your brother. He did it. And I know it. And, he's going to pay for it!"

"I didn't do it," Sam says.

"He didn't. I did," I plead.

"Well, if you took it, where is it?" Fran asks.

I lower my head. "I chewed it."

I can't contain my shame.

"All of it," I add.

My father, visibly disappointed that it wasn't my brother, looks at Sam and then at me. With hate and disappointment, he releases Sam and slams his chair against the table. Then, after charging up our environment with his vitriol, he turns and walks out of the kitchen as if nothing ever happened.

I am not punished.

I am not anythinged.

I stand trembling as my father pushes by me on his way to the living room. My father was ready to rip Sam limb from limb, and then, on a dime, dismissed the entire event.

I don't get a scolding for taking Fran's gum. Nor do I get a "that was really brave of you to tell the truth, Connie Sue."

Sam doesn't get a "Sorry I didn't believe you. I didn't mean to get so upset."

Nothing.

Everybody just goes about their business.

Fran refuses to talk to me. She looks at me with utter disgust, goes up to our bedroom, and shuts the door.

I am crushed.

I run for paper and a pen. For the first time, I acknowledge that I know she is Dorothy by addressing her as such in a note of apology. Fully adorned with drawings of Dorothy and Toto, I proudly stand outside the door holding my note of reconciliation and knock.

She doesn't answer.

I try two more times, and then I put the note on the floor so when she opens the door she'll see it. On my way downstairs, I look out the landing window. The snow, falling hard, has already covered the ground.

It's an hour before she acknowledges me, and instead of accepting my apology, she laughs at me.

I don't understand.

I feel awful inside.

After that day, I no longer play Dorothy with her.

That night I have what becomes a recurring dream. While many of my tornado dreams vary in the details, this dream never does. Events similar to the gum incident, which contain the unfulfilled threat of violence, are the harbinger for this dream.

I'm sitting on the front porch swing looking toward the river valley where the Des Moines River cuts through the middle of town, dividing the north and south sides of Forked River. Sitting high atop a hill to my right is the high school. According to my mother, Sac and Fox tribes lived on this hill. From that vantage point they were able to watch for marauders coming down the river.

The summer day is peaceful and warm, absent of both the stench of Morrell's meatpacking plant and the cries of the pigs headed for slaughter. I see clouds starting to form in the southwestern sky. The clouds, wispy white in the distance, begin to gather shape and substance as they move towards town. I stop the swing. A gentle breeze sweeps my hair as I watch the clouds with curiosity.

And then an all-white baby tornado lowers from the cloud. It never touches the ground.

It simply hangs from the cloudbank, dragged the full distance of the sky. The whole time it's moving, I hear a voice deep and ominous swirling down from its tail, "I'm watching. I'm coming," it says. "Not this time, but soon. I'm watching. I'm coming."

EF-1

With winds ranging from 86 to 110 miles per hour, an EF-1 tornado can cause moderate damage to stronger structures leaving roofs severely damaged. Mobile homes can be pushed off their foundations, and cars can be pushed off roads.

It is a Saturday, late in the summer of 1973. It's several months after the gum incident, and thankfully, life has been absent scenes like that since. My father is relaxing in his recliner reading the paper, the boys are playing cards, and Fran is hustling about getting things ready to leave for college soon. I'm sitting on the porch swing reading a book.

Everyone is calm and preoccupied, so it is no surprise when my mother takes advantage of the moment and announces, "I'm going up to relax in a bath." It's a perfect time for her to indulge in this luxury. Something my mother seldom does.

Five minutes later, I have to go to the bathroom.

I hold it for as long as I can and then go upstairs.

I knock on the door.

"Mom, can I come in? I need to potty."

"I locked the door, Connie Sue. You'll have to go to the basement."

"Okay," I say, and slump down the stairs. I figure I can hold it maybe five more minutes. Surely, she'll be done by then.

I don't want to ask anyone to take me to the basement. If

I do, Fran won't. Joe will tell me not to be a baby and to go by myself. I love Sam to death, but he likes to tease me. And I'm obviously not going by myself, this being the year of a cockroach infestation in the town. They're everywhere, and I'm certain all over the basement.

A few minutes later, I try my mom again, and get the same result.

I go downstairs, stand in front of my dad, take a deep breath, and say, "I need to go to the bathroom, and mom is in the tub. She locked the door, and I can't get in."

"Well, go up and tell her to let you in," he says, without moving the newspaper.

I leave my body for a moment, and my spirit-self goes high up in the corner of the room. I look down and see myself standing in front of him, the newspaper between us. I have on my favorite outfit this summer: pale green shorts and a matching halter-top with a frog sitting on a lily pad on the front. A purple lotus flower adds color to the various shades of green. My spirit-self, who feels older than my actual self, knows something is missing in this home.

Back in my body, the need to go is more urgent. I don't want to bother my mom, who is just trying to relax, so I ask Joe.

He is, as I expected, dismissive and tells me to go the basement by myself. "Don't be so afraid. There's nothing down there," he says.

Now I'm on the verge of wetting my pants, and I'm getting nervous. If I wet my pants, we're all in trouble.

Hesitantly, I tell my dad that no one will take me downstairs.

"Go tell your mother I said to let you in." I can hear the frustration in his voice.

As I run upstairs, it crosses my mind that it's odd he tells me to do this instead of ordering someone to take me to the basement.

"Mom, Dad said to let me in," I call from outside the door. I constantly move to keep from going.

"Tell him I'm in the tub, and the door is locked. Just have someone take you to the basement." My mother is exasperated.

Icksnay on the elaxingray athbay, I think as I run down the stairs.

"Mom said the door is locked, and to have someone take me to the basement," I tell my dad.

I'm frantic. I need to pee, and bad. I'm terrified of the basement and I can tell right now that everyone is annoyed by the seven-year-old in the house.

"That's it. I'll take care of this!"

In a fury, my father throws the paper aside and stomps upstairs.

Joe, aware everyone has let this go too far, grabs me. We head for the basement.

"I really have to go bad Joe," my voice is full of panic. I don't have to tell Joe how awful things are going to be if we don't make it in time.

"I know," Joe says. His voice betrays both his worry and his compassion.

We can hear my father yelling and cursing on his way upstairs.

Down in the basement, I pee like a racehorse. I cry and pray that no cockroaches skitter across my feet.

Upstairs my father is screaming at my mother, "Why couldn't you unlock the goddamn door?"

I finish, wipe, and pull up my shorts. Joe tells me to run upstairs and let dad know I went.

I run up the stairs. My dad is outside the bathroom door yelling at my mom, "Unlock this goddamn door right now! Or I'm going to bust it in!"

"My God, I'm just trying to take a bath. Why can't someone take her to the basement?" justified ire fills her voice.

I try to get his attention. His rage has acquired a momentum that has overtaken him. He doesn't see or hear me.

He marches past me to the boys' room yelling, "I'm going to take care of this once and for all goddamn it!"

"Daddy, I went. Joe took me to the basement. I don't have to go anymore," I plead, but I'm invisible to him.

He stomps out of the boys' room, head down like a bull. What I see frightens me. He is carrying one of Joe's larger hand weights. What is he going to do with that?

Before the question is completed in my head, he starts pounding the doorknob with the weight. All the while yelling, "If you're not going to unlock this goddamn door, then I'm busting it down."

My mom screams, "Stop! I'll open the door."

My fear is heightened by her fear.

I hear her foot slip on the porcelain bottom of the tub as she frantically tries to get out.

Immobile, I watch as my father, who is not a small man, raises and lowers the hand weight once, then twice, onto the glass doorknob. The metal against the glass rings out between his yelling and my mom's pleading screams. I can do nothing but watch.

With an athlete's studied practice of follow through, he lifts the weight and lets it complete its downward pass before lifting again. On the forth blow, the knob breaks and drops to the floor.

In an immeasurable instant, my father's countenance returns to normal. He throws the weight on the floor behind him. It drops with a startling thud, which shakes the floor. He doesn't display any awareness of either, and, as calmly as if he were saying, "Let's go out for ice cream," he looks at me, and says, "There, no one will lock that door again."

I have another tornado dream.

I am walking down the Locust Street hill to my house. The entire neighborhood is calm and still. Mr. McDavitt, who is always out in the street playing fetch with Thumper, his black Lab, is nowhere to be found. Thumper isn't in his pen.

As I walk across the driveway into our backyard, I stop. Suddenly, I am aware that I'm having a tornado dream. Dread washes over me. That's why it's so quiet. The tornado is coming.

I run to the front of the house. Sure enough the clouds are beginning to gather in the distance. I run around to the back porch and fly into the kitchen. Without stopping, I race through to the living room, and by the time I reach the front door, the tail has dropped. The tornado is rolling forward, headed, as always, directly for our house.

My throat begins to constrict, my heart is about to beat out of my chest, and I know what I have to do: warn everyone so we can get to safety.

Only this time, I can't find anyone. I race upstairs: no one. I half fall down the stairs into the living room: no one. The kitchen, the dining room: no one. I go back to the living room door. This time, I walk out onto the front porch.

A green hue has colored the air, and it smells rather metallic. It feels as if the oxygen is being sucked out of every corner of the world, and then BAM! . . . I am blown back against the porch wall. The screen is ripped out of my hand and off the house. It literally flies away. I shake off the blow I took, and dart inside.

I try every room one more time: still no one.

The wind is loud.

I hear tree limbs banging against the house.

I hear glass shattering.

I don't scream. I clear my head and think.

Get to the basement.

Get under the stairs.

That's where they say to go.

The basement side door is ripped off the house as I turn on the landing. I jump down the last five steps, run around the corner, and make a beeline down the dark room towards the gargantuan furnace. It looks like a many-armed monster in the dark with its ducts reaching out to the ceiling. I pass the toilet, go behind the wall that backs it, and tuck in under the steps. I hold my knees tight to my chest, and bury my face into them.

And then it ends.

The tornado is over.

My eyes go from side to side as I listen acutely for any evidence of it remaining.

As I come out from under the stairs, I see light coming in from behind the furnace. A limb is halfway through the window. The sky is blue. The sun is shining.

I go upstairs, and while the house is still standing, it's a mess. All three of the living room windows are shattered, the door is gone, and debris litters the floor.

"Mom? Dad?" I call out. No one answers me. I assume they were someplace safe away from home.

I walk through the kitchen. The door is missing here as well.

I walk outside. A dog bowl is upside down on the steps. I pick it up. I laugh when I turn it around and see THUMPER on the front.

"I hope you're okay, Thumper," I say, and put the bowl down.

The sun is so bright, it is almost blinding.

I shield my eyes as I walk into the backyard. Something unusual is happening.

My eyes adjust. I stand in awe of the scene before me.

It's as if all the homes in my neighborhood were made only of doors. Doors are everywhere. Our bathroom door dangles from the now tornado-ravaged maple tree in our backyard. Below it on the ground is a multitude of shattered and semi-shattered glass doorknobs, reflecting the sun like diamonds.

Sunny Days

Skies are clear (in the United States) if cloud cover is less than one tenth.

We have a biological need to be loved by our parents. That is one of the reasons my father can manipulate me. Occasionally, he throws me a bone. He offers me hope. He suggests things aren't what I think they are. He tells me, it's only my perspective. He claims a fierce loyalty to me while creating an almost religious loyalty in me towards him. He does this by transforming the definition of love into the definition of loyalty. I owe him my loyalty if I want his love. Therefore, when I don't do what he wants, I'm displaying my lack of loyalty, and that lack renders me undeserving of his love.

And, generally, what he wants me to do is agree with him. No matter how absurd his assertion is.

Every summer Sunday for the majority of my youth, my family gets up, has breakfast, and goes about happily preparing to go to the Izaak Walton League for a day, simply put, of fun in the sun. The "Ike's," as all the members fondly refer to it, is about ten minutes from our backdoor. Within minutes, we're out in the country, going up and down hills, and then at the top of the highest rolling peak, the Ike's appears on the left.

The clubhouse, a one-story yellow building with a large open meeting room and a restaurant-sized kitchen, sits atop a green grassy hill with the woods and the country expanding out behind it. Off to its side is a firing range. On most mornings, the clay ducks are already flying by the time we arrive.

My dad turns to the right upon entering the lot, and stops in front of a padlocked gate straddling a single lane gravel road. He passes the key to whoever happens to be sitting behind him. That person jumps out and opens the gate. After my dad pulls through and the gate is locked, we begin the journey down the curving, rutty gravel road to the lake.

The further down we go the more embedded in the small woods we become. My father takes the last turn, and light hits the car as a glade opens before us. The lake, a large crescent moon, sprawls out in front of it. We drive by the few campers that are parked for the weekend. I look to see if I recognize any of them as we pass. Selfishly, I enjoy the lake better on days when there are fewer people here.

My dad stops at the end of the gravel road and the fun begins. We all help unload the car. Boots and Margaret, our neighbors and friends, have already shoved together two tables. Margaret has covered them with classic red and white checked tablecloths. I say hello, put down my load, and dash to the water. I love the feel of the warm sand seeping through my toes as I run across the beach.

"Look out for pull tabs," my mom yells. I should, but I'm too excited to get in the water, so I don't. A couple of times a day, the adults will comb the sand looking for the pull-tabs from soda cans.

"Why can't people just throw them in a garbage can?" the adults always murmur when they find one.

The water is clear and warm. The sky is blue and cloudless. It's a perfect day. But even if it isn't, as long as storms aren't in the forecast, we still come.

I dog paddle (my best, and only, stroke) out to the dock and begin my endless rounds of jumping off the dock until my friend the turtle, a three-year resident, shows up.

Raised three feet out of the water, the dock has nine support poles extending down into the lake's sandy bottom to anchor it. Not long after I arrive, the turtle arrives, and together we race around the dock poles. More than once, we'll swim around a pole and stop, turtle face to human face, and smile at one another. I love my turtle friend.

I swim until lunch. By this time all the families who join us have arrived, and the potluck is complete. My dad grills up our burgers or hot dogs, or in the case of him and my brothers, both.

"Cheese on mine, please," I say as I pass by him to fill my plate with chips, slaw, corn (either on the cob or creamed), baked beans, and fruit. I crack open an A&W root beer as my father places my cheeseburger on my plate. After adding ketchup and pickles, I eagerly bite into it, letting ketchup dribble down my pinkie.

Often after lunch we take a walk in the woods. This small break from swimming alleviates my mother's fears of someone drowning from post-lunch cramps.

My whole family walks up a small hill to the swinging bridge that connects to another small wood. We swing as much as possible on the crossing in an attempt to topple each other over.

Sometimes, I come to the middle of the bridge by myself, and sit down just to enjoy the sun and watch the fish swim by. After we cross the bridge, we hike up into the woods following the path that leads out to the back edge of the lake. My eyes always squint from the bright sun upon entering the clearing. We walk along the bank until we are in the middle of the lake standing between the two woods that surround it. A large cornfield is behind us, and off in the distance to our front is the beach and the picnic area.

It's absolutely perfect in every way. The only sounds and views are people and nature. These are the best days I have with my family.

Once back from our hike, it's Frisbee time. This is when my dad, and one or two of the other dads, throw the Frisbee to anyone who wants to jump off the dock and catch it. The line is never short, and the fun is endless. It seems like no one, even the grown-ups, get tired of doing this. One time, Joe acts like he's going for the Frisbee, but then moons us.

As the day wanes, our energy does too. Some of us walk up the road to the clubhouse to see what's going on, or we build a sand castle, or just lay on the beach. As suppertime approaches, we load up on another round of food before packing up and heading home.

These days are the most enjoyable familial times from my youth. They last until I am ten. They are days when everything and everyone is carefree. They are days when my father is predictable. He is not annoyed. He is not anxious. He is not put out having to be with us. He has tempered his hate. We feel like the family everyone thinks we are. Happy, close, and stable.

But even given that, most Sundays start the same way.

After finishing breakfast, my mother goes about packing the cooler. One of us is sent to the basement to collect six of the milk cartons of water she has frozen. My father beats them apart with a hammer letting the ice spill over the contents of the cooler. Once this job is over, we all go upstairs to brush our teeth and get on our suits while my mother finishes packing and cleans the kitchen.

As my mom finishes cleaning the kitchen, my dad picks up the cooler, tells us all to grab something, and marshals us to the car.

"I'll be there as soon as I get my suit on and brush my teeth," my mom says as we go out.

Once we're in the car, my father begins, "What is taking her so goddamn long? Your mother can never just walk out the door. She always makes us wait, god dammit!" his tone implies that she does so with nefarious intent.

I sit in the back thinking, 'she's upstairs brushing her teeth and putting on her suit.'

"Son of a bitch," he yells, and lays on the horn.

"Every weekend it's the same thing. Don't you guys get tired of waiting on her?" He pauses.

"We're ready to go. What the hell is she in there doing?"

He pauses again, and then, "Jesus Christ, it's gonna be lunch before that goddamn woman gets out here!"

Again, he blares the horn.

My mom comes bouncing out of the house, this time in my favorite suit: kelly green with white polka dots.

She gets in the car, smiling until my father says, "What the hell took you so long? We've been out here waiting on you."

She can only answer with a defensive tone, "I was putting on my suit and brushing my teeth." He's intimidated her, and her answer sounds more like an excuse than a reason.

But then, with my father, there are no reasons, especially if his actions have anything to do with it. And, over time, even the clearest mind grows suspicious of others' motivations.

EF-2

Causing considerable damage to framed structures, with winds ranging from 111 to 135 miles per hour, an EF-2 tornado can uproot trees, turn light objects into projectiles, and completely demolish mobile homes.

The blizzard is getting worse.

Just a few moments ago, the white-lined edge of the other lane visibly raced along with us as we sped down the road to Forked River. Now, even the yellow centerline is lost in the snow. I look over at Fran. She is head down in a book. Not legally confined to a seatbelt, I easily stretch across the car to look out her window. The snow is a wall against the glass. Annoyed, she pushes me back in the seat.

It's the same when I look out the back and front windows. I can no longer feel the motion of the car. We are surrounded by white as if we've parked inside an igloo garage.

I know we must be moving though. It's a strange illusion messing with my senses. I lean forward and look at the speedometer. Seventy miles per hour! I stifle my gasp. I look out the windshield and see the yellow-white headlights shining two truncated beams into the storm. The snow is falling fast and hard. My dad's line of vision is maybe ten feet in front of the car. To say that I'm nervous is an understatement.

The ride home is silent, not because we are all relaxed and have enjoyed ourselves while visiting Joe at the University of

Northern Iowa, applauding him for a job well done for being one of two seniors picked to have their artwork displayed in the professor's annual art show, but because we have been stunned into silence. Humiliated. Muted.

My father offered no positive recognition of Joe's piece. No show of pride. No, "son, you did great." No patting him on the back, "I'm proud of you, boy."

Instead, while pointing at one of his professor's pieces, my father boisterously announced, "What's that piece of shit. Connie Sue could have done that. Who are these idiots teaching you anyway? What a waste of my goddamn money! If these are the people telling you that you have talent…" and on it went through the whole gallery.

My father walked past the doorman of the gallery with his head high and his shoulders back. The rest of us tried to be polite and rise above the circumstance while thanking the doorman, but our stooped postures betrayed our humiliation and shame.

The doorman's heartfelt look of pity as I walked out the door crushed me.

I felt awful for Joe. The enthusiasm and fast talk he greeted us with faded almost immediately upon entering the gallery.

We dropped him off in the barren semi-circular drive of his dormitory, the storm having driven everyone indoors. With his hand resting on my dad's car door, he stooped down to see through the window. He uttered a barely audible good-bye.

Speeding down the road with the blizzard wrapped around us like a blanket, I can still see his downcast face. He glanced back at me, and I hoped he could sense my compassion. Unable to mask the disappointment that poured from his pores like the snow falling from the sky, Joe turned, head down, away from the car. He walked like a man of eighty towards his dorm. He seemed a shell of a person, and I feared the blizzard would sweep him away.

The original plan had been to go to UNI on Sunday, but late in the week a snowstorm had been forecast for overnight Saturday into Sunday with blizzard conditions likely resulting in several inches of snow, as I informed my junior high from the audio visual room on the Friday morning announcements.

I arrived, along with the rest of the A.V. crew, Friday (yesterday) at 7:00 a.m. After a week of working the cameras and the sound booth, I was assigned to the weather. After reading the Forked River Courier and Des Moines Register, I made notes for my forecast. Then, I set about displaying the predicted high and low for the day on the felt board, along with a sun since yesterday's forecast was clear. Under the words FUTURE FORECAST, I placed snow and wind cutouts for Saturday and Sunday.

Once live, camera A was positioned on me, while camera B stayed on the felt board during the forecast.

"And now, here's Connie with the weather," my news desk crewmate cued.

"A very strong blizzard is predicted to begin around ten Saturday night lasting through the day on Sunday," I said after giving Friday's weather. "We might be lucky and have a snow day on Monday, as two to three feet of snow are predicted from this storm."

As I said this, camera A stayed focused on me while camera B switched to the sports desk. Once camera B was locked in place, I said, "And, now, to Steve with the sports."

It's exactly because of the storm's predicted start time that my parents decided to come to UNI today confident we would beat the storm home. But the storm came out of the Rockies sooner than expected, and began around two in the afternoon.

I sit back in my seat scared upon scared. Like always, there's no talk or acknowledgement of what happened in the gallery. The silence is somehow heightening my fear. And now, the man who once again has rendered us all dumb with his bile-laden verbal dump is speeding down a single lane Iowa highway at seventy miles per hour in the middle of a whiteout blizzard.

I move forward and look at the speedometer again: still seventy miles per hour.

I look over at Fran who is nothing short of gone. I scoot a little closer to her. I move my hand along the seat so my dad can't see me getting her attention. I scratch the side of her leg with my index finger. She turns towards me, sighing. Agitation is all over her face. I lean the side of my head against the back of the front seat, thank God it's not bucket seats, and lip, "Look at the speedometer."

"What?" her annoyance hits me like an off-pitch bell.

Quickly, I put my finger to my lips and shush her.

I point towards the front seat, and lip again, "Look at the speedometer."

My sister's eyes focus. She looks around, sees how bad the storm has gotten, and finally senses the speed of the car.

Fran sits up, elongates her neck, and looks at the speedometer. She shoots me a wide-eyed glance as we both move back into our seats.

Fran is clearly reasoning things out.

"Hey Dad," she says, affecting nonchalance as much as possible, "you're going kind of fast in this storm."

"Don't worry about it," he is on edge and dismissive.

Feeling brave, and really, really wanting him to slow down, I chime in, "But Dad, you're going 70."

"Don't worry about it I said," he glares at me in the rearview mirror. I pull back and look at Fran.

Our inquires bring my mother back from wherever her thoughts and humiliation had taken her, and she asks, as if she just walked in a room, "What's going on?"

"Dad's going a little fast in this storm," Fran ventures, but there is reserve both in her tone and posture. She looks like someone expecting to be smacked.

"Why don't you all just read a goddamn book or something, stop worrying about how fast I'm going, and leave me the hell alone!"

As with Fran, once my mother is brought out of herself, she senses the speed of the car. She looks back at Fran and me. The clueless look on her face proves she just became present.

She leans towards my dad, still looking bewildered at us. She turns her head, her eyes trailing the movement, and looks at the speedometer.

"My God. Why are you going so fast?" she blurts.

Her question: reasonable.

Her tone: appropriately full of concern.

Her reaction: natural.

But it's all a big mistake.

"I'm not going fast. Everybody just shut the hell up."

"Bob, slow down," she says. She leans forward on the dash, adding, "You can barely see in front of the car."

Her tone is more adult than I am accustomed to. I'm amazed at how reassured I am by it. Surely, he will listen.

"I said not to worry about it, goddamn it," his voice has surpassed angry.

I've learned, as well as my mom and Fran have, that things don't go well when he is like this. I think pressing him is a bad idea, but at the same time I desperately want him to slow down. There is no doubt at this speed he would rear-end a car before he saw it.

She looks back at us, I know for reassurance. Someone has to stop him.

She takes a deep breath, Fran and I both give her a reassuring nod, and with an inexplicable calm, she says, "C'mon, Bob. We have nowhere to go tonight. It doesn't really matter when we get home. It just matters that we get there."

Well put, Mom. You did good; it was, in my opinion, beyond reasonable.

But no.

Suddenly, I am thrown across the seat towards Fran. She slams into the door as my dad furiously jerks the car into the oncoming lane. He slams his foot on the gas, and speeds forward into the blinding white of the storm.

He's in this lane long enough for me to recover from the throw. I am behind him fighting to stay seated.

All of my energy is flying out the top of my head. I press against the roof in an attempt to not fly away.

My eyes, frozen wide in shock, stare out the windshield waiting for a vehicle to emerge out of the white, allowing me to glimpse it in the last split second of my life.

Panic grips my throat, suffocating screams of immeasurable length and volume.

Every second is laden with the anticipation of what can only in this moment be assumed as the inevitable.

Not a breath escapes me.

I am horrorstruck.

Then, with an equally unexpected jerk as the first, I'm thrown into the window. Fran is thrown into me smashing my face against the glass. We are quickly uprighted when he straightens the wheel.

The jerk is so abrupt I think we stop moving. I feel like Dorothy when her house lands in Munchkin Land. Her bed pops up in the air, and everything stops when it lands back on the floor.

The extreme whiteness of the storm suspends time and motion, but my father is still barreling down the road.

"Now, goddamn it, you can either shut the hell up, or I'm pulling this car over right now, and you can get out and walk your ass home."

None of us say a word.

"That's what I thought," he says. He continues down the road to Forked River at seventy miles per hour.

I'm in a state beyond shock as I stare straight ahead into the bald head of the man who just tried to kill my mother, my sister, and me. There is a scream lodged in my throat that I will not permit under any circumstances to escape. The fact that I'm still alive is impossible for me to comprehend.

The urge to leap across the seat and beat him, hard and violently, begins to bubble inside me. I am incapable of wrapping my mind around ever looking at this man again.

In my mind, the debate is now officially over as to whether or not he cares about us.

About ten miles outside of Forked River, the snow lightens as we've come to the front edge of the storm. And, now, like a harbinger of our future, it chases us.

We pull into the drive, and oddly my father doesn't put the car in the garage. Fran, without saying goodbye, heads across the street, brushes the snow off her car, and leaves. How I covet her position in our family right now: twenty-three and living on her own.

Once in the house, my mother takes off her coat. Dazed, she begins chopping vegetables.

"I'll make some vegetable soup," she says. Her ability to act as if we've just had the most normal day both stuns and infuriates me. But her nervous hands and tightly rounded, lifted shoulders suggest she feels differently.

I don't know why she's even thinking about food. In this moment, I'm certain I won't eat for at least a week. My stomach is brick-hard, wrenched into knots as tangled as tree roots.

I hang up my coat and collapse on the sofa. Sam is in the living room watching *Wheel of Fortune*. Sam lucked out. His Saturday bowling league championships kept him home.

I can see by the streetlight that the storm is setting in.

Looking out the living room windows, I can normally see the neighbor's house across the street, but now even the edge of our lot is lost to the ethereal white that surrounds our house.

I sit watching the wheel go around while listening to the water from the shower my father immediately went up to take. What the heck?

Twenty minutes later he comes downstairs dressed, shaved, and smelling of Old Spice.

He puts on his coat.

As he opens the kitchen door, my mother meekly asks, "Where are you going in this storm."

"Kiss my ass. I don't have to tell you every little goddamn thing I do," he yells at her with so much hate it stings.

And then, just in case she didn't hear the hate, he slams the door with violent force. I'm surprised the window doesn't break.

I go to bed early.

I lie in bed staring up at my ceiling, praying. In my mind, I'm sitting on the red-carpeted steps leading up to the altar of our church. I love our church. And I often go there in my mind. I know the universal energy I feel so attached to is there. And that energy of pure love, pure compassion, and pure light cleanses and enlivens me. It makes me feel eternally safe. But that energy is being drowned out in my house. My father's energy, filled with hate, indifference, and darkness soils and weakens me. I feel trapped in the lair of my most dangerous predator.

Even though he has moments when these attributes seem to be at rest, they are always brewing right under his surface. They define his character.

Two pews run along either side of the walls from the podiums at my side. Beautiful stained glass edged in a deep brown wood rises behind the altar. In my mind, the choir stands in the pews singing my own private hymn as I kneel and speak to God.

"I don't understand," I whisper. "I thought we all came here knowing the same thing. I thought we all knew to love and be kind. If that's the case, what's going on with my father? Why is he so mean?"

I stay quiet a long moment.

The choir stops singing. In the silence, I am brushed by a reassuring energy. I am left feeling that I will be okay. That ultimately, I am okay. But I'm stuck between this understanding of a spiritual world where I feel love and trust, and my immediate physical world where I live with a father that seems to be at war against that understanding, or, in the least, is attempting to expunge it from me.

Back in my room, I'm angry that I am lying in my bed, and that my mother is in hers. Sam is sound asleep, completely unaware of the day's events because, of course, mum's the word. How is it that in my father's absence, my mother has not, with great speed and rage, made us pack our bags and taken us from this house? Why will she not rescue us?

I consider running away the following morning before anyone wakes up. But none of my friends' parents will believe this story. And my father will just deny it.

I can go to the police. But what then? Foster care? I'm certain my father will be the one believed there as well. I've heard too many stories about his family, and it seems there's some rather shady dealings going on that they are never made accountable for. They seem to be protected, and I have no reason to believe my father won't be as well.

I don't trust my father. And I know my mother is paralyzed by an omnipresent state of shock, and therefore can't protect me, which means, sadly, while I trust that she loves me, I don't really trust her either.

Big question. How do I hold onto that larger sense of love and protection, while living in its absence?

I sigh.

I know I can't escape my earthly reality, which I'm thrust back into when I hear the kitchen door open.

My bedside clock reads eleven. My father shuts the door. I hear him drop his keys on top of the microwave. I hear the fabric of his coat brush against itself as he takes it off. I hear him drape it over a kitchen chair. He gets a drink, and then heads upstairs.

My first thought is how dare he ever come back here again. My second thought is not a thought really, but instead a paralyzing fear and sense of dread. I am suddenly afraid of him discovering that I'm awake. I don't know what I would say if he came into my room. At this moment, I never want to see him again. Something intrinsic tells me that you run, and run fast, from people who so ruthlessly endanger your life, even if they are (and maybe most definitely when they are) your own blood. But no one is running. And at twelve, if my mother isn't going to run, how can I?

He goes into the bathroom, which is right next to my room, brushes his teeth and pees. I put my hands over my ears. The sounds are too intimate. And in this moment, as he is a person I desire never to see again, they are abhorrent.

He turns out the light and walks down the hall. I exhale as quietly as possible. I hear him change into his pajamas. I hear him pull the blankets back. I hear the mattress give as he crawls into bed.

How is she lying there? How is she not ready to beat the shit out of the man who just risked her life and that of their children?

I want to scream.

I picture her: her back to him, rigid and frost-covered as if she has been frozen into a permanent state of shock.

I cry myself to sleep because I know in the morning we will all be seated around the kitchen table acting as if none of this ever happened.

The prolific nature of my tornado dreams after this event is downright stunning. I don't have them every night, but enough to begin to feel like it is almost the only thing I dream about. The only other dreams that come are often dreams of me taking flight in order to escape something or someone, or to simply feel the freedom from and independence of this place. All it ever takes is one motion of my arms, and I lift off. My favorite place to soar is above the Rockies.

My tornado dreams begin to include all my family members, like one I had shortly after the blizzard incident. *We've just come home from the Ike's, (a now sad pastime in my family), and, as soon as I step out of the car, I'm aware of the change in pressure. And I have come to recognize a certain metallic odor that precedes the tornado. I drop my beach towel and run to the front of the house. There it is, the tail already dropped. The tornado is moving faster than I've ever seen it move.*

I run to the backyard, "You guys, a tornado is coming straight for our house. We have to get inside."

No one responds to me.

"Come here! Look. It's getting closer. We have to get to the basement."

Joe walks by me, "What are you going on about?"

"There's a tornado, Joe. Look!" I shout.

"I don't see a tornado," he mocks.

"You're not even looking. Of course, you don't see it. Why won't you believe me?"

"Connie Sue, pick up your beach towel, and come in to take your shower," my mom calls from the back porch.

I run inside, "Mom, there's a tornado coming. We have to get to the basement."

"There's no tornado, Connie Sue. Just go take a shower."

"Mom," I bend over to look out one of the windows. "It's right across the street. Just look!"

With her head down as she unpacks the cooler, she says, "Well, then just shower in the basement." She looks up at me with a mocking smile. I'm unnerved.

Wind blows through the house. I hear what sounds like the front door come unhinged.

"C'mon everyone," I shout, my voice silenced by the wind. Debris is now circulating like little Frisbees throughout the house.

As I run for the basement door, I cannot grasp what I see. Sam and Joe are setting up a game of Monopoly on the dining room table, my mother is still unpacking the cooler, my father has settled into his recliner with the paper, which is being whipped by the wind, and Fran is switching through television stations. Shutters are banging on the house, pieces of roof are flying by the windows, and I almost laugh when our car, appearing as light as a toy model, goes rolling down the street past our dining room windows.

Okay, so they won't look, but how do they not notice the wind, or all the objects flying through the house?

A huge branch from our tree crashes through our garage. I laugh.

"At least the car wasn't in it," I yell.

Now, there is no time to lose.

I turn and run for the basement door. I assume everyone will come to their senses and follow me as I go through my routine.

Through the door. Jump the stairs. Down the dark hall. Pass the furnace. Tuck in a tight ball under the stairs.

I start rocking.

I practice my recital dance in my head until the air is silenced in the tornado's aftermath.

I emerge from the stairs. All the basement windows are shattered. I carefully step over the glass and make my way upstairs. A full two-thirds of my house is gone: scattered, it would appear, from here to the McDavitt's down the street.

I can't find anyone.

I step across the threshold of the now gone back-porch door. I walk over downed tree limbs. Our maple tree has fallen into our neighbor's garage, which has only half a wall standing. Leaves, limbs, papers, books, clothes, a box of Frosted Flakes, the cooler,

Fran's broken White Album, the TV, all litter the yard where I'm standing.

I see something shining under a shirt. I move the shirt and discover it is my diary, its gold lock having caught the sunlight. I pick it up and walk out of the yard. I have no idea where I'm going. I head up the Locust Street hill. As I step over debris, I try to identify my neighbors' unrecognizable homes.

Where is my family? I wonder. Why is no one else out?

Holding my diary close to my chest, I walk on as a voice whispers, "You're okay."

Downburst I

A localized area of damaging winds so severe it can be mistaken for a tornado, a downburst is caused by downdrafts of unusually high speeds penetrating close to the ground. The winds in a downburst flow outward from straight-line or divergent winds as opposed to the circular, converging winds of a tornado.

"She's paralyzed from her neck down. They don't think she'll ever walk again," he says.

A thick fog encircles my head, "What? Who's paralyzed?"

As my vision clears, my dad's face looms large in front of me. He peers under my canopy. I feel his thick hand wrap around my bicep. He gives me a shake.

"I need you to get up and eat breakfast. She's at the Des Moines hospital, and as soon as everyone's ready we're going up."

"Who's in the hospital?"

"Your cousin, Susie."

Everyone, I realize as I sit brooding in the backseat, staring into the same bald head that risked my life just a few months before, means my mom and me. Somehow Sam wriggled out of this one too. I believe for another bowling tournament.

"I'm certain Dale was driving drunk," his self-righteous tone grates my nerves.

"Weren't they going home after a party?" asks my mom.

"Yep."

My dad begins a boy-did-they-have-this-coming-to-them speech followed by a just-goes-to show-how-stupid-people-can-be tirade.

I lift my book, so my eyes are covered from his sight in the rearview mirror.

I roll my eyes and stifle a sigh. We're all to blame for everything that happens to us. Never are we a victim of circumstance, but yet he, on the other hand, is. In fact, everyone's function in this world, according to my father, is to actively and intentionally act against him, to keep him from doing whatever it is he wants to do (even though that's about all he's ever doing), to wrongly accuse him, and if nothing else, to just piss him off. More often than not, it's my mom, my siblings, and me that somehow are the greatest offenders.

In fact, his common refrain of, "I wouldn't be that way, Connie Sue, if you (or your mother, brothers, sister, my boss, co-worker, friend, or the goddamn clerk at the grocery store), weren't the way you are," sums up his response anytime I question his behavior.

I try to focus on my book, ignoring his condemnation of my cousin, Susie, who is much older than I am. I can't picture her face. I've only met her once at my uncle's house. In fact, I can only recall meeting all four of his children once. And that was when I met his new wife. I don't recall ever meeting my cousins' mother. My father has never said anything nice about Susie. In fact, upon reflection, I've never heard my father say anything nice about anyone.

Since my father has made it clear he doesn't care for her, I wonder why we are going to visit her. My father has never struck me as the kind of person who willingly puts himself aside during exceptional circumstances.

I doubt my cousin is the awful person my father makes her out to be. I've learned that my father speaks of everyone in his world as someone with deep character flaws by creating lies about their nature. My mother, for instance, is a liar, she uses people, and she is nice only to make other people think he is not. He has this convenient way of turning others' foibles into character flaws, while turning his own character flaws into mere foibles.

I sigh, look out the window at the passing snow-covered cornfields, and wonder what this all means for my cousin. I understand that she is paralyzed, but what does that mean, really. Her life is forever changed, and I think that must be so scary.

I return to my book.

Soon, we are walking down the corridor to my cousin's hospital room. Susie is the oldest daughter of my father's oldest brother. She has children, whom I don't recall ever meeting, who are around my age.

"Here it is," my dad says.

The room is momentarily blocked from my view by my parents. I have no idea what to expect, and I most desperately don't want to be here. I shove my hands in my pockets and shiver. My nerves rattle my system, leaving me untethered and chilled.

I fight to keep my feet on the ground.

Unexpectedly, my parents move further into the room, exposing the enormous hamster's wheel my cousin is in. Cutting a straight line through the middle of the wheel is my cousin, lying on her back strapped to a board. I jump when a motor kicks in. I watch, wide-eyed and nauseated, as the human-sized hamster wheel rotates Susie from a face-up to a face-down position.

I'm flooded with panic of what it must feel like to be her. I realize she is going to be strapped to this board with nothing between her and the floor. She is awake and alert. How then, I wonder, will she deal with what I can only imagine is a natural reaction. How is she overcoming the anxiety of free falling? She's paralyzed. She can't feel the straps that are securing her. Empathy overwhelms me.

I jump again when the wheel locks in place. The motor shuts off, leaving the room weirdly quiet.

I realize no one has noticed I'm here. I bump into a chair to my right, and decide my best option is to sit quietly until I'm relieved of this trip through hell.

"Susie, Uncle Bob is here," her father says.

My dad walks down the far side of the wheel. He looks into a mirror angled upward, positioned slightly to the side of Susie's head.

Susie looks into the mirror and says, her voice childlike and afraid, "Hi, Uncle Bob."

I am transfixed.

And then, my breath is arrested.

My blood stops pulsating through my body.

I watch as my father takes his hand out of his jean's pocket, and with the utmost love and tenderness, strokes my cousin's back and her hair. His hand, so gentle and kind, doesn't stop stroking her.

I don't know what I'm witnessing.

Never, in all my life, have I seen him extend even an ounce of this amount of compassion and kindness to my mother, my siblings, nor me. Never. Not once.

And then, for the coup de grace, he begins to cry.

Through tears, still stroking her back and hair, he says, "I'm so sorry, Susie."

I'm shattered and blown into a million pieces right there in front of everyone. Only no one notices because I am a self-contained explosion.

The room fades to black, transforming into a large movie screen. Three scenes in slow motion unfold before me.

The first: I am thrown from a car and severely injured.

The second: I am in a hospital bed, dying from some terrible sickness.

The third: I am on my bike and hit by a car.

Somehow I stay seated, while my body goes wild with awareness. In my mind, I scream *I will not make myself sick or get injured to get your attention! I don't want your love. I don't need your love. Not if it's under these conditions!*

In this moment, I make a pact with God not to injure myself for my father's love.

While I have other dreams like flying or falling and waking before I hit the ground, my tornado dreams are pervasive. They always begin with a beautiful, sunny day.

I am in the backyard, playing by myself. I'm calm and relaxed. The green of the grass, the blue of the sky, the yellows and reds of the tulips, the pink of the peonies, and the lavender of the lilacs are vibrant and alive. I'm trying with much tenacity to find a four-leaf clover among the weeds that have crept under our neighbor's fence when the colors are dimmed.

I look up.

A menacing cluster of clouds is forming in the distance.

The maple tree in my backyard becomes motionless, and all the birds disappear.

My entire body is gripped in panic. I know this dream. I've been here several times before. The clouds start to roll. Downdrafts begin to meet updrafts, and the conspicuous tail begins to drop towards the ground out of the bank of cumulonimbus clouds.

I force my rigid body to move and run inside.

My mom is passing through the kitchen on her way to the dining room.

"Mom, there's a tornado coming. We have to get to the basement."

"There's no tornado, Connie Sue," she dismisses me entirely.

"But there is. Go look out the front door."

"I don't need to look. I'm sure there is no tornado."

"But Mom," I plead.

She shrugs me away.

I run into the living room. Sam and Joe are there. "Guys. There's a tornado coming. We all have to get to the basement."

They laugh at me.

"I mean it. Go look out the door," I beg them.

I run to the door, and sure enough, it is near the river and raging towards our home.

According to my mom, "tornadoes, they say, won't travel along water, or is it jump water? Either way, that's why there has never been a tornado touchdown in Forked River."

In my dreams, I learn, tornadoes can do whatever they want.

The wind flattens the bushes lining our walk. A kid's plastic pool flies across the street. It looks like a giant's blue discus. I jump when it smacks into the side of a parked car.

Frantic, I try one last time to get someone, anyone, to look out the window. If they saw, they would believe, but they refuse.

My dad walks in the room, "See what you're all doing to me," he says.

I wake with a jolt.

The hopelessness evoked by my dream makes my heart beat wildly in my chest. My eyes dart back and forth in the dark in an attempt to re-establish my reality. I struggle to slow and elongate my rapid, short breaths.

Gustnado II

I am what I am: a social animal who longs to be loved by my parents.

My biology leaves me vulnerable; and, when in the midst of a predator, it is wise for one's senses to be sharp and finely honed. Because I am a developing child, it is inevitable that there are times when my deeply rooted desire to bond with my father will overcome my senses and the wisdom I have gained thus far. When my father is smiling and feigns enthusiasm towards me, I am sucked in. I am hopeful that maybe, just maybe he has changed. I hope that he has finally seen me in a light that has stirred something paternal in him. I hope that he is moved to let his natural desire to love me be trumped by his need to emotionally and mentally abuse me.

And so, from time to time, I relax my senses. I cave to my hope. But always the outcome is the same.

I am 14. It is summer.

While looking through the S encyclopedia, I come across the entry for sign language. It includes a picture of the hand positions for each letter of the alphabet. I am surprised, and elated, when my father sees this and suggests that we learn the alphabet together.

This is new territory for me. He is actually interested in spending time with me to learn something together. So, together we memorize the hand signals and test each other until we have them down pat. For a couple of months, my father and I communicate almost entirely in sign. I'm amazed by how proficient my ability to both sign and to read my father's signing has become.

There is something elevated in communication through signing, I come to think. Perhaps it is because it required a commitment on both our parts to learn the language. Or it is because different senses are required in order to understand what is being said. At any rate, it definitely makes me feel connected to my father in a way I haven't before. I begin to feel our bond is special in part because it is exclusive.

This makes me feel both good and awkward at the same time. I'm not a fan of leaving people out. Especially people I care for.

I'm lying on the sofa, my dad is sitting at the far end, and we are watching *Mutual of Omaha's Wild Kingdom*. During a commercial break, I look outside the window into the hazy cloudless sky. Thick humidity lays heavy in the air.

My dad taps my leg. I look down the sofa.

"Boy, is it humid today," he signs.

"Yeah, and Morrell's stinks," I return, enjoying the ease with which my hand works together with my brain communicating my thoughts, one letter at a time.

"It's always worse when it's humid," he replies.

"Did you hear the pigs squealing yesterday?" I ask.

"Sure did. I was working on a pole down behind the hardware shop this side of the tracks. I was high enough I could see them being herded up the catwalk."

"I think Gramps is right. They know they're going to their death. Yesterday, I could smell it all the way out at Sarah's house."

I am mid-way through signing how surprised I was, because normally I can't smell the meatpacking plant at Sarah's, when my mom, in a jovial mood, comes bouncing down the stairs.

"You two look quite comfy," she says. Sometimes my mother is simply radiant, and today is one of those days. It's hard not to smile when she's like this.

My attention is brought back to our conversation, when my father taps me on the foot.

"Your mother is such a god-damn," he signs.

I stop watching.

I have no desire to know the end of his attack.

It's so clear in this moment that his vitriol is unwarranted. That he is simply being mean-spirited is recognizable and indisputable.

I stare at his face. I'm sickened.

The cruelty coming from his eyes frightens me, even though it is not directed toward me.

Insight overwhelms me. It hits me, in a flash. As if someone just threw cold water on my face, I shake my head, sit up, and move back into the arm of the sofa like an animal avoiding a predator.

This was all one great big manipulative set-up. He strings me along for almost three months, and right when he thinks he has me, when he believes I'm too far in to get out, he exposes his truth.

His mistake.

My stomach constricts when I realize how he's methodically brought me to this moment. This moment where we can collude in mother-bashing. This is the special bond he was creating between us? How thoughtful of him to give me a private-behind-her-back way of expressing what he hopes are my real feelings.

I've been used.

And, worst of all, he believes I'm that low of a person. And, maybe even worse than that, if he doesn't believe it, he believes he can break me down until I am.

I'm about to retch.

I have to get out of here.

"I have to go to the bathroom," I say through puckered cheeks. A tell-tell sign I'm about to vomit.

"Okay," he signs.

While running up the steps, my mind travels back to a night before we started signing. I overheard my father (after having showered, shaved, and splashed on some Old Spice) say to my mom, "When your kids are all grown up, they won't want a thing to do with you. Look at the way Connie Sue talks to you. She hates you now. They all do! The little bastards!"

"Bob, kids will be kids," her defense ends. He preyed on her worst fears, and now she's thinking, questioning, and she doesn't even know it.

But, to my surprise, she squeaked out, "How can you call our kids bastards? They're not bastards. We have great kids, Bob."

As always, when appropriately questioned, he gets mad and turns it back on her, "all they do is use you, and you're too goddamn dumb to see it. Nobody can talk to you. You're always so goddamn right about everything."

Then, he slammed the door and left, no mention of where he was going or when he'd return.

He continues to sign with me for about a week, but I always speak my response. It is obvious he's mad at me. His inability to confront me, since it would expose his intended agenda, only adds to his rage.

He can't force me to sign with him.

Nothing angers my dad more than his victim establishing a boundary.

Eventually, he concedes and our false bond breaks.

Bow Echo II

"This was a great class," I say to a fellow dance student. "I love having class on Saturdays. I'm not so tired." *And I'm out of the house*, I add in my head.

"For all of you attending Alwin Nikolais' workshop tomorrow, I want you dressed appropriately with your hair up. Be sure to eat well this evening, and get a good night's rest. I worked very hard with the University of Iowa to get him and his company down to Forked River for this class, so I expect the best from all of you," Miss Milly's reproachful glance lets us all know we'll be in for it if we don't do as she asks.

This is my first-ever workshop and I'm a super-charged bundle of adrenaline. I am so grateful to Miss Milly for getting Nikolais to come here. I don't think my parents would've taken me to the U of I for the student workshop he held last night. I don't fault them for that. In their world that's an unnecessary extravagance.

I run outside expecting to find my mom smiling at me through the windshield. Instead, I find my dad.

"How was class, Babe?" he asks as I shut my door.

His "Babe" lands with so much inappropriateness, and his tone is so disingenuous, that my automatic cringe response, or ACR as I like to call it, begins to take control of me. But I'm in a good mood, so I suppress it.

I fire at him, "Miss Milly says Alwin Nikolais is one of the biggest influences in modern dance. He's respected all over the world. She told us about some performance he did in France a few years ago, right in the streets. Performers were hanging from ropes in trees, and all sorts of wild stuff. The dance was called something about bird people. I can't remember. But you know what? She said she pulled in some favors with people she knows at the U of I to get him down here. It helps that she's acquainted with him. This is so big," my hands are wide-open, shaking to the gods in thanks.

I can tell by the look on his face that my father thinks Milly is full of it. If I were anyone else in the family, he would let me know that, but instead he pulls into a convenience store parking lot and destroys my mood in a different way.

"Just wait in the car, Connie Sue. Your mom wants me to get some milk," he says, and shuts his door.

"Okay," I say.

Relieved of his cynical energy, I daydream about what the workshop will be like. I have no idea what to expect, but I'm hopeful it will be wonderful. If nothing else, it will be outside of any experience I've had before, and that makes it exciting.

I realize I've been lost in my daydream for some time. I've watched at least five people come and go in the time I've been waiting.

"What's taking him so long to get the milk?" I ask the air.

Another five minutes pass. Confused, hungry, and somewhat concerned, I get out of the car.

Big mistake.

The clerk's attention is turned my way when the door

signals my entrance with a two-tone bell. I smile awkwardly at her. I don't know her by name, but she's often working, so we recognize each other. She knows exactly who I'm looking for. I sense both skepticism and pity from her as she gestures with her head to the back of the store.

At the end of the center aisle, next to the bathrooms, my father is on the pay phone in what appears to be an involved conversation. His back is to me.

"Dad," I say.

He turns around. His face turns red, and through clenched teeth asks, "Why are you in here?"

"It's been about twenty minutes. You said you were just coming in for milk. I'm getting hungry, and I want to go home."

"Go back to the car. I'll be there in a few minutes," he fumes. He turns around. For a moment, I can do nothing but stare at his back.

His few minutes turns into at least another ten. Why didn't I just walk home? It's only about five minutes away.

He comes out of Casey's as if he just walked in.

He gets in the car. No sign of anger.

Hmm?

"Why were you on the phone in Casey's?" I believe it's a legitimate question.

"Because sometimes I need privacy, and I can't get that at home."

"Privacy? For what?" I'm not trying to be insubordinate, but I know he's not talking about "privacy." He's talking about concealing and subterfuge.

"None of your damn business, Connie Sue." Under normal

parenting conditions, his response is not out of line (although I feel his swearing always is). But my life doesn't exist under the umbrella of normal parenting conditions.

I look out the window so he doesn't see me roll my eyes. I want to comment on how obvious he is when he goes to the basement to use the phone when my mom is gone.

The question that is beginning to bubble to the surface, to knock upon the door of my consciousness, is one that I can't yet allow myself to form into audible words, but I can no longer distract myself from its whispering inquiry inside my head. "Who's your girlfriend, Dad?"

Instead, I couch my suspicion in accusation, "You know, I spend a lot of time at Sarah's house, and her dad never has to have private conversations on the phone."

"Well, if you like Sarah's dad so much, why don't you go live with them," he gets out of the car.

"You two have been gone a long time," my mother says as we enter the kitchen.

"Where's the milk?" she looks at my dad.

I stifle a mocking ha-ha-Dad-busted-big-time-busted laugh.

He storms out of the room.

I eat lunch, and then I walk to Casey's to get the milk.

Sunny Days II

The next day is glorious.

It is my first experience truly outside of the world I inhabit. It's a world where people have dreams and visions and make them come to life. I am pushed beyond all my limits, both mentally and physically. I'm challenged. And I'm pushed and challenged by people who push and challenge themselves. They are fearless in their willingness to try, knowing they will fail more times than they will succeed, and they ask no less of me. They teach what they know and they know what they teach. They are vibrant and alive, and I want to be immersed in their energy.

After an arduous class that makes my muscles ache but yearn for more; after a class that teaches me that I'm made of more than I believed when I walked in the door; after a class that makes me realize I've only scratched the surface of who I am and what I'm capable of, Alwin Nikolais sits us down and talks to the class in a way I've never heard an adult speak to kids. His compassion and understanding of where we are both as dancers and developing people is astounding. He is neither demeaning nor overly praising of our abilities. He gives us hope that life is not confined to our beginnings, and that with hard work, commitment, and integrity, we can do great things with our lives.

I am mesmerized.

His face is so warm and kind. I believe the man never frowns. The wrinkles on his face suggest a state of contentment and wonder. He so obviously loves dance and people, and that love radiates from him. He is white haired with longer, wider sideburns than I'm accustomed to seeing. They add a charm to him. His nose is slightly hooked like a parrot's beak. His hands are full of emotion, one constantly resting on his cane, which he sometimes picks up and turns into an extension of his gesticulations.

I don't want to leave him. I don't want to leave the world he has invited me into.

But the workshop comes to an end, and we must go. Before we do, Miss Milly has us thank him as a group, and we applaud. Many students just leave.

I take a deep breath. I walk up to this juggernaut of modern dance, still sitting in his chair, and say, "Thank you Mr. Nickolais."

It is a loaded four words.

He grabs my hand and puts it between both of his. "You, my dear," he says through a tender smile, "have a lot of potential."

I look him straight in the eyes. I get lost for a moment, touched and bewildered by his words. His eyes are like my grandfather's: deep and ancient. This is a man whom I believe I can have faith in.

I'm moved beyond words. I humbly smile. On the verge of tears, I leave.

Thankfully, my mother picks me up. As always, she eagerly listens to me. I share all the wonderful new things I experienced.

How it was scary at first, but then exhilarating to just let go and dive into all they asked us to do.

I don't, however, tell her or anyone about how he made me feel. And I don't tell anyone what he said.

I hold his words close inside where no one can spoil them.

Downburst II

"Get in here, Connie Sue," he calls from the bathroom.

I pull up my leotard, put on my sweats, and go to the bathroom. Oh, how I hate this. I don't hate many things, but this I hate.

I find my dad sitting on my mom's little vanity stool in front of the mirror, "Hook up my hair," he orders.

I let my ACR pass over me. I can't resist saying, "You know, I'm trying to get ready for dance class." I want to add, *I don't ask you to put my hair in a bun*, but I walk behind him instead, and lift up the back edge of his toupee.

"Well, it's just a lot easier for me, if you do it," he says.

His aunt gave my parents a sizable chunk of money for Easter last year. My father applied part of it to a high-end toupee, which requires him to go to Des Moines, to the high-end toupee salon, every so many weeks to have it washed and styled.

"You know," he reports to me and my mom shortly after getting it, "all the ladies down at the diner tell me I look just like Burt Reynolds."

He expects us to be happy for him.

I overlay the toupee edge about a half-inch into his hairline. As I'm snapping shut the seven little barrettes sewed onto his toupee into his hair, he says, "Make sure you get it nice and even, Connie Sue."

Oh, how I want to make it crooked.

I notice that he's showered and shaved, and that Old Spice once again permeates the air.

The whispering slides further up into my consciousness, "How does it feel to get him ready for a date?" it asks me.

I come downstairs to find my mother, already in her pajamas and robe, sitting in her rocking chair. Her posture and demeanor give her the appearance of warm over-kneaded dough.

Obviously in a hurry, my dad pushes me out the door.

I lose myself in class for two hours. My toes thank me when I free them from my pointe shoes at 8:45.

"How's it feel," Lori asks me.

"Great," I smile at her. "Thanks for asking."

"I've been working so hard on my fouetté turns, and tonight you made them look so easy."

"Something just clicked. At least tonight it did. I finally got the rhythm of the whip," we both laugh, and pick up our things to go.

We're the last two to leave class. We walk outside with Miss Milly, who says goodnight. Soon Lori's mom arrives, and I'm left alone standing outside the YWCA.

It's a cold fall night.

"Good night," the YWCA receptionist says to me as she crosses the street to her car. The pity I sense in her voice humiliates me. It's not the first time she's left me here.

The Y closes at 9:00 p.m., and my dance class ends at 8:45. The time is intentional. It allows for all of us to be picked up before the building closes.

As is often the case when my father picks me up, I'm left standing outside the locked building.

At the moment (and for about another month), we're down to one car. This leaves my mom stranded at home, and generally alone, for three nights out of the week. My dad almost always drives me to and from class. And during that time, he almost always goes to some secret destination that is never questioned.

I jump up and down in an attempt to warm my muscles. The cold air is not good for them, especially since I'm wet with sweat under all my layers. The barren street starts to play with my senses. The whole town feels dead, but then a car comes down the street and begins to slow down way before it's necessary. I start to plan my escape route. Cold or not, I trust my muscles and my strength. The man driving the car eyes me as he comes to the stop sign, but luckily he continues on.

Lately, my father has been very paranoid, and, in this moment, standing on this empty street corner, I'm not sure if my paranoia is legit or just a result of his.

The fact that he hasn't left the house in the last six months without a loaded Derringer in the right pocket of his pants could have something to do with it.

He obviously doesn't feel anyone is going to get him in our home, however, because he routinely leaves the loaded gun on top of the microwave next to the kitchen door. A door I can easily break into with my driver's license. I often go to bed at night thinking how lucky a random burglar would be if he chose our house.

Finally, I see our car coming down the street.

I get in the car glaring at him.

"Hi, Babe," he says.

The hairs on my sweaty neck rise. ACR. ACR.

"How was dancing?" he asks.

I don't answer. Instead, I ask, "Why can't you ever be here on time? The building closed at least fifteen minutes ago."

As par for the course, he turns it all back on me. "If you don't like it, walk your ass home. You know the way."

"Were you even at home? What were you doing?"

"That's none of your goddamn business."

"Do you really think it's fair to always leave Mom at home without a car?" I challenge.

"If you don't like it that your mom's home alone, then stay your ass home with her. Why should I have to stay with her?"

I wonder if other people would hear the petulant teenager tone in his voice like I do.

He finally starts to pull away from the curb.

"Oh, I don't know. Maybe because you're her husband? Maybe because it would be nice to spend time alone with her? Maybe because she would like to go somewhere?"

I'm fully aware of my insubordination. I'm also aware I'm pushing and pushing and pushing him at every turn to be accountable for his actions. She won't, but I will. I hate clipping in his god-forsaken toupee, and I hate being played with.

I am blown back to the present from this small digression of thought as he slams on the brakes and throws me head first into the dashboard.

"How dare you question me! If you knew what the hell I was protecting you from, you'd thank me!"

His words take a moment to register.

He leans forward in a predatory manner ready to pounce on me. He is all aggression.

His comment is such a non sequitur that I can only respond in one way.

"Just who or what are you protecting me from?"

"None of your damn business."

I might be seventeen, but I feel like I'm dealing with a juvenile delinquent and I'm the adult. I feel like I'm doing and saying what my mom just can't bring herself to do or say. It's all wrong.

So my rational mind asks to be relieved. "What do you mean? Since you're the one with the loaded gun, and I'm not with you all the time for protection, it would be helpful to know what or whom I should be looking out for," I say.

He says nothing.

He guns the car, throwing me with an equal force into the seat, flies around the corner, and speeds up the hill.

I have two thoughts on the way home. One, things are possibly worse than I expected, and two, why would my father, who believes he has to protect me, suggest I walk home alone at night from downtown?

My first thought, I'm certain, is correct, but I have no way of predicting the degree to which things are worse, and what exactly that means for my family or me. But the second point, I'm certain, is meant to scare me. It shuts me up, moves the focus from him to me, and makes me appear once again to be an ingrate not appreciating his magnanimity. But I pause… there is, after all, the Derringer.

What follows is my biggest misstep to date.

I arrive home furious. Once again, I contemplate an escape. My body reacts as if a bomb exploded at my back when he slams the door. After I recover from a near tumble, I walk into the living room. There is a hiccup in my step when I hear him put the gun on the microwave.

I consider, not for the first or last time, going to the police, but this is equally as frightening because I don't really know what my dad is involved in. Then there are those stories about his family. Something just tells me that he will be protected rather than me. I run up to my room, close the door, and violently pace the floor. I've never been so grateful for a walk-in closet. It adds at least six steps to my pacing. Fury, frustration, and the need to escape him rattle me to my core.

"Eight months," I mouth. "Eight months and you're in college, away from him."

I don't speak to him or look at him for three days. My mind is set on never talking to him again.

By the third day, tension is omnipresent in my house. My mother can't bear it, and like me, she knows my father will never apologize. In fact, at this point he would flat out deny that anything ever happened. "I'm over it," he would say, and that would be that.

While making dinner, my mother begs me to apologize to him.

"What?" I'm out of my mind. "You've got to be kidding me."

She bumbles and fumbles her way through some kind

of rhetorical nonsense about me needing to let go of what it means to apologize, and how I need to take the high ground.

"You know and I know he was in the wrong, Connie Sue." At least she is struggling a little with the absurdity of her request. "But it will break the tension if you do it," she adds.

She continues pleading with me to remove the responsibility from him. In utter disbelief, I stare at her. I don't understand her. I've never understood her when it has come to this. She is so afraid of this man that she's willing to have me do the most self-defeating, demoralizing thing any human can do: apologize to their abuser.

Then I almost laugh. Of course she is. It's what she's been doing for thirty-some years.

I am resting on the kitchen floor, something I never do, when I hear my father open the screen door. He takes off his boots and comes into the house.

I'm unable to make myself stand up.

Prostrate before him, I apologize.

I hate myself.

I am furious with my mother.

His smug face smiles down at me, and his eyes say, "Ha. Finally, I broke you."

Now I stand up.

I leave the kitchen ready to retch. I am mad beyond mad at myself for caving.

But his belief that he has broken me is an illusion. He doesn't understand that I gave in to her, not him.

Squall Line

Forming along or ahead of a cold front, a squall line can create strong straight-line winds when it is in the shape of a bow echo.

It's two days later, on a Friday night.

My mother and father are sitting across the dinner table from me. We're having dinner, chatting. We do that again now that I caved and broke the tension.

The phone rings. It's on the wall right beside my father.

My father has, for the last several months, refused to answer the phone. So, while all he needs to do is reach out to grab the phone, he instead says, "Connie Sue, answer the phone."

I do the unexpected and refuse, "You're right beside it. You answer it."

"Goddammit, I told you to answer it. Now get up and answer it."

"You're right there. You answer it."

There is a mirror that runs the length of the sink and countertops directly behind them. I watch my mother's shoulders curve inward from her back. I look at her face. She is catatonic. She has left the room.

The phone keeps ringing.

"Goddammit, answer the phone," he yells at me.

"No," I calmly say, and take a sip of my soup.

He stands up, nearly rips the phone off the wall, and says, "Hello."

He listens for several seconds before hanging up. I look to see if my mom is as perplexed as I am that he said nothing. All I see is the expression of fear frozen on her face.

I'm about to ask who it was when he slams his chair into the table.

My whole body quakes, and a ping rings through the room when I hit the side of my soup bowl with my spoon.

He starts to leave the kitchen, but then turns back, anger spewing from every pore of his body.

Up comes that stubby index finger. "If you find me dead in an alley someday, it's all," jab of the index finger, "your," another jab, "fault!" He fists his hand, and punches the air towards me. In a whirlwind of undefined rage, resentment, and paranoia, he storms out of the room.

My mom, now hyper-catatonic, has completely closed in on herself. I stare at the table, my mind scrambling to make sense of what I just heard, and, oddly, I find myself thinking about my dad's mom: the table is one of the few items from her house bequeathed to my dad after her death. I can't see the table without thinking about how she was bedridden for three days after Elvis Presley died. She was so devastated and incapacitated by his death that everyone thought for sure she was about to die as well. Clearly, the woman was in love with him. And, none of her sons could live up to him, or so it seemed from her constant praise of Elvis and the implication of his superiority over his entire gender.

For a hairsplitting second, a connection starts to form in

my brain, but like a needle being quickly dragged across an LP, the thought is rudely stopped.

He just accused me of being responsible for his possible death. I don't assume the burden that I will be, but who was on the phone? What did they say to him? What if we do find him dead in an alley somewhere?

Bow Echo III

During my senior year in high school, my dad takes a painting class. It meets one night a week. It's no surprise to me that Joe is artistic. My mother is very good at what I would call folk art, and my dad is actually a decent painter.

As winter slowly fades into spring, my father begins coming home from this class in an irrational state of agitation. On this night, I'm sitting at the kitchen table having a bowl of Frosted Flakes and toast after a long night at dance. I'm worn out.

Until . . .

BAM! The door slams behind me. Startled, I nearly tip over my bowl, and accidently land the side of my hand in my peanut butter toast.

My mom comes into the kitchen, "My God, what's wrong?"

"It's that fucking bitch, Meg Smith!" he yells, as he throws his gloves on the table.

Here we go again with this Meg Smith. For reasons unknown, she has graduated from "that goddamn Meg Smith" to "that bitch Meg Smith," to the now "fucking bitch Meg Smith," all in the course of two months.

"Oh," my mother says.

"She walks in that room, and can't sit her ass down until she makes goddamn sure everyone sees her."

He looks at us expectantly.

He gets nothing.

"The whole time I'm trying to paint, she's sucking up to the instructor."

The same expectant look.

"I don't know why you let her bother you. Just ignore her, and take the class," my mother says.

This is not what he expects or wants.

"You know, what is it with you? The woman is completely annoying, and you act like I'm the one who needs to change or something. Ignore her? Who could ignore her? I know she does it just to bother me. I can't talk to you about anything, goddammit." He throws his arms up in exasperation and storms out of the room.

Ten minutes later, he's back in the kitchen putting on his gloves.

"Where are you going, Bob?" my mom asks.

"Kiss my ass. It's none of your goddamn business." He bookends his brief stay with another slam of the door.

I ask, after our stunned silence passes, what has become a routine question of mine, "Why do you let him talk to you like that?"

She answers with what has become her routine response, "You know, Connie Sue, your father's a good man. He goes to work every day, and he always brings home his pay check." Her eyes plead with me to accept her answer.

"Who is Meg Smith anyway?" I ask. "What about her makes him so mad?"

"Come with me," my mom says.

I follow her upstairs.

"Stay here," she points to the top step.

I sit down. I watch her disappear into her room.

She comes back, sits down on the step next to me, and shows me a picture of a girl who looks to be my age with a '50s style hairdo.

"Who's this?" I take the picture from her.

"This is Meg Smith's senior-year picture."

"What are we doing with it?"

"It's in a little keepsake box of your dad's. He dated her in high school. In fact, I think he broke up with her to go with me."

I look at her. I finally understand why my father, quite emphatically, didn't want her to take the painting class with him.

Does she?

Gustnado III

I'm poised to go upstairs.

I hit the first step running, desperate to change out of my sweaty dance clothes, but I'm stopped.

My mother slams open the closet door beside the stairs. Through a series of frustrated grunts and sighs she enters into what appears to be a futile fight with the vacuum cleaner.

She wrestles its bunglesome body from the closet only to have its long handle become entangled in a knee-length winter coat. Eventually, the vacuum pulls the coat off its hanger. The hanger clangs as it hits some loose neighbors, and my mother, who never swears, says as politely-mad as possible, "Shit." She untangles her coat from the vacuum, throws it in the closet, slams the door, and begins mindlessly vacuuming.

I know she's nervous about her hysterectomy (she's had her fair share of surgeries due to kidney stones, and is scared of being put under), but this is something else.

My 'something else' suspicion is immediately corroborated when my dad comes joyfully down the steps, freshly shaved and showered, smelling of Old Spice and smiling, and asks her with no particular air of concern, "What time do you need to be at the hospital tomorrow?"

"Ten," my mother says. Her right hand violently argues with the vacuum's cord.

Take it out on him, my internal voice yells. *Not the vacuum.*

Since her surgery is at the University Hospitals in Iowa City, he says, "Well, we should leave here by eight then."

He turns to leave.

I can't take it. "Where are you going?" I ask.

"None of your damn business," he sets his beady eyes on me. Clearly, he wants me to stay out of it.

"Why are you going anywhere?" I ask, depriving him his wish.

"Who are you to ask me where the hell I'm going?" His face becomes a flame.

I pull a Bob, and turn it back on him, "She's having a major surgery tomorrow, and you're not staying home with her tonight?"

"If you're so goddamn concerned about her, you stay home with her," his words dump bile in the air. He looks and acts like such a spoiled little brat. I feel like I'm fighting with Sam over who's going to take out the garbage.

My mother throws the vacuum cord on the floor. She is crying.

"Don't worry about it, Connie Sue. It's okay," her strained words sound somewhat feigned to me. She looks, and acts, like someone who believes everything is beyond her control. Or, as a slippery little thought that emerges in my head suggests, she wants *me* to believe everything is.

"No, Mom. It's not okay. Nothing about this is okay." Why won't she stick up for herself? Ever!

"If he doesn't want to be home with me, then I'm not going to make him stay here," she says. There is something so pathetic in her tone, something needy, yet claiming not to be needy, something that makes me want to shake her until she wakes up.

My father, with a victorious smile, says to me like an eight-year-old who just got his way through unscrupulous means, "See, she doesn't want me here anyway." His mocking air taints the house as he leaves.

My parents go to Iowa City the next day. I've never been so thankful for a history test in my life.

I struggle to find a way to understand her. My father protects nothing about any of us, least of all her. He does not inspire trust or love, but rather fear and suspicion. In fact, anytime he is trying to make you feel safe, it's only to set you up and then exploit any vulnerability your hope allowed you to expose. Then he comes in for the kill. He transfers vulnerability into gullibility, and once again, any pain or hurt feelings you might have are your fault for trusting him and opening up. You're the idiot. You're the fool. And, therefore, you deserved to be used. But as he always makes clear, it is my mother, Fran, Sam, Joe, teacher, preacher, or best friend who does this to me, not him. And how dare I accuse him of doing something so hurtful and low.

What I don't understand is how she doesn't see this. The list of examples demonstrating just this one dynamic with my father is longer than all of my Christmas lists combined (and I'm talking several pages by this point). Her tenacity to cling to denial is impressive. And mind numbing. And staggering. And infuriating.

I'm stuck at home with him for three days.

On the second day, I ride to Iowa City with him to visit my mom. The car ride is excruciating.

"You know what Joe's problem is, Connie Sue?"

I say nothing.

He offers his unsolicited answer, "He's a taker. He's a user. He doesn't care about anyone but himself." (Uh, that would be you, Dad.)

"You know what the problem with Sam is, Connie Sue? He's not as dumb as everyone thinks. He's a con man. He's a liar. He couldn't tell the truth if his life depended on it. Everything he does is to either use you or get your money." (Uh, yeah, I'm going to have to go with you again on this one.)

"And, Fran, you know what her problem is, Connie Sue? She's a giver. She would give the shirt off her back. Problem is, she'd give it to a mangy dog who's going to use her. She's so dumb and desperate that she allows herself to be used. Sam and Joe use her the most. (Uh, again, I think that's you.)

"But your mother. That's where they all get it from. She's so manipulative. You know the only reason she tells you she loves you is to make you think I don't. And she's so god...damn... controlling," he draws the words out, and allows his contempt to fill the spaces between.

"She thinks she's right about everything. I can't stand going anywhere with her. She can't walk in a room without everybody stopping her to say hi. You know, Connie Sue, that's the only reason she does things like be the president of the PTA, or run her business. All these women she's helped to start their own businesses. Boy, does she have them fooled. They think she cares about them, but your mother just cares about herself. She just does it all for the attention. (Wow! That's some textbook projection right there.)

And, if Sam, or Joe, or Fran would've been in the car instead of me, they would've heard, "You know what's wrong with Connie Sue?"

What are the things he uses to poison their love for me?

I don't respond. Eventually, he shuts up, putting an end to the torture.

My dad receives the discharge information for the following day from the nurse while I visit with my mom. I wonder why she even wants to come home. She's not going to be allowed to properly recover. The emotional stress alone disallows that. But she does come home, and life moves through my senior dance recital and graduation. Both events seem to lack the ritual and significance I had hoped for.

Two days after I graduate, we all head east for Joe's wedding. It, too, lacks any substance. The event has no teeth. There is a desire for his wedding to have meaning and depth, but it can't. Our family is already falling apart, rendering it impossible to carry forward something intact that offers a foundation of love and support to a fledgling couple.

EF-3

Severe in its destructive force, and packing winds of between 136 and 165 miles per hour, a tornado of this scale can tear roofs off buildings and cause major damage to structures. Cars can be tossed in the air, trees can be uprooted, and trains can be derailed.

"C'mon," she says, hanging up the phone. "That was the Dittmers. They said the police phoned them, and the car's been parked on Jackson Street for a couple of hours. We have twenty minutes to move it or they'll tow it."

I think for a minute. Why were the Dittmers phoned? And then I remember. My parents recently bought the car from them (a Cadillac DeVille that my parents would've never been able to afford new), and the title hasn't been transferred to us yet.

"Jackson Avenue?" I say, confused. There's nothing there. It's just a semi-circle street off Pennsylvania Avenue. I thought it was used for turning around. Why would our car, which my dad left in over two hours ago, be parked there? Where is he?

"Sam. Get down here," she yells upstairs.

We get in the Buick, and my mom heads up Locust Street. She explains one of us will have to drive the Buick back, since she'll have to drive the Cadillac home.

It's a dark mid-July night. All the summer bugs are singing, the humidity is thankfully low, and while it's not the case, I feel like there is not a single soul about. We come up the hill, round the corner, and there, appearing abandoned, is our/Dittmer's car sitting in the middle of Jackson Street, which is no more than a narrow gravel path. To its front is Pennsylvania Avenue. To its back is a steep hill with a small neighborhood nestled below in its valley.

My mom pulls up beside the Cadillac, gets out, and says, "Go straight home."

Sam gets in the driver's seat, and I roll myself up and over to the front passenger seat. Once my mom starts the car, we leave for home.

Sam turns into our drive, but my mom turns up the alley across the street.

"What's she doing?" Sam asks.

"I have no idea."

Then, she comes around the front of Old Lady Carlson's house, turns up Locust Street off Ash, drives up over the curb, and pulls the car as far into the backyard as she can. I'm surprised by how far that actually is, considering the DeVille is the size of a boat.

Having executed this brave bold maneuver, she gets out of the car. In a panic, she orders us to go in the house.

"I swear I saw someone coming out from the bushes as I was leaving. I know it was your father."

I can tell by the wringing of her hands and the nervous shifting of her eyes that fear has replaced any pride she might have felt.

None of us knew what was coming.

"Did you hear that?" I say, and rush over to the dining room window.

My father is leaning over the passenger side of a green Pontiac, saying something to the woman driver who just dropped him off.

We all see this.

The car drives away, and it's obvious that he is not coming in the house, but going to the car. It is also obvious from his gait that he is furious.

My mom does another brave, bold thing: she rushes outside.

Sam and I run up to my bedroom. We dash to my windows (thankfully, they are open), and watch the scene unfold below us in the backyard.

"Bob," my mother says. I don't recognize the strength in her voice.

"You are not taking that car anywhere!" she says this as he reaches towards the door handle.

I give her credit. She is out there alone, and I know she's scared. She's giving it the best shot I have witnessed to date.

And then...

"Who the fuck do you think you are, you goddamn bitch? You can't tell me what to do. If I want to take this fucking car, I will goddammit!"

"The police called Dittmers and said they were going to tow the car. I didn't know why it was on Jackson. You said you were going to the Club. They told me they were going to tow it if it wasn't gone in twenty minutes," she finishes with diminished strength. "What was I supposed to do?"

"You goddamn lying son of a bitch. The police didn't call here."

"No, Bob, they didn't! They called Dittmers, and Dittmers called here," her embarrassment by this fact is unmistakable.

He continues annihilating her character. He is so loud that it makes me think he is putting on a show.

"We have to do something," I say to Sam. "He's out of control. Who knows what he's going to do?"

"Should we call the police?"

"I don't know." As is always the case, I'm leery of that option.

"Fran?" Sam belts out.

"She won't believe us, or she'll say it's no big deal."

I think for a moment, "I'm calling Joe."

Luckily, he answers on the second ring. I explain to him what has happened, and just as I finish explaining I hear my dad yell, "You better get out of the way!"

He slams the door and floors the car in reverse leaving ruts in the yard as he flies backwards into the street.

I'm right by the window. Joe hears all of this.

"I'm not letting us stay here Joe. He's absolutely nuts. There is no telling what he'll do if he comes back. I'm making her go to Fran's."

Joe says he and Kathy will be down first thing in the morning.

I call Fran and tell her we're coming out to spend the night. "I'll explain when we get there," I add.

The tone of my voice is obvious, and without question she says, "Okay."

Sam and I run down to the kitchen. I'm not sure how my mom is holding herself in a vertical position, but she is. Her face is drained of its color. Her eyes show a soul wounded beyond repair.

She temporarily resists my plan until I say, "What are you going to do if he comes back?"

Her eyes widen. "Go get your stuff," she says. Flooded with urgency, she pushes us towards the stairs.

I run up to my room and pack an overnight bag. As I run out to the stairway, the gun cabinet stops me.

Terror overwhelms me.

He's been outed. Not only to my mom, but to the Dittmers as well. His behavior in the backyard suggests that he's out-of-his-head mad.

And it's not his fault. He made that very clear just moments before leaving, "If you would've left the son-of-a-bitchin' car alone, everything would be okay. This is all your goddamn fault."

There is no way to predict his behavior.

I send a seeking hand under my bed, locate my red duffle bag, run back to the cabinet, and open its never-locked door. Quickly, but with care and caution (oddly my father has taught me how to dismantle, clean, and reassemble his rifles, and I have done target shooting with his automatic), I take out his two handguns. One is in a holster attached to a fully loaded ammunition belt. I take out all the boxes of bullets in the bottom of the cabinet. The un-holstered pistol is loaded. I push out the chamber, empty the bullets into the bag, and then carefully put the pistol in my bag. Since I have all the ammunition, I leave the rifles in the rack, hoping that will be enough to make it look normal.

As I zip up the bag my reality gets all messed up because this surely isn't real. Is it? I'm just paranoid? Right? This isn't my life?

All I know is he's out of his head, and he can't lie his way out of this one. No one knows what he will do.

We spend the night at Fran's. I don't tell her I have his guns with me. There is some conversation about what to do, but nothing is talked about in any concrete terms. Eventually, exhaustion forces sleep.

The next morning is different. My mom is weary. She's unable to act as if nothing happened last night. This is good. Now I'm certain my mother will leave him.

We change, and tentatively head for home. This is all new territory. He is outed, and I believe that this Pandora's box can't be closed.

The house is still and hollow when I enter. The morning sun fills the rooms with brilliant light. I walk into the living room to find him waking up on the sofa. He is toupeeless. He sits up, and with both hands shoves the bottom of his white terry-cloth bathrobe between his bare legs. He looks like a child who is wondering if he is in trouble or not.

I can't look at him. I go upstairs.

"You don't have to talk to me if you don't want to, and I don't care what you think about me, but I'm still your father, goddammit," he says to my back.

I stop and turn to him. Struck by the fact that this is his response after his actions last night, I wonder what on earth he means by the word father.

Without responding, I turn and go upstairs. I walk by the gun cabinet. My breath is arrested, and I gasp. I hadn't thought about putting them back in the cabinet with him home. What if he comes upstairs and catches me doing it? How do I explain to a madman why I took the guns?

I decide to hide them for the time being. I tuck my loaded duffle bag under my bed and pray that I will be presented with a safe time to return them.

I don't come back downstairs until I hear Joe's voice.

I stop on the landing.

Joe is on the sofa next to my dad. Joe rests his elbows on his knees. He is slumped over rubbing his balding head. My father still has his hands between his bare legs. He has a scared but expectant look on his face. His jig is up, and he doesn't know what that means.

"Why was the car there?" Joe presses.

"Buck met me there, and took me to the Club," my father says, as if his friends always meet him in strange places and he abandons our car to go with them.

"Dad," Joe says. "You don't expect me to buy that. Why wouldn't you just meet him there?"

"I don't care whether you do or not. It's the truth," he says. He never looks at Joe.

"Well, then who was the woman who brought you home? Connie Sue said there was no mistaking that it was a woman."

My father pulls a non sequitur on Joe.

"No one understands me," he pouts.

"What don't we understand, Dad," Joe says. "Tell me. Please. Because I really do want to understand."

"I can't. You wouldn't understand anyway."

Joe, in utter futility, slaps his hands on his forehead. Once again, my father refuses any ownership of his actions. We just don't understand. How pathetic.

My mother walks in the room. Her face is so war-torn I barely recognize her. She stands silently pleading before him. She's waiting for something, anything, from him to show the slightest bit of remorse. Any sign of acknowledgment that it was embarrassing for her when Dittmers called. And who was the woman in the car?

My dad sits on the sofa awaiting sentencing. I'm certain if she told him to get out, he would. In this case, he doesn't have a leg to stand on. He might blame all of us on the way out, but he has no defense. All the power is in her hands.

All the power *is* in her hands. Why then won't she call him out? Why will she not take advantage of this opportunity? What in this whole universe is she waiting for?

She was so brave last night. She's been given visual proof. What more does she need?

Trapped in the middle of their staredown, I wait. My gaze goes from one to the other, like I'm watching a tennis match.

Is he going to acknowledge what he did? Is she going to draw a line and kick him out? The battle of their two wills is agonizing. Our entire family is stuck in this incorrigible competition of wills they are waging.

And then, my mother, without saying a word, turns and walks out of the room. Just like that, it's all over. Just like that, in a moment absent any true communication (which should have happened privately between the two of them to begin with), it dissolves into an unresolved metaphorical puddle in the middle of the room.

Two weeks later, life becomes a new normal because things are never quite the same after this event. It's not talked about, which is normal. Everyone acts like the tension will pass, which is normal. But the tension takes on a low-level hum. It is now omnipresent. The tension exists whether my father is in the house or not, and this isn't normal.

And, there's something else: an alteration in the energy. I search all my senses in an attempt to define this change. There was something in that moment when he was on the sofa and she was standing there. Something that suggested the future could be altered, right then and there: that the tornado of my dreams could be averted. That this was her last chance to see the tornado, to act.

But once again, she chose not to look, and I fear the winds will begin to blow.

I run upstairs to use the bathroom. I see myself in the glass front of the gun cabinet. I look at my watch. It's 4:45. I have about twenty-five minutes before he'll be home from work. I quickly go to the bathroom, and then retrieve my duffle.

Careful to put everything back just as it was, I wonder if he has noticed the near-empty cabinet. It seems strange that over two weeks time he wouldn't. It also seems strange that he wouldn't want to know where they were if he did notice.

Suddenly, I'm wracked by the absurdity of this moment. Here I am, putting guns and ammunition that I hid under my bed for fear my father would do what, kill all of us in a crazed man's rampage? Actually, I don't know exactly what I did think he would do, but I am and was certain that a crazy man and a gun is not a good combination. I still feel like I did the right thing. But what an awful right thing to feel one must do.

I count up to five on my hand. Five weeks, and then I'm gone to college.

I am somewhere in the living room. My family is scattered about the house. I look out the opened front door. I see a tornado headed right for the house. It is unmistakable that it will hit our house. I frantically run from person to person, telling them I see the tornado.

"We have to get to the basement." Each word shortens my breath further.

Everyone ignores me or mocks me.

"Really. It's there. Just come in the living room, and look out the front door. It's headed straight for the house."

No one will listen. No one will look.

I continue to run from person to person, begging them, "If you don't believe me, go look for yourself!"

I'm shouting. I'm imploring. I'm pulling on clothes. I'm trying to turn my mother's head around. If she would only look!

I run to the living room. The tornado is moments away from hitting the house. I try one last time to get everyone to go to the basement with me.

Now everything in the dream is arrested. I am the only thing animate other than the tornado. While it is no longer moving forward, it continues to spin in place.

I walk to my brothers. They are frozen in a game of Monopoly. Sam's arm is extended. In his hand is gold and tan money. Joe is celebrating: he is in mid-action of pumping his fists up and down.

I go in the kitchen.

My mother is hunched over whatever she is chopping up for dinner. With her body frozen like this, I notice her shoulders are elevated and rounded. She clenches her shoulders inward. Her neck disappears into her shoulders towards her ears. She white-knuckles the knife, and her elbows squeeze into her sides. She looks like what she is, a woman fighting to hold it together.

My father is sitting in the lounger reading the paper, conveniently unavailable to everyone.

I find Franny brooding in her room.

Strange, Fran and Joe don't live at home anymore, but they're here in my dream.

I tell myself that I love them all. And I do. But I know the tornado is real. I trust my judgment.

I look.

I see.

I believe.

And, intuitively, I know this dream is about them not wanting to see, them not wanting to believe and how their denial of what is right in front of them will so dramatically impact my life.

I feel so sad for all of us. My father has made feeling, and definitely expressing, fear a major character flaw, while at the same time imbuing us with large amounts of it.

When I realize I have done everything I can to make them look, and that I cannot do a thing to change their unwillingness, full motion is restored to the dream. The wind and the rain pummel the house, the tornado continues on its forward surge, and I run towards the basement door just as the vacuum created by the tornado begins tugging at me. I fling the door open and run down the basement stairs. I get myself under the steps, tucking my knees tight under my chin. I forget my fear of spiders and bugs that are surely creeping around in the small corners of the underbelly of the stairs.

I curl up in the tightest ball I can, and cover my ears. The noise is unbearable. Pas de bourrée, glissade, chassé, jeté, I repeat over and over again. I have no success distracting myself from the knowledge that my home and my family are being destroyed. Then, suddenly, it's all over.

I know I have survived.

I'm certain I am alone.

Bow Echo IV

I sit across the table from my mom.

My dad and Lydia (my mom's lifelong best friend, someone I've never fully trusted) sit across from one another. My father looks at Lydia. His pulled brow suggests annoyance; her lifted brow suggests a collusion that makes me very uncomfortable. I look around the crowded restaurant at Field's hopeful we can shop some before heading back to Lydia's daughter's condo.

"How did the audition go, Connie Sue?" Lydia asks.

"Well," I pause.

"They really gave her a raw deal," my dad interrupts, and highjacks my story.

My parents brought me over to Chicago to audition for a summer gig at Disney. Upon walking in the audition hall, I spied three upperclassmen dancers from ISU. Being a freshman, I hadn't felt comfortable asking to ride along with them, but now as my dad tells his exaggerated version of my false persecution, I wish I had risked the rejection.

It was such a simple combination: just a short 16-measure tap dance. I knew all the steps, and the tempo was surprisingly reasonable. I was third to audition in the first group of 100 dancers. We auditioned in pairs. When called, we stood about five feet in front of the judges' table. The four judges sat with note pads and pencils at the ready. We stood, confidently still while they scrutinized everything about us, and then the choreographer said, "5-6-7-8."

I was doing great until somehow I got on the wrong foot in the middle of a time step. I stupidly tried to correct my mistake, and in so doing lost my focus.

Then, the female judge looked to the man at her right and said, "She's really good, if she would just get on the correct foot."

With that, it all fell apart. I just wanted to finish the combo and get out of the room. I was so mad at myself, and embarrassed. One of the other dancer's facial expressions confirmed my feeling: I was nailing it, and totally blew it.

I didn't make the first round of cuts.

I fled the room in humiliation.

My parents were sitting in the back row of the auditorium behind three guys assigned to the second grouping. I threw myself in the seat next to my dad. I put my feet on top of the chair in front of me, and hid my face in my knees.

"What's wrong," my dad asked.

"Nothing, I just want to go."

"You look very upset, Connie Sue," my mom said. She leaned past my dad accidentally hitting the shoulder of one of the guys.

Why did my parents pick this moment to notice my mood?

"Did they do something to you?" my dad's accusation turned the heads of the three guys in front of us.

I didn't, I couldn't, respond to such an absurd question.

"What did they do to you?" he demanded.

"Nothing, okay. They didn't do anything to me. I blew the audition, okay. I just want to go."

"Wow, is it that hard?" one guy asked.

"No, it's not hard at all, if you know how to tap. I just blew it, and I'm really mad at myself."

"Oh, man. I'm really sorry," another offered.

"Thanks," I tried to smile.

Then my mom, "You're a good dancer, Connie Sue. I can't believe you would mess up. What did they do?"

God bless these three guys. First, they understood what blowing an audition means, and they were truly empathetic; second, they knew the last thing anyone wants in this moment is to be with their parents.

"It really is easy. Good luck, guys," I said, and left.

But it was the taxi driver who brought us to Field's who redeemed my day. As soon as we were in his car, I started to cry. The release, after all, was imminent. Seated directly behind him, we could see each other in the rearview mirror.

"Ah, just come from an audition?" the driver lifted his chin and looked at me in the mirror. He looks like a grandpa LeVar Burton. His deep brown eyes are intense and kind. They suggest age and wisdom, and like my grandfather's they have the quality of deep long rivers.

"Yeah," I said with a shrug.

My father started a similarly twisted explanation of the events to the one he is now reveling in telling to Lydia.

When he finally shut up, I looked up at the driver, and said, "I just blew it, that's all. I got on the wrong foot and messed myself up." And then, a mistake, "One of the judges said I looked good, if I could just get on the right foot."

"Why is a judge talking while you are trying to audition?" my mother asked, happy to find a place for blame.

"Because she's a judge, and that's what judges do," I said.

"Well, how loud was she talking?" My father's accusatorial tone embarrassed me.

"Not loud at all. She didn't have to be." Another mistake, "I was only about five feet away from the judges' table.

"Well, it seems to me they would put you further back so you wouldn't be distracted by them."

I quietly cried as the taxi driver maneuvered the streets of downtown Chicago. Something about my parents' reaction made me feel like I was being robbed of my experience. Why couldn't it just be that I failed? Why couldn't they just pat me on the back? Why couldn't they say something like the important thing was that I tried, and I'd do better next time?

And then, a wave of nausea washed over me. If we weren't in public, my father wouldn't be acting like I was a victim. He would want to know what I did to screw up and possibly use it as an excuse to remind me of all the money spent on my lessons.

"Hey," LeVar said to me.

I looked toward the mirror and uncontrollably smiled when I saw his kind face smiling at me. "You know I drive a lot of people around after they audition here in Chicago, and you know what?"

Between his eyes and his deep, warm voice, I could have looked and listened to him forever. He felt like a lullaby.

"What?"

"I can tell by looking at you that you're gonna be famous one day. You might have blown this audition, but I just know you won't the next."

"Thanks," I said, and began to cry for an entirely different reason.

Unaware of where my dad is in explaining to Lydia my audition experience, I interrupt him.

I look at Lydia, "I blew the audition, and I was mad at myself. The dance was super easy, I got on the wrong foot, and I couldn't straighten myself out."

It dawns on me that had I not reacted to messing up, the judges would have never known. They were all only looking at my face. I could see them perfectly: their faces smiling. They were being entertained, and none of them were even looking at my audition partner. It was my reaction to my mistake that made them look at my feet: tip to self to keep in my hip pocket.

"Oh, sorry to hear it," Lydia offers, and pats my shoulder.

"Thanks."

"Lydia, do you know where the restrooms are?" my mom asks.

Lydia directs her. They are on a wall straight behind her.

I watch my mother move around the crowded tables. When she is halfway there, my father startles me with a sigh that is full of disgust.

"I just don't know how much longer I can take this, Connie Sue" he says my name, but is looking at Lydia.

"I understand," she returns.

What does she understand?

"What can't you take much longer?" I ask, figuring the attention had been focused on me long enough.

"Your mother, Connie Sue," he looks me in the eye.

Before I say anything, I search the last two days in an attempt to identify the source of his annoyance.

"What are you talking about?" my audition is a long lost memory, and has been trumped.

"Well, you know what she's like. Even Lydia knows what she's like," he gestures towards her.

I glare at her because it's now clear they have been talking behind my mother's back.

"No Dad, I don't. You'll need to be a bit more specific," I say. My tone is that of a peer, not a child.

"Her constant nagging. I suppose you can't know what it's like to be married. To always have your spouse wanting to know where you're going, and when you'll be home."

I'm stunned speechless.

"Your mother is just too perfect, Connie Sue. She expects way too much of everyone," Lydia says.

Who are you? How dare you? I want to ask.

"I just don't know how much longer I can put up with this," my dad reiterates.

"I can understand, Bob," Lydia says with conspiratorial compassion.

Before I can say anything, my mom returns.

With such innocence, she sits down and says, "What a beautiful bathroom."

Both my father and Lydia sigh and sit back. How does someone saying something so innocuous create such disgust?

I don't eat.

Not surprisingly, no one notices that.

I can't handle my mother's naïve, happy approach to the rest of the trip. How has she not sensed their disgust? Why hasn't she asked what's wrong?

We spend the day shopping on Michigan Avenue. My father and Lydia roll their eyes at my mother's back every time she speaks, no matter the subject or context.

We spend the night at Lydia's daughter's and head back to Iowa the next morning.

"Thanks so much for letting us stay here," my mother says to Jess.

Jess, whose genuine affection for my mom is apparent, gives her a big hug, "It's my pleasure." She extends a specific invitation to my mom to come and visit anytime she likes.

"I'm really sorry things didn't turn out so good," she says to me.

"Thanks," I say.

The ride back is unbearable.

My dad and Lydia dominate the conversation. She is in the backseat with me. I look out the window to keep from vomiting. I never want to be in her presence again. How dare she call my mom her friend.

While I can't determine the full implication of my father's conversation in Field's (Is he going to leave? Are he and Lydia having an affair?), I become determined to never blow an audition again.

I close my eyes. I see the taxi driver, chin lifted, looking in the rearview mirror. "I'm certain you're gonna be famous," he says. I fall asleep envisioning myself performing on the world's largest stage.

My dad pulls up to my dorm. I'm out of the car before he comes to a complete stop. Relieved to be free of them, I take a deep breath. The cold air fills my lungs and revives me. At least I have two weeks before break to live in my world without them. I'm always more relaxed in their absence.

My tornado dreams come fast and furious. I seldom go a night without finding myself frantically trying to get everyone to look out the window before I head to the basement alone, praying that everyone is okay, and that I'll be okay.

Our house is always completely demolished. I emerge from the basement to find nothing and no one. Debris is everywhere. The maple tree is twisted and uprooted. I start walking away from the yard with no clear destination in mind, trusting that I will be shown the way. I'm flooded in sunlight, and awash with a sense that in the end everything will be fine.

Gustnado IV

It's finals week. My bliss is rendered impossible to hold on to. The phone rings.

"Hey, are you alone?" Fran says, sitting in her kitchen back in Forked River.

"Yeah. Why?" It's a question I'm not sure I want answered.

I love Fran for her frankness, but it's generally coupled with a harsh tone that makes me wonder what she is so angry about. Today, she sounds a little pissy, but cuts to the chase, which I appreciate.

"I'm just calling because your father (It's never Dad or Mom. It's always your dad or your mom, or Bob and Arlene) told me last night that he is leaving your mom."

She hasn't suggested I sit down, but I drop into my desk chair. The implication of my father's conversation over lunch in Chicago is no longer a mystery.

I don't speak. I need clarification, but I'm too nervous to ask for it. Do I really want to know? I've wanted them divorced for years, but on my mother's terms, not his. Something about him leaving her conjures up C-3P0 in my head, and I lip, "We're doomed."

"He says he's gonna leave before Christmas, but I don't really buy it. I think in the end, he's too much of a chickenshit. I just thought I should let you know, though."

I muster, "Thanks. I'm glad you did," but a huge part of me wishes she wouldn't have. The information is all too vague, too heavy.

When is he leaving, exactly? Why did he tell Fran behind our mother's back? Is she the only one he told?

We hang up.

I sit alone, weary in the silence.

Calm Before the Storm

As a storm builds, it pulls warm, moist air upwards through the clouds.
This air then shoots out over the top, and travels back down. On its
downward journey, the air becomes warmer, drier, and calmer,
stabilizing the air on the ground.

It's Thursday night. Three days after Fran's call.

I have a final tomorrow morning at 8:00. Campus is virtually empty. My roommate left late Wednesday, so I have been alone to study, which I haven't done. Joe and my dad are driving up in the morning to take me home. Does Joe know? I can't imagine Christmas: all of us together after the events of this past summer, my trip to Chicago, which I've told no one about, and now Fran's call. I don't want to go home, but I have nowhere I can hide.

I fall into a deep sleep. In my dream, which I cannot readily identify as a dream because it is so real, I bolt upright in bed with that desperate sense that a tornado is coming. I'm on the fifth floor of my near-empty dorm building unaware in this moment of where the basement door is, or if the dorm even has a basement.

And then terror from the most unexpected source sends me, feet pushing hard against my bed, into a ball in the corner. I try to press my back through the wall so I can run.

A pale yellow curtain, lit by the parking lot outside, covers the one window in my room. Pacing back and forth in front of the window is a man carrying a rifle, poised to pull it into place to spec a shot at any moment. Backlit from the parking lot lights, I know this shadowed, imposing figure is looking for me. I know he knows I'm inside.

He stops.

He turns towards the window.

He pulls the gun into position, and points it directly at me.

Knowing it's not real, but needing to escape the dream, I start screaming to myself to wake up.

I bolt up in my bed, screaming, sweating and shaking.

This is my first gun dream.

My clock says 6:15. I take a shower and pack my bag for home. At 7:15, I'm one of twenty people sitting in the commons having breakfast. It's my last doughnut for a while, and that is probably a good thing. While my professors aren't neurotic about weight, we were encouraged to pay attention to our eating habits over the holiday.

I sigh. My last final is now over. I try to relax as I walk back to my dorm. It begins to snow, adding to the quiet of the deserted campus. I tell myself everything is going to be okay. It's Christmas after all, and he hasn't left. I cut to the side of Curtis Hall towards Ross Hall, the quickest route back to my dorm.

Then I stop.

I stand dead still. The snow is falling to the ground in beautiful, big flakes. I watch two people coming toward me. The snow, swirling in all directions, blurs their images.

Our proximity wanes, and suddenly, I'm thrust into the grips of terror.

One of the men has the same posture and energy of the man from my dream.

I feel like a small animal exposed on the blanket of snow.

My predator is approaching.

My eyes dart about, looking for a place I can hide.

"Connie Sue," Joe calls out.

I gasp. I'm totally freaked out. They appear to emerge from behind a scrim.

My dad's demeanor changes from the man of my dream. He smiles and removes a hand from his pocket long enough to wave at me.

I haven't seen him since Chicago, and for the umpteenth time in my life, I never want to see him again. And, for the umpteenth time in my life, my heart breaks with that realization. This is not how one is supposed to feel about a parent.

"I'm all packed," I say as naturally as I can muster. My voice echoes off Ross Hall.

"Great," my dad says.

"How'd your final go?" Joe asks.

"Oh, you know. It's a final. I can't really say. Right now, I'm just glad to have them all over."

I sit in the backseat. Somehow Joe is capable of making conversation with him.

I can't figure Joe out. He's like my mom. He acts oblivious. Has he already forgotten the events of this past summer? Maybe Fran didn't say anything to him? I haven't said a thing to anyone about Chicago.

I'm unnerved by how not unnerved everyone continues to be around him.

My dad is unusually relaxed and jolly during Christmas. This creates a weird sense that perhaps he has had a change of heart. I can't believe that he has, but I also can't explain his actions.

It reminds me of days at the Ike's. We feel like a family. We feel, and act, like everything is okay. Everyone, including me, takes a huge sigh of relief. I don't know this man, but he is nice, seems to enjoy all of us, and doesn't take a verbal dump on anyone clear through New Year's. We celebrate his birthday on the first, and two days later, I'm back at ISU for rehearsals.

I'm amazed at how much better I dance. I feel like burdens have been lifted. I feel normal. We've always had large Christmases in my family, due in part to my mom, but this was different. This didn't have the illusory feel to it that others have had.

Maybe Fran was right. He is too much a chickenshit, and maybe his actions are a reflection of the fact that he's decided to stay and make the best of it.

EF-4

With winds ranging from 166 to 200 miles per hour, the level of destruction is devastating from a tornado this powerful. Large homes are completely leveled, cars are thrown, and large objects can become small missiles when thrown by the high winds. The area of the debris field increases.

I look at my watch: 1:45. I finish my reading just in time to make a mad dash to my 2:00 class.

The phone rings.

"Hello."

"Hi, Babe," my ACR goes off.

"Hey, Dad, what's up?" I ask, while trying to put on my coat.

"Well, I have something to tell you."

I know immediately what it is. I take off my coat and sit down. I move away from the mirror. I don't want to watch myself go through this.

"What's that?" I say with negative curiosity.

As if he were saying, "I'm going out to shovel," he says, "I've decided to leave your mom."

I say nothing. I assume since he called to tell me, he's going through with it this time.

"I just can't take it anymore, Connie Sue. You're mother is just too difficult to deal with."

"Oh," is all I can say. I want to ask, how is the person who never questions anything and who takes care of all the responsibilities in the house the difficult one to deal with?

I tune out all his justifications and character attacks against my mom, and then, "You know, Connie Sue, I'm through with the obligations of parenthood."

"Excuse me?" I'm not sure I hear him correctly.

"I'm through with the obligations of parenthood. I've been held back by you kids and your mother for far too long. I really think I deserve a lot more than this. I could've done a lot more, if it weren't for all of you."

Now with ire, "Excuse me? You could've done more?"

"Well you should understand better than anyone."

"Huh?"

"Well, you're in college. You get to do whatever you want. Whenever you want. You know what it's like to be free. I deserve that same thing."

I am in utter disbelief. My fifty-five-year-old father just compared our situations as if we were peers.

What *Twilight Zone* episode am I experiencing here?

"Yeah, Dad. But I'm eighteen. I'm not married with four kids. It's what I'm supposed to be doing right now."

"Well, you'll understand, when you're married and have kids."

"No," I say with more certainty and maturity than seems possible for my age, "I won't. Not if what you are insinuating is that I would tell my child that I deserve better than her, and I'm done being her parent. No Dad, I will not *ever* understand that comment."

I look at my watch: 2:00. Now I'm really pissed. I'm missing my favorite class. I have no idea how I will even begin to explain this absence to my professor.

My father informs me, with so much magnanimity dripping from his tongue, "I'm going to make sure you and your mom are taken care of. I'm going to let her keep the house, and my attorney told me the other day that now that I'm divorcing your mother, you can get Pell Grants."

Before I can wrap my head around this, he drops in an oh-by-the-way way, "There's a woman I've been talking to. She's been very supportive of me while I've been going through all of this. She's a really nice person, Connie Sue, and I think the two of you would get along. I'd like you to meet her."

I don't even have to ask. I suddenly know it's not Lydia, but Meg, the woman from the art class.

"No, Dad, I don't want to meet your mistress!"

Then he blows.

"I wouldn't walk across the goddamn street for a piece of ass."

"And, by the way, what is it you're going through?" I add.

He tells me he's leaving my mom, and I will have to deal with it however I do because he's not responsible for my feelings. He again states how deserving he is of a better life and then, more or less, hangs up on me.

Two days later, on Valentine's Day 1985, the spring of my freshman year in college, my father leaves my mother. Meg leaves her husband on the same day. Together, in what I'm sure is a very celebratory mood, they leave town for a romantic Valentine's Day rendezvous.

Four days later, I come home from class to find my mother,

who has gotten the RA to let her in my room, curled up in the fetal position on my bed, crying.

I find I have no tolerance for this. I try to be understanding and compassionate, but I just can't figure out why she is so upset. The man has been nothing but an asshole for my whole life, and a class-A one for the last three years. Why is she acting like she's just been used, taken advantage of, and then dumped by someone who was actually worthy? She had, after all, plenty of opportunities, and reasons, to leave before this.

I sit down on my roommate's bed, "Mom, I'm a little confused. How can you be so upset by this? How can you be surprised? Especially after this past summer?"

"I don't know, I guess it's because I'm going to be alone," she says maintaining her fetal position. "I just didn't think he would really leave and throw it all away."

The combination of shock and complaint in her voice is stunning.

My mind is like a scattered jigsaw puzzle because all I can ask under my breath is, *Why were you waiting for him to leave? He's treated you like shit. He threw it all away years ago, and then shat all over it. And now, he leaves you after how many times the universe has tried to get you to open your eyes, and you're confused and hurt by his actions, while lying in an infantile puddle on my bed? Why aren't you mad?*

I say, instead, "But Mom, you've been alone for the last," I throw my hands up in the air and roll my eyes trying to calculate the number, "God knows how many years. Now at least he won't be there shoving it in your face. How does this not bring you relief?"

"You just can't understand, Connie Sue," she says. She looks at me with the eyes of a teenager who's just been dumped by her first love.

I sit looking at her. All I can think is, this is going to be a bigger mess than I expected because, right or wrong, she is wounded. But, I think, for the wrong reasons. She is reacting as someone who had a happy marriage, and truly didn't see this coming. She is reacting as if my father never did anything to betray his true character.

And this has danger written all over it.

My nightmares are now split between tornado dreams and gun dreams. Always something or someone is chasing me. The tornado, however, is trying to tell me something and force me towards action, whereas the person in the gun dreams is stalking me to silence me and force me towards inaction. Both fill me with dread and deep anxiety as they both suggest that if I don't act with readiness and prudence, I will die.

Microburst I

There is a possible threat to life and property when there is a downdraft (sinking air) in a thunderstorm. These downdrafts, known as microbursts, are not as widely recognized as tornadoes, but in some instances, they can cause comparable, and even worse damage, than lower-rated tornadoes.

I'm home over spring break.

My dad picks me up for lunch. The meal is awkward to say the least.

As he's dropping me off, he begins to tell me how hard all of this is on him, "You know, I'm staying down at Buck's."

"But what did you expect? You're the one who chose to leave."

Somehow my question renders me incapable of understanding his situation, and thus, I am an ingrate.

Two days later I'm sitting in the dentist's office for my check-up. At my feet is the dental hygienist, who happens to be the wife of my dad's attorney. She is staring at me rather contemptuously. I don't understand. Outside of this office, I never see her. In short, I don't know her.

"I'm curious, Connie," my dentist says. He removes the little extend-a-mirror and his hands from my mouth.

"Why aren't you talking to your dad," he reproachfully glares at me.

"And why is that any of your business?"

My world is shrinking. Now I can't even go to the dentist.

"Well, it's just that your dad has been so great to you. He doesn't deserve to be treated this way," he says with the utmost confidence in his assertion.

The hygienist now has her arms crossed staring down at me, waiting.

I feel on trial. They've obviously colluded in this attack. I feel as though the goal is to entrap me. I know they don't expect me to reason this out. My father must have forgotten, while bragging about how wonderful he is, that I have what seems to be an inherited bullshit detector from my maternal grandfather.

For the first time in my life, I swear at an adult.

I pull myself up in the chair, look him in the eye, and say, "You might want to know what the fuck you are talking about before saying something like that to me."

Stunned, he goes back to checking my teeth, claims that I have two cavities, and books an appointment to fill them.

I tell my mother it's a lie. "I don't have any cavities," I say. "He's pissed that his little plan to set me up didn't work. I think the hope was to get me to say you were keeping me from talking to Dad, or something like that, but it didn't work. Now he's going to gouge you for money."

The act never ends.

"Connie Sue, there is no reason why he would lie about your teeth. He's been our dentist for over twenty years."

"Yes, Mom, there is. He's pissed off."

The following week, he did nothing to my teeth and charged my mom for filling two cavities.

Microburst II

Two days later. I'm walking out of the bathroom.

I stop.

I cock my head sideways, and slightly forward. What am I hearing?

My mother is sucking in small gasps of air between sobs. I take the first step to go to her. I'm strong enough tonight to put myself aside and comfort her. She is, after all, a woman whose illusions have been shattered. It must be hard for her to find her grounding, being someone who so deluded herself. These last few weeks have forced her to see that the reality of her life is very different from the fantasy she created.

I stop before my big toe touches the step. Frozen in a tendu, I hear a muffled male voice. I can't understand the words but the berating tone is unmistakable.

What is he doing here?

And then he yells, "You goddamn bitch."

I fall backwards. There is one thing my mother is not, and that is a bitch. I've never met someone so un-bitch-like in my life. He seems to be taking some mysterious delight in shattering her illusions. In fact, in the last few weeks I've witnessed this same kind of odd pleasure from Lydia and my mother's two sisters.

"She always was such a goodie-two-shoes," I overheard one of her sisters say to the other.

"She's always right," the other returned. I smiled, wondering if she was aware of the fact that she left "thinks" out of her judgmental retort concerning my mother's behavior. In my experience, especially when it came to things like how unhinged my aunt's children were, and the lack of parental supervision she placed over them, my mother *was* often right.

He continues yelling. I'm incapable of comprehending what he is actually saying because it is so baseless. What is he doing here? He left her. She didn't stop him. She's not stopping anything. So why the attack?

"Please, Bob," her feeble voice cuts through.

I don't know what to do. I want him to stop. Again, I think of calling the police, but the dentist showed me who will be protected.

I get the wooden baseball bat my mom keeps by her bed. I sit on the top stair resisting the urge to go bash him in the mouth. *Shut up! Leave her alone!* I scream in my head.

I hear him slam his fist on the table. I'm going insane trying to discern any reason for this unprovoked attack he is leveling on her character.

Prone on the hall floor, I white knuckle the bat in one hand, and unwittingly pull a small clump of hair out of my head with the other. It's taking everything I possess not to intervene in some manner.

"Meg is out in the car waiting for me right now. A woman who is ten times the woman you've ever been." The whole house shakes when he slams the door.

I rush downstairs and wrap myself around my mother. I'm not saying she is a perfect person, but nothing about her deserves such abuse. This has been going on to some degree her entire married life. How has she continued standing?

Microburst III

I'm back at school, and I'm a mess.

Blessed with my mother's tenacity, I'm still standing.

I come back to my dorm from class, and I am confronted by a good friend, who has taken some unspoken issue with me.

"Okay, I can't take this anymore. What gives?" I ask my friend, whose father is a close friend of my dad's attorney (the hygienist's husband).

"I know about the money," disappointment in my character oozes from her.

"What money?"

"The three thousand dollars you stole from your dad," she says with heightened confidence. She believes she has the upper hand.

"What?" now I'm just pissed. "What three thousand dollars are you talking about?"

She informs me that my dad's attorney told her father that I had stolen this money from my dad.

"And how do you propose I got my hands on his money?"

"I don't know and I don't care. I just know you stole it."

I'm surprised by how easily she has been manipulated into believing something so nefarious could be in my nature.

"Look, I have no access to my father's money. And if I did, I would never steal it. And if I did steal it, given the shit storm that my life has become since February, you and I would be enjoying ourselves on a tropical beach somewhere."

Microburst IV

"I never promise a woman anything nor let her know what I'm going to give her. That's the only way to manage them. Always keep them guessing. If you can't think of any other way to surprise them, give them a bust in the jaw."

The ringing phone robs my attention from *The Sound and the Fury*.

"Hi, Babe," he says when I answer.

I roll my eyes. He's up to something. The casual tone of his voice betrays his intent to manipulate me. To what end is the only question.

"Hi, Dad," I look at the clock. I have an hour before my seminar on early 20th century literature. I smile every time I think of the professor, Papa Hemingway's doppelganger. I doubt, however, that Hemingway was the fan of William Faulkner that my professor is.

"Did you know your mom is stealing my money?" he doesn't waste any time.

I roll my eyes. Last week, I was the thief. Now she is.

"Can't say that I did. How's she going about that?"

"She's hiding my money in the attic at home you know."

I repeat my question, "How is she stealing *your* money?"

I tap Faulkner's book on my knee. Sometimes I think only he or Flannery O'Connor could fully understand my life.

"Well, she's cashing my pension checks," he says, like his word is credible.

135

"Dad, how dumb do you think I am? Or maybe it's that you think I'm gullible."

"I don't understand what you mean, Babe. In fact, I think you're really bright. The smartest one of all you kids. That's why I'm telling you this. You need to know the truth."

I can't contain my sigh, "Dad. You have a separate checking account from Mom's now. Correct?"

"Yeah."

"And, your checks, even if they were still delivered to the house, which they are not, have pay to the order of Bob Walker on them. Correct? Not pay to the order of Bob Walker or Arlene Walker."

"Correct," he answers, seemingly unaware of the trajectory of my questioning.

"Well, then," my measured tone evaporates, "How the *hell* is she cashing *your* checks, and therefore, stealing *your* money?"

My dad, poor man, never expects logic and reason from his prey. He's accustomed to them becoming defensive and muddled. The older I am, the more I hone in on my Vulcan-like powers of logic. And he is the king of misleading definitions, like defining manipulation as generosity and obligation as gratitude. He is not happy with me when I try to point things like this out to him.

Sensing defeat, he, like Jason Compson, gives me a bust in the jaw, "You and your goddamn mother are just alike, Connie Sue. You're so goddamn selfish. Do you know what I've been through? Do you know what in the hell I've put up with?"

"What you've put up with? You're the one who left, Dad."

"You're goddamn right I left, Connie Sue. Who could put up with all of you?"

He slams down the phone. The noise reverberates through my head.

Microburst V

Sam and I sit around the kitchen table eating lunch. It's a beautiful summer day in June. The humidity is at a comfortable level. The breeze gently billows the curtains. The scent of lilacs wafts through the air. The midday sun fills the kitchen. I feel good.

We are now a year past the divorce. My dad had the divorce bargained, signed, and sealed 90 days after filing. My mother, more or less, fought for nothing.

"If he wants a divorce, I'm not going to stop him. I don't want to make someone live with me who doesn't love me anymore."

Anymore? The word rang in my head like a gong. I try to imagine what my father ever did that made my mother believe that at some point in time he loved her.

There was a brief holdup in the proceedings, however, due to my mother receiving a letter from the Arch Duke Ferdinand Bishop of Canterbury (whatever the heck his title is) from the Catholic home office in Des Moines. The letter requested that she sign papers of annulment so that my father and good ole Meggie could get married.

"We weren't even married in the Catholic church. And I have four children. He wants me to say you don't even exist. Not only that, the reasons he's given for leaving is that Sam has a genetic disease, which both of our genes are responsible for, and that I've been sickly. I suppose he's talking about all my kidney stones. And he didn't even get a single one of your birthdays right."

When you yourself are floundering, trying to deal with absolute absurdity and the reality that many things in your life were never true, you don't make particularly good counsel. Especially for a parent who is suffering from the crashing and smashing of all her illusions, and who should be seeking counsel elsewhere. In other words, I was a bit insensitive.

"Just sign the paper. Who cares? I know you have four children. That paper doesn't render me nonexistent. Sign the thing, and get this over with."

On this morning, though, things are calm. We are adjusting to our new reality. The divorce and dad are starting to take a backseat to conversation more grounded in the present.

The porch door opens.

My back is to the kitchen door.

I look up from the paper into the mirrors behind the sink.

Expecting to see Fran, I am a deer in the headlights when my father crosses the threshold behind me. His demeanor reflects someone returning home from running errands.

He's smiling.

He appears open.

My body involuntarily presses into the table to get my energy as far away from his as possible.

"Hey, Babe. Hi, Sam," he strikes a familiar tone. There is an expectation for Sam and me to behave in a manner that suggests nothing has gone on, and that he has been the best dad in the world. And if we don't, something is wrong with us.

Instead, I'm pissed.

"How dare you just walk in here."

My tone strips him of the desire to play nice.

His face reddens.

An all-too-well-known malevolent presence inhabits his eyes and posture.

"Where's your mother?"

"In the basement," Sam answers. I fight the urge to kick him.

Absent any compunction whatsoever, my father pushes past me and goes downstairs.

Out of my head, I pace the kitchen and berate Sam at the same time.

I rip the paper in half, and then I hear, "Bob. I can't take this. Please, stop."

"That's it. I'm putting an end to this," I say, and scowl at Sam.

"Why did you tell him where she was?"

I throw the paper at him and go downstairs.

I stop on the landing. My father is just past the bottom of the stairs. I'm unable to see him.

He is talking quietly.

Pathetically.

His tone is awash with victimhood. I can't make out everything he says, but all I need are the bits and pieces. He is complaining about Meg.

"She's impossible to live with" I hear. And then, "You can't imagine what I'm going through."

Saying I'm in a state of disbelief is beyond understatement. No hyperbole can adequately explain the degree of disgust, repulsion, and nausea flooding my system.

"Oh, Bob. Please stop," my mom weeps. Her voice is faint and vulnerable.

I can take it no more. Even I can hear the authority in my footsteps as I go down the stairs. Said authority drains from me when I enter the room.

My father, his eyes wounded and downcast, stands slumped. His wrists bend out of the pockets into which his short stubby fingers are stuffed.

My mother, her skeleton liquefied, her soul emaciated, slides down the pale blue wall. Her knees are on the ground, and, with her right arm extended above her head, her palm pressed flat against the wall, she has the appearance of drowning.

This scene is added to my situations-a-child-should-never-witness-their-parents-in file.

Both are unaware of my presence.

"I don't know what to do, Arl. I just don't think I can take her any longer." He looks at the floor and shakes his head.

"Bob, please," she sits on the floor.

"That's it!" my returned authority startles them.

"Get out of this house. How dare you come up here looking for sympathy after everything you've done!" I'm all fight.

"This is none of your damn business, Connie Sue. Go back up stairs," his victimhood evaporates.

"Oh, this most certainly is my business. You've made it my business, and she's in no condition to protect herself. How dare you come up here looking for sympathy."

After a few similar exchanges, I help my mom up, and we all go upstairs. My father refuses to leave.

He has the gall to sit down at the table next to me. He tries to tell me how awful his life is.

"You act like someone made you leave. You act like someone made you lie and cheat. You do understand, don't you? It's not possible to feel sorry for you! You're not the victim here," and with that I crossed a line.

"You know, Connie Sue, you don't hold a candle to Meg's daughter Katie. She's a far better daughter to me than you've ever been. She calls me. Checks up on me. And is concerned about how I'm doing. She's ten times the daughter you ever were!" he says this looking me straight in the eyes.

What is it with his 'ten times?' I think as I stare at him. His words have one purpose: to hurt me into submission. They don't succeed.

I push my chair out from under me with the back of my knees.

I consider saying, *"Perhaps you haven't been the asshole to Katie that you've been to me,"* but he's looking for a fight.

He has constantly maintained: "I never throw the first punch. But if someone hits me, I'm sure as hell am defending myself, and hitting back."

Time, life, and experience have proven to me that while he might not throw the first punch, he is always provoking it. What a great way to maintain innocence and victimhood. "They punched me. What was I supposed to do, just sit there and take it?"

I turn and leave the kitchen.

With rare exception, I don't see or talk to my father for well over a year.

EF-5

Incredible and total devastation results from winds that are over 200 miles per hour. Homes are leveled and blown off their foundations. Cars can become airborne missiles flying through the air in excess of 100 miles per hour. Significant deformation can occur on high-rise buildings. Incredible phenomena have been known to happen.

"Operator. How may I help you?"

"I would like to place a collect call," I say.

"What number, please?"

I give her the number and say, "Thank you."

I stare at the calendar above the pay phone while the operator punches in my mom's number. July 28, 1987. Wow, time is flying. Just two more weeks of the camp, and then it's back to Iowa.

On the third ring, I stop breathing. What if she did have a heart attack? But she answers on the fifth ring. An audible sigh escapes me as oxygen returns to my lungs.

"Yes, I'll accept the call," she says.

"Hi, Mom. I'm just calling to see how you're feeling."

"Well, I did go to the hospital last night after I talked to you. They took me through a series of tests and found nothing wrong with my heart."

"I was worried," I shift the phone to my other ear. "I've tried calling three times today. Where were you?"

"I decided to stay home today, so I had to run down to the office and put a note on the door saying I was closed. Then I stopped by the grocery store. Now I'm going to have some lunch and rest," she was noticeably exhausted. Then, "They suggested that I was having a panic attack, but nothing has happened lately to make me panic."

Oh, yeah, not aware of anything in the last two years to cause any panic, I think.

"Well, it's a good idea to stay home and rest then," I say. "It's a little after one here, and I need to eat before I teach at two. I'll check in later this evening."

"Okay, Sweetie," she says.

I echo her I love you and goodbye, and hang up the phone. I don't let go of the receiver. I stand staring at my hand. Why am I white-knuckling the receiver?

Something's wrong.

I release my death grip on the receiver and turn down the corridor to my dorm room. I have a great dorm room for my temporary stay at North Dartmouth College where I'm the dance director, and a counselor, at a camp for overweight girls. Freedom overwhelmed me when I saw the ad in the ISU newspaper: six weeks out of Forked River for the summer. What a blessing. Plus, this allowed me to see Joe and Kathy, since they now live in Boston.

The sun fills my room, and because the dorm is settled in a small wooded area, my room never gets unbearably hot. My attention is drawn to my letter sitting on the desk. I grab it. I sit on my cot-bed and my eyes begin to water as a recurring conflict surges up inside. The letter, addressed to Joe, is a five-page purge of the internal struggle I'm suffering due to the guilt I'm feeling for not talking to or seeing my father for the past several months. This guilt is smacked up against the fact that, minus a feeble attempt by showing up unannounced at BARJCHÉ (ISU's annual dance performance) this past spring expecting me to act as if nothing has gone on, my father has made no attempt to reconcile, God forbid console, any of the emotional wounding his betrayal and abandonment has caused me.

My attention is drawn outside, as many noisy girls cross past my window on their way to the commons for lunch. As I watch them, I pat a corner of the letter on my palm and try to recall when, if ever, my father has asked me how I'm doing. How all of this has affected me? I cannot recall a time before, during, or since the divorce that my father, with sincere interest, has asked about my well-being. After all, if I'm not well, that's my fault and my problem.

Whenever I've asked him about his lies, his cheating, and his betrayals, which have caused more than an impasse in our relationship, his response is always, "I'm really sorry for you, Babe, that you just can't get over the divorce. I've moved on. I'm not sure why you can't. I think your mom is making that hard for you. You know, she's brainwashed you against me."

I'm not a psychologist, nor have I had any therapy, but I'm quite certain that when deep fissures have happened between two people, especially when one has severely wounded another, that relationship can't move forward until some kind of reparations have been made.

A small laugh escapes me. I see my dad, sitting on our sofa, after a time when I caught him in a lie that was corroborated by other adults.

"How dare you accuse me of lying to you," he said. His tone imbued with hurt, his eyes, crestfallen.

And then, for his Oscar-perfect performance, "You know, Babe, you've really hurt my feelings," he said as tears began to fall down his cheeks. "I think you owe me an apology for suggesting I would do something so awful to you."

Did he really think the tears would work? He appeared to read the bewildered look on my face as victory: his lip curling upward at one side. A less narcissistic person might have read it for what it was: disgust. He, however, read my silence as success in putting me in my place. Ultimately, this was my father's greatest downfall with me. While that might have been an accurate read of most people he dealt with, it wasn't of me. But he continued to treat me as if it were, which sadly heightened the side of my personality that wanted him to know he was wrong, thus causing me to become more and more defensive in an attempt to justify my position, this being my greatest downfall with myself.

I look at the clock: 1:45. Well, so much for lunch. I grab a breakfast bar, a pear, and an Evian. I leave for class grateful my workday will be over soon.

Walking from the rec building back to my dorm, I'm soothed by how quiet campus is. A little unusual, but it bodes well for an afternoon nap.

Once inside, I pass the pay phone, pause, and lift my head to the side to focus my hearing.

Nothing.

No one.

I press up against the window. The sky, a beautiful blue, fills my vision along with the wooded path across the way. But where is the usual gaggle of girls, arm in arm and giggling as they practically skip down the path to go flirt with the college guys tending the grounds for the summer? Where are the younger girls jumping rope? Where are the counselors tanning in the grass? The quiet has become, well, disquieting.

The silence is jarred when I hear a familiar voice in an unfamiliar pitch and tone say, "Connie Sue."

I jerk around to see Joe in front of me as Kathy and the camp director go back down the hall.

His lean, generally erect frame is clenched inward. He wrings his hands, gives a nervous laugh, and asks, "Is your room nearby?"

"Sure," I gesture for him to follow me.

"Is everything okay with Mom?"

He stumbles on his words but in essence lets me know there is nothing wrong with her health. In other words, she hasn't had a heart attack since I spoke to her a couple of hours ago. Nice that we've ruled out that scare.

Once in my room, I sit on the bed. Joe pulls out the desk chair. His shaking hand causes the chair to undergo a brief tremor. I notice his bicep bulge from under his t-shirt sleeve. It's nice to know he's still fit for a twenty-nine-year-old struggling artist. He's smart, funny, manic, and in this moment, afraid, concerned, and, as his pinched brow and pallor suggest, upset and sickened by the information he is about to share. His countenance is disconcerting to say the least.

"I'm not quite sure how to tell you this," he catches his breath. He looks down and rubs his bald head. This is his typical contemplative posture.

"Obviously, something bad has happened," I say. "Just tell me straight out. It will be easier for both of us."

I breathe deeply and brace myself.

My brother's face registers relief. Neither of us had ever dealt well with the beating-around-the-bush approach to anything.

As Joe unleashes the news that irrevocably alters my future, I listen, incapable of grasping the magnitude of his reveal.

"Around noon today, Dad was shot," his words mechanical and dry. "He's alive, but he was helicoptered to Des Moines. He's still being operated on to remove the bullet. They don't know yet if he will live," Joe pauses.

I look at Joe. The question, what does it all mean for us, is spinning through my brain like a top. And then, as the top slows, wobbling and losing traction, I wonder, in more specific terms, what it means for me.

For a brief moment, I feel immense relief, thinking my father is dead. This thought brings about a violent dust devil that whips my thoughts around, depositing guilt in one corner, ramming relief into another, blowing fear up into the third, and flinging my entire body head over heels into the abyss of the fourth.

Joe's demeanor lets me know there's more to come.

He takes in a breath before continuing. What is left to tell me? Isn't what came before all of this enough? Isn't Dad being shot enough? Apparently, in my family, in my life, it isn't.

"He was supposedly," he drenches the word in sarcasm, "having lunch with a woman in a park out on the west end of town when they were shot."

He pauses.

My heart stops and holds onto Joe's "they."

"She's dead," he lets it hang.

Comprehension becomes very slippery when news of this nature is given to a person. I'm certain Joe is still dealing with his own slipperiness while giving me the facts. Technically, I understand the words I've heard, but I can't comprehend their full context. So, as I try to grab onto their meaning, I slip and lose all traction from the absolute absurdity of where life has just launched me.

Finally, my head still muddled, I ask, "Who was she?"

"We don't know. It wasn't Meg or Mom."

My brother and I look at each other. We both *know* why our father was in a park with a strange woman. I am crushed for her.

She's dead.

She's DEAD.

SHE'S DEAD!

Breathe. Freeze. Think.

And somehow, he's not.

Someone died while in the park with my father. Someone, I'm certain, my father found some vulnerability in and exploited is dead.

My curiosity kicks in, "Where was he shot?"

"Right between," my brother leans forward, and while punctuating his statement by tapping his index finger on his forehead, his eyes wide, his expression hysterical and comical all at once, blows me into the stratosphere with, "the fucking eyes."

"The bullet lodged in his skull, Connie Sue," Joe gives a nervous high-pitched chuckle.

The bullet hit the man in his third eye and lodged there. I always knew the man was hard headed, but my God.

I look at Joe in disbelief of our reality. Slowly, I grin and chuckle too. Soon, we are laughing, and for the first time, but most definitely not the last, I laugh so hard I cry, but I'm not crying from laughing. I'm simultaneously laughing hysterically and sobbing uncontrollably.

And then it hits.

My entire body is sucked upwards with force: gravity is no longer a downward pull, but rather an upward push. Only the ceiling keeps me from flying out into the atmosphere. Everything inside me starts to violently spin. And while I have no idea what this all means, I'm certain it's going to be bad.

"I have some medication the doctor gave me to give you. I think under these conditions it might be a good idea for you to take it," he says and hands me a tiny envelope.

My brother knows I'm medication-averse, but he's right. Under these conditions I need assistance finding the ground again. I open the envelope and down the two tiny white pills.

"We have a flight back to Iowa in the morning. Let's get you packed up."

Kathy walks in the room. She hands me my final check, "Your contract is terminated, and we can go whenever you're ready."

"Thanks, Kathy," I take the check.

"How ya doing?"

I look at her perpetually sad hushpuppy eyes. She must wonder what the hell she got into. Two months after her wedding, there's the car scene. Before she celebrates her first anniversary, my father leaves, and now this.

"I don't know yet. How about you?"

She shrugs, and we both smile at each other. It all sucks. What can really be said about anything?

"That's it," I say as I zip my duffle.

Joe takes my suitcase. I fling my backpack over my shoulder. Kathy offers to take my duffle. In single file, we walk down the corridor and leave the dorm.

The emptiness is unnerving.

No one is about.

Where did everyone go?

I look back over my shoulder as we turn down the tree-lined drive. I didn't get to say goodbye to anyone, particularly the girl who had been crying on my shoulder just last night about all her father's affairs. The irony.

"Why is it parents think kids don't know what's going on?" she asked me through sobs.

"I think if they acknowledge you know, then they have to acknowledge they know, and I think that can be hard for them to do."

"Why?" she asked.

"Well, once they acknowledge it, then they're responsible for what they know. In the case of my mom, she was never ready to take that responsibility. You have to act once you accept responsibility, and my mom just wasn't prepared for what that meant."

I wonder, as I turn back to the front, if she was prepared for what her inaction has resulted in. Not that she's responsible for the shooting. My dad has been pulling that inevitability (or something like it) to him for years. But, I wonder, how different her life and our lives would be had she left my father years ago.

I hear the alarm. Startled and disoriented, I fall off the sofa. This is not my dorm room. My brain has issued a dense fog warning to my system. I have no idea where I am.

My eyes begin to clear when I see the wine glasses left on the table from last night. The fog in my head begins to lift. My consciousness struggles to return from a deep, peaceful sleep I owe to the certainty that followed me to bed: my father, I felt sure, would not survive the night.

I try to stand. I'm in a tangle with my blanket. Claiming victory after a brief wrestling match, I stand and walk down the hall toward Joe and Kathy's room.

He comes around the corner.

We both stop before colliding.

We stare at one another, reflecting grave uncertainty in each other's eyes.

I look to my left. The sun is illuminating the white-tiled bathroom. There are so many emotions swirling through me. I decide there will come a time in the future to sort, categorize, feel, and process them all, but that time is not now. For now, I must put them aside, and deal with the unknown reality that awaits me in Iowa.

"I'll get in the shower," I say as I turn back to him.

"Thanks," he says and continues past me.

Once we arrive in Iowa, life becomes a series of mentally and emotionally warping sights and events. To begin with, there's my mother standing at the end of the gate with none other than Lydia. I had prepared myself for this on the plane, but really? There is no preparation for these kinds of events. The woman's ex-husband of only two years, and after thirty-six years of marriage, is in a hospital bed still unconscious from a gunshot wound to the middle of his head, and she is not the one who is allowed to be by his side. (Why she would want to be, I can't reason.)

She collapses into my arms like my child.

I comfort her as such.

My brother insists on going to the hospital before going home.

I have no desire to see my father. There are too many unresolved emotions between us, constipating my ability to have compassion for him. I don't want something like this to happen to anyone, including him, but I can't help thinking his lifestyle led him to this moment. I can't offer him the victimhood he is always seeking.

I know with every fiber of my being that he will demand my forgiveness, and use this situation to excuse himself from any obligation of remorse or apology for the things he has said and done to me. A near-death experience is not going to reform him, I am certain. It's going to embolden him.

I can't abandon myself. And a voice inside me is echoing throughout saying, "Walk away. Walk away. Walk away."

I run into Meg's son and her sister, who have just come from talking to the investigating officers.

He's a wreck.

She smiles at me as if we bumped into each other at a restaurant. Odd. Not only because of the circumstance, but I've never met her.

"First thing tomorrow morning the Des Moines intelligence officer wants the two of you to go down to the police station," my mother tells us on the way to Forked River. "I told him you would be there at nine."

My night is fitful: I'm scared about the meeting tomorrow morning, I don't want to be in this house, and I keep wondering what the dead woman's family is going through.

Finally, I drift off to sleep.

I'm in my dorm room. The air is hot, but I am cold and nervous. I can't find a reason for either, and then the phone rings.

"Hello," I say.

"Hi, Babe. It's Dad. What are you doing?"

"Oh, just studying," I say, wondering why he's calling me. I haven't talked to him for months.

"What's up?" I ask.

"Well, I just wanted you to see something," he says.

"See something? What do you mean?"

"Well, just look."

As he says this, my dorm room turns into a big screen divided into four squares. My mom, sister, and two brothers are each in a square. I hear Lily Tomlin's voice (as her character on Laugh In) *say, "One ringy dingy," and my mother is shot between the eyes. "Two ringy dingy," says Lily, and Joe is shot between the eyes. "Three ringy dingy," and Bam! Fran is shot between the eyes. Lily clears her throat, and says, "Four ringy dingy," and Sam is shot between the eyes.*

I see all four of them with bullets in their heads. Blood is running down their noses and cheeks.

"I did that, Connie Sue," my father says. With cold dismissal, he hangs up the phone.

I wake up in a cold sweat, shivering. "It's only a dream. It's only a dream," I tell myself over and over again.

I thank God the sun is beginning to illuminate the eastern sky.

"This is unreal," I whisper to Joe, as we are waiting to be called into the investigator's office.

"Too much like a movie for me," he returns.

We're ushered into a rather discombobulated office. Papers are strewn all over the desk and piled on filing cabinets.

"Please sit down," the investigator motions to two seats in front of his desk.

We find out we have been asked down to give character references on our father.

Joe and I both chuckle.

We learn, as the investigator holds up a yellow legal pad with names filling almost every line, "We've been traveling southern Iowa, interviewing women your dad has had affairs with. We're not certain how he covered so much ground." Then he makes some crass comment about how ten men couldn't have screwed as many women as our dad did.

I might not like my father, but that doesn't give this guy the right to be funny about the whole affair. I quietly pardon my own pun.

"The important thing to know," he says right before he gives us leave, "is that the killer is still out there. We have intentionally withheld the fact that your father survived from the press in the hopes of pulling the person out. We believe this to be a crime of passion, and therefore, the person will want to know if he's alive or dead. No one in your family should go anywhere alone. They've already killed one person, so they won't be afraid to do it again."

I didn't just hear that, did I? This is not for real.

I stare at the investigator, as he continues, "If anything out of the ordinary should happen, call me immediately."

He hands me his card.

Joe and I decide on the way home not to tell anyone about this, and to make sure no one goes anywhere by themselves.

At lunch, my mom informs us that shortly after we left, someone called the house posing as me, asking about my dad's condition.

"I asked her if she was okay because it didn't quite sound like you. She said she had a cold. It was no big deal. I didn't remember you having a cold when you left. Then I asked her where she was, and she said she was at ISU. I asked how is that since you just walked out the door. And then she hung up. Isn't that all very strange?"

"Call the investigator right now," my brother demands.

"I don't want you to leave your home, be in your yard, or walk by any windows until I come to your home and tell you in person that you're safe. Do you understand me?" he says.

"Yes," I say. I hang up the phone, certain my face is sheet-white.

I share what he said. Joe explains about us not going anywhere alone. I spend most of the next six hours prone on the living room floor reading. I'm literally afraid to stand up. I go to the bathroom as little as possible, as doing so forces me to walk by three windows. I crawl everywhere I go.

Around eight, the investigator is in our kitchen. I listen from the living room. He informs my mother they have the suspect in custody, and that we are all safe now. I'm once again free to move about the cabin. I'm not free, however, of the magnitude of the ransacking of my life.

I go to bed.

I have the most violent, menacing tornado dream yet.

I'm napping on the sofa. As the sun begins its slow descent into the western sky, an orange-yellow hue fills the living room. It's late Sunday afternoon, everyone is home, and like in most of these dreams, I am around the age of nine.

The smell of meatloaf awakens my senses; with much reluctance, I attempt to open my eyes. My dad is in his usual position reading the newspaper. I can hear Joe and Sam in the dining room. "Yes! Boardwalk!" I hear Sam exclaim. "That'll be, let me see, with a hotel, you owe me two thousand."

I smile. Sam is unbeatable.

Fran, I'm assuming, is up in her room blasting her brains out with her headphones on while drinking Mountain Dew.

Calm is the pervading feeling.

I close my eyes and breathe. I'm thankful for the moment. As I continue breathing, the delicious smells of the meatloaf are overtaken by a different smell. I grimace. It's the meatpacking plant. A huge wind has wafted the stench of death up from the river.

The wind blows it through the house and replaces it with another odor.

I inhale.

My eyes fly open wide.

I sit up.

I know this smell.

I can see the rolling cloud in the far distance.

Okay, great. There's time for us all to get in the basement. I know where everyone is. This should be easy.

"Dad. There's a tornado coming," I say, rushing past him to the door.

"Leave me alone, Connie Sue. I'm reading," he says, nonplussed by the upticking wind.

I run upstairs, "Fran," I shout. I know she's blaring the volume. She's on the floor reading a teen magazine.

"Fran," I say, shaking her shoulder. "There's a tornado coming. We have to get to the basement!"

"Get outta here," she grumbles. With force, she pushes me away.

I fly down the stairs, lose my footing, and butt-bump down the last four steps, landing on the living room floor. I look over my shoulder. The tornado tail is dropping.

My heart rate escalates but I have time. It's still on the other side of the river.

"Mom, there's a tornado coming. We have to get to the basement," I shout at her back. The wind is getting loud.

"Not this again, Connie Sue," she sends me a reproachful look over her shoulder.

"But Mom, there's a tornado. We have time to get to the basement. It hasn't crossed the river," I tug on her shirt in hopes she'll turn around.

"The meatloaf is almost ready. Go get your sister," she dismisses me.

"Mom," my plea rolls out on the exhalation of my breath. "Please. Please, just come look out the front door. You'll see it."

"Connie Sue, I'm trying to get dinner ready. Leave me alone. There's no tornado."

I dash into the dining room. Joe picks up a wad of money and throws it at Sam. Sam rocks back laughing. I watch as the money slows down and separates until it stops mid-flight. Sam is frozen on his return roll. His head coming forward, mouth wide from a guffawing laugh. Joe's arm is extended, hand open from the money's release. His face expresses what all faces express when we play games with Sam: frustrated defeat.

My father is unchanged in the living room.

I find Fran unchanged in her room.

I walk, methodically, down the stairs, my hand trailing on the banister. I stop on the last step. Wooden slats are flying in a tangle through the air and smacking against our house as the garage across the street disintegrates. A book flies through the living room window. Briefly, I ponder its title. Shattered glass follows the book like a comet's tail. I involuntarily jerk back when it lodges in the plaster wall above the archway into the dining room. The wind muffles the clinking of the colliding glass as it hits the floor. I hear the crack of a large branch meeting its end on the pavement.

Can I change the TV station? Maybe I've been dropped inside of Fahrenheit 451, *and we were a lucky family able to purchase all four TV wall screens.*

I realize I'm in a dream. I tell myself to grab hold of the ball at the end of the banister. Yes, it's a dream, no reason to be afraid, and then I hear...

"What's the matter, Connie Sue?"

I turn towards the sound. The tornado, which fills my entire view, is rotating in place right outside the porch screen door.

At first, I jut my head forward and squint my eyes. I can't be seeing this correctly. I straighten my body and walk to the door.

My vision is confirmed.

Bemused, I cock my head to the side, still questioning what I'm seeing.

"Oh, your eyesight's fine all right. No problem there," *the mouth in the tornado says to me. His eyes twinkle as he scrunches up his nose.*

"Excuse me," *I say.*

"Excuse you," *he returns.*

"Why are you mocking me?" *I ask.*

"Because you still don't get it, do you?"

I cock my head the other way. A tornado is talking to me.

"For years, you've tried to get your family to believe I was coming, and no one would listen to you. Today, I'm the wrecking *ball on your life. You have a choice to make. Do you stay up here and die with them, or do you run to the basement and save yourself? It's a choice you know."*

In a dream's instant, I'm revisiting a real life experience. I'm seventeen, sitting at a desk in my English honors class.

"I just want a good grade on the project, and my team members aren't exactly pulling their weight," I say to my teacher.

"But that doesn't mean you do their work for them," she returns.

I look up at her thinking she doesn't get my dilemma. "I know there's an individual grade, but you've put a lot of weight on the group grade as well," I say.

"Connie," her voice rings with authority. "The world doesn't need another martyr."

Her words devastate me.

Then...

"Why don't you trust that I see what's going on?" she asks so simply and plainly that I almost unwittingly reveal, Because no other adults around me do.

At whiplash speed, I'm back in my dream.

"I don't understand why they won't look. You're right here. You're always right here waiting," I say. A tear rolls down my cheek and slips between my lips. I taste the salt.

"Oh, but I'm not waiting anymore. And it's not important why they won't. They're not going to. So, what is important is what are you *going to choose?"*

I roll Mr. Tornado's question around in my head.

"That's it. You get one more try. Run, Connie Sue, run," his menacing voice deafens me. All motion is restored.

Seized in panic, I run upstairs, downstairs, in the dining room, in the kitchen. I plead. I yell. I physically turn heads. No one will look.

"5," Mr. Tornado roars.

I go back to the kitchen, "Mom, please!" Our long hair is being whipped about our heads.

"Connie Sue, will you stop it about the tornado. I'm trying to get dinner ready."

"4," Mr. Tornado continues his countdown.

I knock Joe over and grab Sam's money from his hands, "Listen to me. A tornado's going to destroy the house." They yell at me for interrupting their game.

"3."

Back up the stairs. Fran's asleep on the floor. I rip her headphones off, "We have to get to the basement. A tornado's coming."

"For the millionth time, leave me alone!" she yells, taking her headphones from my hand.

"2."

I jump down the stairs, skipping multiple steps at a time. I knock my dad's paper away from him. "What the hell," he yells. If looks could kill...

"Look. Right there, Dad," I frantically point at the door. "It's a tornado."

He scowls at me before shaking the paper back in place.

"1. Ready or not here I come!"

He winks at me. He makes a clicking sound as he offers me an ominous sideways smile. The noise cracks my soul as he begins to move. Oh, God, I should've never watched The Shining. *Why doesn't Mr. Tornado just say, "Wendy, I'm home."*

The boards of the porch floor begin to splinter and fly away.

What to do? I pause for a nanosecond, and then my survival instinct overcomes me.

"Oh, God! Oh, God! Oh, God!" I yell-pray as I dash for the basement door.

The wind makes it hard for me to move, but I get myself to the steps and jump the full five steps to the landing, turn and jump the remaining ten. I hit the third to the last step, stumble, and somersault onto the basement floor. Without missing a beat, I'm up and around the corner. I tuck myself under the stairs and count 1-2-3-4-5-6-7-8: first, at an allegro's pace, and then at an adagio's, until my breath slows.

And then...silence.

I unfold myself from under the stairs. My torso and legs are longer. I sit for a moment and internally scan myself. I emerge from the dark underbelly of the stairs to find my dream age chronologically synched with my real age: twenty-one.

I cover my eyes and blink away the bright sunlight crashing through the broken window. The same tree branch has shattered it, but the branch is larger since the tree is now twelve years older as well. The branch has downed one of the furnace's many vents. A leaf brushes the top of my head. I look up to see a large portion of the ceiling blown away. A peaceful, endless blue sky betrays the destruction that has occurred.

I walk up the stairs. All walls disappear once I emerge on the ground floor.

There is no house.

There is only debris.

I am the only survivor.

Again, Thumper's food bowl is upside down on the porch steps. Again, I turn it over, and hope he and the MacDavitts are okay.

My neighbor's house is demolished, exposing the church that is next to it. The steeple is now a pile of bricks in what was once a beautiful garden.

I walk through the yard and view my life commingled with that of who knows how many neighbors' lives.

My system nearly collapses when I see Fran's headphones wrapped around a branch.

I bend over to pick them up but decide otherwise.

I know my entire family is gone. I decide to take with me only what I have inside.

I walk across the yard, trying not to trip.

The MacDavitt's house is a splintered pile. The tree in their backyard, where all the neighborhood kids use to meet to decide the day's play agenda, is completely gone. The ground where it once stood is a jagged open wound.

About ten feet in front of me a splintered piece of familiar, gold-painted wood attracts my eye.

I'm not sure I want to look, but with cautious feet, I approach it.

It's the only family picture we ever took. Its golden frame is mangled. The picture itself is shredded. Only shards of its glass covering remain.

We are a broken family.

We are a family torn asunder.

I look back towards my home. I will never see it again. I will never see my family again. I fall on my knees and weep. My sobs spread out away from me as there are no longer any structures for them to bounce off and echo back.

I cry until I am spent.

It's only then I feel the pain in my knee. I pull a small shard of glass from my skin, grab a dark blue t-shirt from the ground, and tamp the blood.

One does need an external scar, I suppose.

I stand, not afraid, but terribly, terribly sad.

I am empty. Barren of all thought. But something tells me this is good. Something tells me to have hope.

I blow a kiss in the direction of my house.

"Good bye," I whisper.

I turn away.

I step over a kitchen sink and God only knows how many pieces of clothing, books, and photo albums strewn about as far as my eyes can see. A familiar noise turns my head as I pass the Pickerings' house. Reflecting a rainbow of light, water gushes from a broken pipe.

The gentle breeze, and the sun, feel good against my face as I, one determined step followed by another, walk up the Locust Street hill in search of my life.

Part II

Debris Field

"The most extreme agony is to feel utterly forsaken."

– Bruno Bettelheim

"All changed, changed utterly;
A terrible beauty is born."

– W. B. Yeats

"You know, I'm the victim here, Connie Sue."

– My father

"But you will admit it is a very good thing to be alive."

– L. Frank Baum

My life is in ruins.

My father miraculously lived. "A bullet was removed from his brain and he survived," one paper reported.

It's odd to have a sense of fear and dread over a parent living. It's also odd, that while he lived, I felt like I died.

I spent the two weeks between his shooting and the beginning of my senior year at home staring into space I no longer recognized, surviving like a cat hanging from the screen with my claws popping through the small holes awaiting my rescue in a tremulous state.

My vision, blurred from constipated tears, made everything fuzzy and opaque. In fact, everything about me felt backed up: my ability to express my feelings, my ability to speak in general, my ability to breathe, and my desire to be in public.

Where do I go from here? Where do I begin? Who am I now that this is my story? How will it play out in my life?

Lost and disoriented, I could only ask questions to myself, to the air, to God. I couldn't, after all, ask one of my family members, who were lost and disoriented themselves, to help me find my way back home.

The Munchkins gave Dorothy direction, "Just follow the Yellow Brick Road," they sang to her. They didn't predict for her the trials she would face along the way, but at least she knew there was a path, and believed it led to help. Glinda even gave her those shiny, red shoes.

All I had was what I was certain everyone could see: my humiliation. The story of my father's shooting, and the murder of that sad, innocent woman, was all over the news in print, on TV, and on the radio statewide. And, according to a good friend who called me from her home in Wisconsin, it was on the news there as well. How, I asked myself, do I face a campus where I was certain everyone who knew me (and due to my campus involvement there were a lot of people who knew me whom I didn't know, which only added to my paranoia) knew my father had been in the middle of a deadly love triangle?

And his picture.

God, his picture.

His eyes have that everybody's-out-to-get-me wounded look coupled with the pleading of a sad little boy who just needs to be loved. Does everyone else see this in him? I believe they do.

So, while Dorothy, with Toto in tow, took a deep breath and extended her lovely red sequined toe onto the place where the yellow brick road began, I brushed off the metaphorical debris from my ISU Cyclones t-shirt of the same colors and kissed my mom good-bye.

While Dorothy pas de basque-skipped into her future, I stumbletumbled into mine.

I shut off my car, take a deep breath, and screw on a smile. I walk up Sarah's driveway wishing I had just called her. I could have told her on the phone that I would see her next week, and avoided this visit altogether.

I briefly lament the loss of our easygoing summer days spent swimming or playing golf and tennis. I've spent most of my summers since sixth grade doing that, except for one odd year when I was thirteen. For some strange reason my mother made me spend almost every day of July at her office. I still don't know why. Neither does she. But something had her bothered, and she didn't let me far from her sights. I was really mad at her, but I started writing that summer. It's how I passed the time, and I fell in love with creating stories and poetry. I graduated high school torn between dance and writing. I decided to go with dance first. I can't put on pointe shoes at thirty, but I can pick up a pen.

Sarah and five of her family members are sitting on the porch. They pounce on me before I barely finishing saying hello.

"Did you read the paper this morning?" her mother asks.

"No," I reply. I don't want to go wherever it is they're taking me.

"Well, it said that if the current suspect isn't charged there are seven other suspects they're considering. We figure your mom and Fran are two. Do you have any ideas for the other five?"

My mom and Fran have alibis. Why are you counting them? I want to yell-ask, but instead I say, "No, I don't."

As they continue to speculate about the possible identity of the other suspects, I wonder if they think at all about how this makes me feel. Just because I'm estranged from my father doesn't mean I want to gossip about this. They seem callous and overly enthusiastic in their ponderings. Okay, they're not that callous, but I'm all on my sleeve right now, and I don't feel like anyone is concerned about how my father's shooting is affecting me. In truth, I don't think they care. All they want is the latest news, and since I'm the closest person they know to the story, they believe I have the inside track. I notice interest is quickly lost anytime I try to talk about the details of what I went through when Joe told me the news.

The story of the supposed love triangle that led to murder is all over the state news outlets. I cringe every time I see my dad's picture on the TV or in the newspapers.

It's a headshot. It appears to be an ID photo.

He's wearing his toupee, and has a rather suspect looking thick, full moustache. He looks smarmy and desperate all at the same time. I feel dirty and ashamed, as if I picked him to be my father, and now my poor judgment is exposed for everyone to see. I look at his picture and my skin crawls as I think about him hugging me and calling me Babe. There's not enough soap in the world.

And, oh, God, rescue me from these awful, hideous feelings I have towards my father. I silently beg.

But then, a gentle little whisper blows past my ear. "It's okay," it says. "These are the feelings he's created in you, trust them."

Then there's the murdered woman's picture. She is pretty, smiling, and looks vibrant. How is she the dead one? What's her story? How did she end up lunching with my father in the park? I don't have to ask that question, I know the answer. He saw someone who was vulnerable for whatever reason, preyed on that vulnerability, even commiserated with her, and then started telling her all his woes until she was stroking his ego with pity and concern saying, "Oh, Bob, you deserve so much more."

And, finally, there is the picture of the woman who is the suspect. She simply looks unhappy and used. Once all the pictures are arranged on the screen in a nice triangular formation, a reporter says, "Love triangle in Forked River leads to murder."

All five members of my friend's family are talking over one another. The cacophony of their voices brings me back to the present. Tired of this conversation, I say good-bye, tell Sarah I'll see her next week, and go home.

On my drive home, I distract my troubled thoughts by reflecting on the many things my mother has done.

My mother has been self-employed since I was three. She did bookkeeping, filed tax returns, typed and edited doctoral theses, opened a Manpower branch that covered all of southeastern Iowa and northeastern Missouri, started a secretarial training school, taught typing in the summer to high school students, helped other women open their own businesses, and, for three years, wrote, edited, and did the layout for her own local newspaper.

My mother was the only person I knew who owned a

mimeograph machine. Most of my friends didn't even know what one was. I would watch my mom type up the stencils, ink the machine, roll the stencil onto the big inked-up roller, and copy her newspaper pages. I learned how to collate by assembling her newspapers on a long table in our basement, and then, bang, bang, bang, three staples down the side as I quickly moved the collated pages through the automatic stapler. It took two afternoons, but we delivered the papers to all the local business and doctors' offices.

Added to all of this, my mother had been the president of the PTA, and was the only woman to sit on the Forked River Chamber of Commerce board.

So how does a woman as resourceful and creative and as driven as my mother not act? How does someone like her not believe that she can survive in the absence of someone like my father? How does she believe that she can't take care of her kids on her own? Maybe she believed she had, within all of her skills, the ability to change my father.

Once home, I read the article Sarah's family asked me about.

"Supposedly, from what I heard, (We qualify so many things that way these days because everything appears to be rumor, speculation, and innuendo.), a few years ago, Mrs. McNutt's husband caught her and your dad in bed together and left her. I think she's one of the seven suspects that article refers to."

I feel a slight punch to my psyche.

"Now I understand why Carrie never liked me," I say. "Even though she never knew me. We never even had a class together. But I'm assuming that's why she was pulled from dance class," I think out loud.

"Hmm," my mother questions.

"It's been years ago, but this mom came into the studio during my class with her two girls. I know now it was Mrs. McNutt with Carrie and her sister, but I didn't know them at the time. Miss Milly made us all sit down while they talked. The mother was crying, Miss Milly was being very supportive, and all the while her oldest daughter was glaring at me. I asked the girl next to me if she knew what was up, and she said she thought the McNutts were getting a divorce, and so maybe the girls couldn't take dance anymore. I felt awful for the girls. I thought it was all so sad, but I still couldn't figure out why this girl, whom I didn't know, was glaring at me".

I suddenly become very ill. "Oh, my God," I say.

"What?"

"That means Carrie has known all this time that her parents got a divorce because my dad and her mom were having an affair. That also means, she knows my parents, at least then, didn't get a divorce, and I was able to keep dancing. No wonder she hated me. I would hate me too. If this is true, I can't believe she never said anything to me. I would almost expect it just out of spite. Who would blame her?"

I pause. With my forehead in my hands I say, "Just how many people's lives is he responsible for ruining?"

My mom and I look at each other. Day by day, the impact and range of his destructive acts grow.

My mom sits down at the kitchen table. We both stare at the backyard. The maple tree blows in a warm breeze. All the late summer bugs are singing in chorus. Somehow that always makes the day feel hotter than it is.

I remind myself to come home and rake for my mom. Burning fall leaves is a meditative act for me. I wish I could burn some now.

My mom interrupts my thoughts, "Before you leave tomorrow, Officer Stetson wants us to come down to the station."

"What for?" I ask. I feel my throat constrict.

"I don't know. He said he has a question to ask us."

"Can't he just ask us over the phone?"

I don't want to do this.

I want to be done.

I want to run and hide.

"I guess not. I told him we would be down at nine," she says. She pats my hand.

I fight back tears.

Lying in my bed, the ceiling, split by rays from the morning sun, appears slatted like a fence. What on God's green earth could Officer Stetson possibly have to ask us? I'm overwhelmed by the sense of being lost and untethered. This feeling is magnified by the sense that I'm about to go to the police station with my sibling, not my mother. While my mother doesn't try to pretend that we aren't all going through something quite awful, she acts as if we are all experiencing it from the same point of view. As if we are all his injured children. She does, however, accept the part of the oldest in line. It's a much easier role than parent. Collectively, we're all children at the mercy of our abusive parent, devoid of our own agency to act, waiting for someone to rescue us.

I try to name this feeling swirling through me at the

moment. And then I realize my difficulty in naming it. Its reality is too crushing, and I've been crushed enough. But I allow myself a tiny bit of awareness.

I acknowledge before I whisperspeak my truth that this is a very difficult feeling to have towards a parent who has been injured by the same person I have. Who, regardless of it all, never did anything to deserve being treated so meanly by my father, her husband; and, yet, what I feel is . . . is . . .

I let it slip slide through my awareness . . . disgust. I'm disgusted with her.

I feel like she's never allowed anything she's witnessed to register beyond the outer layer of her eyes. She has spent her life turning piles of shit into non-existent rose gardens. After everything that has happened to me (and my siblings, and her) to think she never once looked reality in the face and said, "That's it. I'm taking them away from here. Come what may, it has to be better than this."

I'll ask her about this someday, but now is not the time.

We're silent in the car on the way to the station until I say, "All my bags are packed. That way I can just load my car when we get home."

"Alright," she says. "It'll probably be good for you to get back in the swing of school. It'll take your mind off all this."

I hope she's right, but doubt outweighs my hope.

My mom parks the car. I stare at an officer who sits at a desk on the other side of a large window. In a matter of a few short days, I've learned that the future is completely out of my control and unpredictable. I understand the cause and effect of crossing ripples in a pond on a deeper level. My dad's decisions have altered so many things. For a moment, I feel a ping of selfishness. Like I'm the only one whose life has been shattered and forever altered. Granting that my entire family has gone through this, my empathy is further tugged when I think of the family of the woman who is dead, all because of her affiliation with my father.

We both take a deep breath and get out of the car.

"This room is completely sound proof," Officer Stetson says.

And see-through, I notice, as he leads me into an approximately six-foot square room encased with floor-to-ceiling clear Plexiglas walls. My little soundproof room is inside a big open room full of desks.

"Nothing we say can be heard by anyone in the outer room," he says.

He closes the door behind me.

This is not a movie, I reassure myself.

A few officers sit at their desks, appearing to be preoccupied. My mother has been taken somewhere else in the station.

Officer Stetson interrupts my surveillance of the room, "I understand that you don't care much for your father." He is rather cunning, yet condescending at the same time. His tone is offensive to me, and odd.

He waits for me to agree with him.

I don't. I simply say, "And?"

"Well, if there is anything your father ever did to you that was inappropriate. If he ever, say, touched you in an inappropriate way, I want you to feel free to tell me."

Officer Stetson looms large in this room. He's quite tall, broad-shouldered, and full of his own power. His beefed up chest and ego makes him look bulkier than he is though.

"My father never did that," I say.

"Well, even if he didn't, and you want to get back at him, you could say he did. And, like I said," he opens his arms and gestures around him, "this is a soundproof room, and no one can hear you."

He smiles at me.

I know exactly what he's driving at. His tone, his demeanor, and his suggestion all hit on the offbeat, and now I'm mad.

"Look, I know, and you know, that my father, even though he didn't pull the trigger, is the person responsible for that woman's death. But my father never did anything sexually inappropriate to me, and I'm not going to stand here and lie so you have ammunition against him. Contrary to what you obviously believe, I don't hate my father, and I'm not going to live with a lie for you. You are going to have to build your case some other way."

Clearly this is not what he expected.

"You can go now," his dismissive tone mirrors his posture.

He knocks the door into a nearby chair and marches out of the room. I stare at the officers who now stare at me.

One of the men gets up from his desk.

"Hi," he says. He is being kind, but all I can hear is pity. "I'll take you to your mom."

"Thanks," I say, and follow him out.

In a private office, they asked my mom the same question. Later that day, Fran tells my mom they called her down to the station and asked her the same question as well.

My vocabulary is not broad enough to name what this does to me.

"This isn't really happening to me," I tell myself, first in a whisper, and then a shout, as I drive up Interstate 35 to Ames.

I try to avoid the TV and radio as much as possible at noon and six. I don't look at any of the papers. I try to be cool when a friend hands me one with my dad's picture on the front. It's not, I'm sure, but to me the news coverage is omnipresent, and I feel there is no escape.

Since I'm estranged from my father, and my friends know this, they assume that I like that this happened to him. Like I think he got what was coming to him. But I don't feel this way.

I don't wish this on anyone.

I do believe, however, that he led a life that set up the potential for something like this to happen. Obviously he believed this as well, or he wouldn't have carried a loaded handgun with him everywhere he went.

The truth is, I'm devastated. I want a father I can be proud of. A father I can respect. I want a father who is there for me whenever I need him. As a result of the way he treated me, as a result of the life he led, I'm also denied being the loving, concerned person that I want to be. I'm incapable of feeling compassion for my father.

He is not an innocent bystander.

Yet that's the way he wants to be treated. Isn't this one of those times where you put the past behind you and go to your family member because, as he always told us, family is everything? As I learned, loyalty extended one direction only, and that was from me to him.

And that loyalty was always tested.

Like when he tried to take me in his confidence and give me an outlet to mutually mother-bash through sign language. My refusal to do so meant I took her side, whether justified or not, and therefore, I wasn't loyal to him. This rendered me undeserving of his love, and loyalty. Oh, yes, and my actions proved, as I heard time and again, that I was an ingrate.

Somehow he defined loyalty and obligation as gratitude and respect, which should always be shown to him since he was such a generous person. Generosity was his definition of manipulative kindness with nefarious intent. Always, with him, there was an agenda.

In the process of it all, he owed me nothing.

In fact, why would he be loyal to someone who had denied him having all that he deserved? He was being smart and looking out for himself by cutting loose what was holding him back. And while he was through with the obligations of parenthood, I was by no means supposed to be through with the obligations of daughterhood, forsaken or not. Wasn't I being a coldhearted daughter for not going to her father's bedside after he had been shot?

He is the victim, right?

He is the victim, right?

No!

I am the victim of him!

But I don't get to say this. At least, I don't believe so.

Most people, however, don't say anything. I prefer that because the truth is I don't know what to say. I'm assuming judgment where there may or may not be any. I want to talk about my feelings, but they're so confused and all over the place.

When I do talk to people, I find that they are more absolute-minded than I am, and they don't understand the grays and charcoals and eggshell whites and bone-colored nuances I talk about.

Generally speaking, no one ever asks how I'm doing. But I have to cut everyone some slack. Most days I don't act like anything is wrong. It's my cover, my defense, my protection, to act unaffected.

In reality, I'm paranoid, restless, looking for love in all the wrong places, and sometimes being promiscuous, and then I stop because I really don't like being that way, but I'm all messed up. I stop dating, but the good thing is, I have tons of guy friends. So, I do what I've mastered: I hang out. I'm all my male friends cheapest date. I'm one-beer-one-piece-of-pizza-lots-of-laughs Connie.

Basically I get on with college business while I watch my grades tank, feel my ability to dance slip away, and for the most part, have no idea which end is up.

My tornado dreams come and go with varying degrees of menace, but my gun dreams amp up, haunting my nights with sinister, predatory images. The fear and paranoia these dreams create in me begin to bleed over into my waking hours and are exacerbated by the mystery surrounding my father's shooting. Sometimes my family and I will not-so-jokingly joke that our dad must be in the Mafia or something, because one thing is obvious, there is so much more going on than we know or are being told.

"Hello," I answer the phone.

"Hi, Babe," disappointment overwhelms me. I'm not in the mood to talk to him.

"What do you want?" I'm not nice.

"Well, I'm just calling about your mother taking me to court over her alimony and your child support," he whines, referring to next Thursday when, for the third time this semester, I will be in Forked River dealing with this matter.

"What about it?"

"Well, you know, she's trying to find me in contempt of court," he says.

"Yes, I'm aware of that."

"Well, doesn't that bother you?"

I pause for a moment. *Bother me?* The question snakes about in my head.

This is a man who assured me he would take care of me. Who told me he would make things easy for my mom. Yet, he is now five months behind on the measly one hundred dollars a month he agreed to give me and isn't paying her alimony.

Bother me? What the fuck should I be bothered about you numb-nutted asshole!

(My need to swear has increased ten-fold since the shooting. It's become my knee-jerk reaction to being kneed by a jerk.)

"Dad. You agreed to pay the amounts set, right?"

He stammers.

"Right?"

"Yes," he squeamishly replies.

"And, you're not paying the money you agreed to. The money you said you could afford. Right?"

He doesn't answer. Instead he says, "You know, I can't ask

Meg to take her money to pay for you and your mother. That's not fair."

"That's not fair?"

"And, I really don't see why I should be paying anything to the two of you," now he's getting feisty. "You know, Connie Sue, I don't have a goddamn thing. I don't have anything but a cow down here out in the field. And I think I've earned the right to have a few things of my own."

"Well, that must be one golden cow then," I say.

"What the hell is that supposed to mean?"

"Hmm. Well, if you don't have anything, how did you buy a brand new truck last month?"

Now I've crossed the line.

"You know what, Connie Sue? If they find me in contempt of court, they're going to put my ass in jail. You're going to allow them to put me in jail? You want to see your father in prison?"

"It's this simple Dad. You signed papers agreeing to these amounts and that you would pay them. You're not paying them. If you end up in jail, you put yourself there. Not me. And not Mom."

I stop listening. Instead, while he annihilates my character, I wonder how his conscience allows him to behave and talk as if we're both reeling from trauma. In this case, I'm referring to the divorce. He acts the part of the betrayed and the abandoned. He complains about the effects of the drama and trauma he created, as if he were an innocent bystander who got sideswiped.

A few days after our phone conversation, I leave the dance building and can't find my car. I grumble as I search the lot.

I remember I parked under the big elm tree and turn back in its direction.

I stare at my car.

I can't believe my eyes.

No wonder I passed it by.

I feel like I have been dropped in the middle of a Flannery O'Connor story.

The bird shit covers my car completely.

Yellow specks, the color of the body of my car, are barely visible through the splats of black and white.

Did every bird in Ames shit on my car?

I'm moved beyond laughing or crying.

The symbolism doesn't miss me.

I get in my car, drive to the sorority where I no longer live, and barely maintain a member status, and kidnap two underclassmen. For some reason, I can't go to the car wash alone.

"This one's on me," the attendant says. "I think the third time should finally get it all off," he tries to keep a straight face as he refuses to take my cash.

The underclassmen in the back seat try to stifle their laughter.

"Please, laugh. It was an enormous amount of shit," I say.

We all laugh. Luckily, my tears go unnoticed in the dimmed light of the car wash.

It's the following week.

It's Wednesday.

Tomorrow I go to Forked River for the last time regarding the court proceedings my dad called about. I haven't seen him

since he's been shot. I decide that yes, for sure, I'm dropping my one and only Thursday class, since, including tomorrow, I will have already missed my allotted absences for the semester.

I put on my sneakers and go to Ross Hall. Luckily, I find my counselor in his office.

My counselor is fantastic. He helps me salvage my senior year. Somehow, in the utter bleakness of the moment, he instills in me an optimism that it will pass, and life will, more or less, return to normal. I believe he is able to do this because he fully understands both my emotional and mental intelligence have been arrested by the events preceding the start of the semester. He doesn't pretend with me that my life is okay. I appreciate that.

I walk in his office, practically collapse in a chair, and stare at a poster of William Faulkner with his sad, weary eyes.

"What brings you here?" he asks. He is a not-too-tall, skinny man who is always pleasant. His demeanor makes me feel comfortable and normal.

"I need to drop a class," I say.

"Well, you're a week past the drop date. You'll have to have my signed permission as well as the professor's."

"That's okay."

"Are you sure you want to do this?"

"I've already missed two classes, and I'm missing tomorrow's class because I have to go to Forked River. I'm so far behind, I don't see myself catching up. And, to be honest, I just don't have the energy to do it."

We have a little more back and forth. Mostly it's just him doing his job so he can say, "I tried everything, but she was resolved to drop the course."

He gives me the paper. I have to have the prof's signature first.

"Thanks," I say, and take a deep breath.

My prof's office is straight down the hall from my counselor's. I can see him typing at his desk.

I gather my strength as I walk down the hall. Before going in, I turn and look back at my counselor. He smiles at me as if to say, "Don't worry, it will all be okay. And yes, I think you should drop too."

I sit down next to my professor and explain why I'm here.

He doesn't look at me. He doesn't ask me a question. He just says, "I won't sign."

I look at this man knowing he knows *who* I am, and *what* has taken place in my life over the last several months. You'd have to be dead in Iowa not to know.

"Your life is on fire, it's all over the evening news, all about the fire in your life, on the evening news."

Paul Simon's lyrics have become so personal. I love the title of the song: *Crazy Love II*.

All of my energy pools in my feet.

Now I'm pissed.

This man is a jerk in class, and now he's just being an ass.

"Why?" I ask, not masking my pissiness very well.

"Because I don't think it's necessary," he says.

"How would you know what's necessary for me?" Now I'm thinking he's a pretentious prick.

"You have plenty of time to catch up and pull out a decent grade," he says, not nicely, and definitely not with a tone that suggests he will be helpful in this regard.

"Look," now I'm hot.

"I'm not going to be in class tomorrow again, and I'm not even remotely close to being caught up from the last two classes I've missed."

"Well, you have the time, so I'm not signing."

I really have an issue with people who use their power to be an asshole for the mere pleasure of being an asshole. Of course, being raised by my father makes me super sensitive with zero tolerance for a dick of this magnitude.

I am trying so hard not to say it. Shame stops me. My own inability to believe it, stops me. My how-did-this-become-my-life-shock stops me. But the asshole is making me say it. He isn't signing, and my GPA has already suffered enough. I don't need a D or an F, so out I come with it.

"I have to leave here tomorrow morning to go home and take my father to court because he has refused to pay me the one hundred dollars a month that he agreed to when he left my mom my freshman year. Given the events in July, and now this, I would really like to drop out of college altogether, but I'm not so far gone that I don't know that's a really bad idea. So, if you could find any compassion at all to sign that document and release me from your class, I would really appreciate it."

You asshole! This I scream in my head as I try to smile at the man.

He silently signs the paper.

He holds it out, but pulls it back before I take it, "Since you can't change your circumstance, you need to change your attitude."

It takes everything I have to not hit him.

I rip the paper from his hand and march down the hall.

Seething, I slap the paper down on my counselor's desk. "What an ass," I say.

He gives me an agreeing nod, and signs.

"I hope this is the last time we have to come here," I say to my mom as we sit outside the courtroom. Another experience to add to my unwanted firsts list.

"Well, he and Meg were already deposed, so the judge should make his decision today."

As my mom finishes her sentence, my dad's head bobs up and down through the banisters of the open staircase. He reaches our floor, looks at us with his sad, pitiful eyes, and sits down on a bench about ten feet away. Soon Meg comes to his side and comforts him like an ailing child. Disgusting is the only word that comes to mind.

He murmurs something from across the empty space between us about still being my father. I almost laugh. I don't want a tit-sucker for a dad.

I inhale sharply. I hate these meetings when nothing about anything has been discussed. That is not the way I operate, but it is the way I have been forced to in my family.

He looks so pathetic. And it's all a game to play on my emotions.

"See what you're doing to me," his posture suggests.

I'm so sick of the games.

What I didn't expect is to see the little dent in his forehead where the bullet lodged in his skull.

After witnessing my father's attorney harass my mother,

my mother's attorney relinquish his right to cross-examine her, and, for all intents and purposes, not really examine my father at all, and watching the judge rudely read a book through the entire process, I'm a bit upset.

After the judge's gavel makes its wooden thud, I march over to the table where my mother's attorney is seated and nearly spit in his face, "What the hell was that? Why didn't you cross-examine her after his attorney abused her? And why was the judge reading?"

He doesn't answer me. Instead, he turns to my mother and asks, "Are you bringing her with you next time?"

I look at my mom and wonder where her anger is. Where does she store it? How is her pride so big, or dense, that she won't stand up for herself? Or me? Ever!

In the end, my father is ordered to pay the five hundred dollars he owes me, and he is judged not to be in contempt of court for withholding my mother's alimony.

I get back to campus in time for lunch. I call a friend and see if she wants to join me at Thumbs for a burger.

We sit down. Thumbs is pretty quiet.

Every TV in the bar is on the Des Moines noon news. Here comes my dad's picture.

The waiter distracts me as he puts our lunch in front of us, "Enjoy," he says.

I look back at the TV in time to see all three pictures on the screen in their familiar triangle.

"Can't it just all be over," I say. I bite into my burger.

"Do you think she did it?"

"Who knows? There's no weapon. The only eye witness said

he saw a woman walking out of the park who appeared to be blond, and tall," I pause to lick ketchup off my pinkie.

"The suspect has dark hair, and could have been wearing a wig, I suppose. But she's really short. There's no way she could be confused for someone tall."

I take a drink, eat a couple of fries, and add, while shaking a fry thoughtfully in the air, "The thing is this. The woman accused of shooting them had been having an affair with my dad for most of my lifetime. Supposedly, my dad promised her, after her husband found them in bed together and left, I think he might have taken the kids too, but I'm not sure, that he would leave my mom when I was eighteen and marry her. Or so we've heard. Well, he left my mom when I was eighteen, but married someone else," I eat the fry.

"Also," I continue after a drink of my root beer, "he had supposedly been paying her mortgage, which might explain why he hid money in his pipe tobacco thing and got really mad one day when it was discovered," I'm thinking out loud, but luckily my friend doesn't seem to mind.

"Anyway, this woman would then be very much like my mom."

"What?" my friend is alarmed. "How can you say that? She was cheating with your dad. For years."

"Just wait. This is a woman who has been involved with my dad for twenty years. She's expecting him to leave my mom, and remember her husband has left her. She's been waiting patiently for the years to pass for my dad to leave my mom. She's emotionally committed, and invested. She's been waiting for her life to start. And then my dad dumps her. She's been used her entire life. Lost her husband, her kids, I think, and has been living a life in secret, just waiting. She's emotional. She's like my mother. Out of her head. She's going to stand at point-blank range, look into the face of the man who jilted her, and, with a deft hand, hit the woman in the temple, and my dad right between the eyes? I don't buy it. She didn't do it. Her hand would've been trembling. She's not by her nature a murderer, so she probably would've been screaming as soon as she realized what she did. I just don't buy it. I can't see my mother, if she would've done this, calmly walking out of the park afterwards. Then there's the whole thing about the guns being stolen."

"What thing?" she asks.

I'm on a roll now. All these thoughts have been roaming around in my head doing somersaults and colliding into each other. I've been trying to make sense out of nonsense, which is probably a futile task, but I keep trying. It's my instinct, and need, for logic that is keeping me sane.

"Well, and these are things I've heard, but I'm not sure what the official report is on them. First, Meg supposedly divorced my father shortly after the shooting, and they're remarried now. Second, after he was shot, my dad and Meg told the police they had either a gun or some guns stolen from their home. Remarkably, one of them was the same caliber he was shot with. They told the investigators they had suspected the woman accused of shooting him of breaking into their home and taking the gun or guns. When asked why they didn't report it sooner, they said something about not wanting to get her in trouble. It's all so very odd, if you ask me. Again, things I've heard, so . . . And, then there's the whole thing with the investigator trying to get me to say my father had sexually assaulted or molested me."

I explained that situation, which she didn't know about. Nobody else knew about it until then.

"Well, who do you think did it?" she asks as she slurps the end of her drink.

"I think it was a gun for hire."

"What makes you think that?"

"Well, rumor has it, and the shooting pretty much proves it, that my dad didn't stop cheating after he and his current wife were married. I'm sure that pissed her off. She and her sister were mysteriously out of town on the day it happened. I don't know. There are other things that make me think that, too, but regardless, I don't think it's the woman on trial."

I take my last bite of burger, finish my drink, and continue thinking out loud, "You know, I don't think my dad was having sexual affairs with all the women they interviewed right after the shooting. I don't think the poor woman shot was sleeping with him."

I pause for a moment. Just talking this out is making me feel calmer and clearer than I have for weeks.

"I think he had a series of emotional affairs. He found women in vulnerable situations, built up their ego, and then engaged in a big flip. He started whining and complaining about his life, and soon his affair of the day was stroking his ego. He put them through little tests of loyalty, and when he was finished with them he became very mean and made them feel like a pile of shit, and made it all their fault things weren't working out, so he could dump them and move on to the next."

I start to laugh and almost choke on my soda.

"What," my friend asks.

"I remember this day before my dad wore his toupee,"

"That's a toupee?" my friend says in disbelief.

"Oh, yes indeed. Anyway, the hair he did have was dark. Not as dark as mine, but definitely not orange, which he came home from work with one day. He tried sneaking past me on his way upstairs. I saw his hair and asked him what happened. He got all snippy with me and said the sun had done it. A bullshit response. My dad was a lineman for the phone company. He worked outside all the time, and the sun had never done that to his hair before. Anyway, the next day he came home with his normal color restored. Someone had tried to dye his hair for him, and obviously, it all went seriously wrong. I thought it was hilarious."

Now, I drift away a bit and get lost in another thought I share out loud.

"That damn toupee. He used to put it on the post of our banister going upstairs. I can still see his furry rug-top resting on the ball of the banister. I would hate it when I wasn't paying attention and inadvertently put my hand on it. One day a good friend of mine was coming over. My dad and I were sitting in the living room, and we could hear my mom say hi to her as she walked in the back door. My dad literally freaked out like some vain schoolgirl. He jumped up, grabbed his rug, and maliciously asked why I hadn't told him she was coming over. My God, she knew him before the toupee, so to see him with it off wouldn't surprise her. I told him this, and do you know what he said to me?"

My friend just stared at me in disbelief. I think she hoped that I was making this story up. I wish I were.

"He looked at me, and with disgust and vitriol, issued the most ridiculous non-sequitur I'd ever heard. He seethed, 'If you are so goddamn embarrassed by this house why don't you go move in with her,' meaning my friend."

After that, I realize why I don't want to get started talking about these things. There is so much inside of me that needs to come out, and in the process I exposed something to her that I'm so ashamed of. My friend sees me differently now, and I can't put that genie back in the bottle. I don't think she judges me. I think she feels sorry for me, and somehow that makes me feel worse.

I go to my apartment feeling a mix of release and guilt. My exposure is weighing on me. I didn't want to do that, no matter how much I might have needed to.

It's nighttime. I crawl in bed exhausted and overwhelmed by a tumult of emotions. I'm grateful my roommate is gone for a few days so I can be alone. As I stare into the darkness, I feel the rock and the hard place between which I am lodged. I can't reconcile caring about my father with the fact that I know deep down it's simply dangerous for me to expose my feelings to him; even those, and maybe most importantly those, that show I care. It's simply too dangerous to my well-being to do so. But how do I explain this? When I think about going to visit him at the hospital after he was shot, and I think about this a lot, I know in my core that he wouldn't have received my gesture as one of love and concern. Rather, after gathering the strength to grant him his humanity and going to his side because that's what you do in these situations, especially for family, I would have answered his siren's call. He didn't want my love and concern. He wanted me to abandon myself.

Finally, after all he had said and done to me, I would show, by going to his bedside, that I couldn't bear to not be there for him, his victory shining bright in his eyes. I can imagine his words, "I knew you'd come, Babe."

These would be words of victory, not of gratitude. This is all he would need to prove that he got by with everything he had done to me, and in the end, I wasn't even going to stand up for myself. I was going to hand myself over, and now he had me for life. I would confirm for him I deserved everything he had ever done to me because in the end, I couldn't resist caring for him, no matter how awful he had been to me. I would have telepathically signed a binding agreement that allowed his continued abuse for life.

And then there's the humanitarian in me who grants him that there is a reason for his behavior. I don't know what it is, but there has to be a reason. Right?

I fall asleep wanting a parent's love and comfort. I desire being able to turn to my parents when I have fallen on hard times. It's a little difficult to turn to them when they're the cause of my hard times. It's doubly difficult when one of them acts like I have created his hard times and I owe it to him to be there for him, and the other one is as needy as I am, and is wanting me to parent her.

I'm sickened by it all.

I'm most lost to find an explanation for my mom. Why didn't she leave him? Why won't she stand up for herself? I'm aware that she has a story too. And regardless, whatever her story is that makes her incapable of acting, it is nothing so egregious that she deserved the treatment she received from him. My mother is a kind soul, albeit a stubborn and naïve one.

I am loyal. I am compassionate. I am a person who loves. And yet, I am unable to extend these things to my parents. I am stuck in a dead heat between self-preservation and all-consuming guilt.

The next morning, I dig out the short stories from my creative writing workshop the spring of my junior year. I frantically search for a story I wrote in the third person with my dad, his character named Andy, as the main character. The story opens with him downing a beer and working up the courage to call his daughter. He rationalizes and justifies all his reasons for leaving her mother and the family. I threw in the thing about being done with the obligations of parenthood. "You achieve," as my professor said in her notes, "empathy with the extremely unsympathetic main character. What you do, though, is to make us experience what he is doing from his point of view, and finally we can't really say that he is evil or inhuman, even though what he does hurts others."

My classmates had very visceral reactions to this story and were mad at me. I think for the very reason the professor said. Even the best of us have a difficult time feeling empathy for an unsympathetic character or person.

Why, I wonder, *am I working harder to find his humanity than he is?*

I listen to the leaves crunching under my feet. All the trees are now bare, and campus is unusually quiet today. Turmoil races through me, driving the pace of my footsteps. They are fast, furious, and ambivalent.

The mandatory audition is in two hours and I still don't know what I'm going to do. Pilobolus is an internationally known company. I can't imagine being a member of their troupe. Of course, nothing says I would make the audition, but they've held auditions at the other twelve universities they've performed at this semester and have yet to find the right person for the one spot they have. ISU is the last campus on their schedule. My former director (who is still very involved in the program) claims to know they are hopeful to find the person here.

"It's all coming down to the improv section of the audition, Connie," she says to me with a loaded look in her eyes. In my tenure at ISU, I have become one of the top improvisers on campus.

What I can't tell her is how terrified I am.

I'm so afraid of becoming an alcoholic or a drug addict given my current state, and aren't all performers one of those two things, if not both? I would have to drop out of college at semester and move. My well-being would be in the hands of people I don't know. I'm so fragile. A truth I'm barely admitting to myself. To admit it to a person, verbally, would shatter me.

"That's it," I proclaim as I enter the building, "I'm blowing the audition."

Since I'm being forced to audition, I have to blow it: this from the person who vowed never to blow an audition again. I guess I wasn't considering the possibility of intentionality at the time.

I'm amazing during the technical parts of the audition. In fact, I'm beyond amazing. I think it's because I know I'm going to blow the improv part, so I'm in this weird state of calm and I'm fully relaxed. I know I will soon eliminate any possibility of making it.

I can tell by the look on the former director's face she is happy with my performance.

I grow sick as I wait my turn to improv. Under normal circumstances, I'm confident I would be a contender.

I'm called forward. I walk to the middle of the room. I want to run away, not audition. Why did it have to be mandatory?

I am intentionally awful.

I absorb the surprise and disappointment of the room.

I finish.

I don't stay for the rest of the dancers' auditions.

I walk past everyone and keep going right out the door.

About halfway down the long hall, the former director, a five-foot bundle of mad and humiliated energy comes screaming down the hall.

My neck is moist and hot from the words she spits on it.

I turn to face her.

Tears are rolling down my face.

Shame is pouring out of me.

My favorite professor, an African-American man, is coming up behind her. His face is kind, forgiving, but confused.

"You will never be a professional dancer! Did you hear me?"

I look at her, pleading with her to understand. But how can she understand something that I've never talked about?

Briefly, I wonder why she doesn't ask me why I intentionally blew the audition. Isn't she even curious?

My eyes beg for her forgiveness.

She shows no desire to do so.

In a state of shame that is so complete it ravages my being, I turn and leave the building.

I have let her down so much. I changed my major from dance to literature at the end of my freshman year without telling her. (I went from rising-star freshman to in-the-gutter sophomore. It took me a full year to redeem myself.) I changed my major over another can't-talk-to-anyone-about-this issue. I had to take anatomy in order to major in dance, and my anatomy professor was sexually harassing me. Since I don't talk about things, the only way I could end this was to drop the class, and the only way to not take the class again was to switch my major. Somehow it all made sense at the time.

And now, this.

She must think . . . I stop my thinking. I don't want to know what she thinks of me.

I'm so lost and confused. I call my mom, "Can you come up here first thing in the morning? I need to talk to you."

My voice is desperate and scared.

"I can't take this anymore," I say within minutes of her walking in my apartment. "I need therapy. I need to drop out of school. My grades are tanking anyway, and my student loans are piling up, and for what? Shit grades. These aren't the grades I want. I just want out of it all."

"Please, don't drop out, Connie Sue. You only have one semester left. If you drop out now, you probably won't come back. And no matter what, once you have that degree, no one can take it from you," her eyes plead with me.

While my mom is somewhat selfish in this request (she didn't go to college when she had the chance, and she really wants me to have a higher degree) she is right, and I know this.

"Trust me," she says, patting my leg, "your grades won't even matter in the end." I put some stock in this since she has co-owned a Manpower franchise most of my life.

However, to me they do. I'm not one who sits comfortably in mediocrity.

We go to lunch, I thank her for coming up, and I allow it to slip in, just a little bit, that she was there for me when I called her in need.

My gun dreams become more than prolific. On the nights I'm not hearing Lily Tomlin's voice ringy-dingying, *I'm being stalked across campus by a man with a rifle. He is patient. He is unwavering in his desire to hunt me down. Often, I find myself walking home from a date, alone. I hear footsteps behind me, and I know.*

I turn.

I hear the bang before I see him.

In slow motion I watch the bullet rotating through the air and BAM!

I'm flying through the air, weightless and free. The earth is a small blue thing below me. Suddenly, I'm falling down towards the planet. As I fall, I separate from my body, and sail above me until I am a dot on its surface. I gently float towards the earth and my wounded self, until I'm hovering above me. I watch as they place my body on a gurney. The golden bullet is flush with my skin. The hole it creates is a perfect circle.

I can see an engraving on the bullet's base, but can't read it.

There is a beautiful burgundy red stream of blood running down between my eyes and off to one side of my nose. It rivers down my cheek to its delta, my neck, and pools there.

Thrust into my body, I feel the gurney being lifted. The legs smack against my back as they lock into a raised position. I'm rolled into an ambulance.

I nearly fall out of bed. My pajama top is stuck to my sweaty skin. I listen for predators. It's only two in the morning. I close my eyes and pray for dreamless sleep.

Everywhere I go, I feel paranoid. I start to think there *is* someone watching me, and then, "Hey, Connie has a secret admirer," Jenny says, as I walk into the dance studio.

"Huh?"

"Haven't you seen the Daily?" another dancer asks.

"No," I say, and grab the paper from her hand.

Connie, I've been watching and admiring you from afar. Soon I will let you know who I am, Your Secret Admirer.

I, with shocking speed, completely and absolutely freak out, on the inside.

"Oooh," my friends say in unison. "Connie's got a secret admirer."

"I do not have a secret admirer. The whole tone of this is creepy. I have a stalker," I throw the paper at them.

"Oh, I don't think it's that creepy," Jenny says.

"I think it is. I'm not excited about this," I start stretching. My friends go on about how they wish they had a secret admirer.

"You can have him," I say. They have no way of understanding how freaked out this makes me. No one knows about my dreams. While they know my dad was shot, they don't know about the night I packed all the guns in my red duffle bag, which is currently thrown against the wall with my dance shoes and leg warmers inside.

Mental note, get a new dance bag.

Everywhere I go I'm unnerved. I start asking guy friends to walk me places.

"Hello," I answer the phone.

"Hey, it's Jenny. There's another personal in the paper for you. This time it sounds creepy."

"What do you mean? Read it to me," I say.

The beginning is similar to the other, but this one ends differently. Jenny reads, "I'll be watching you from the wings."

Oh, great. BARJCHÉ is in two weeks. "He's either a dancer," I say.

"Or part of the stage crew," Jenny finishes.

"We know everybody backstage. Well, and all the dancers too. Why wouldn't this person just let you know he likes you?" Jenny ponders.

"Because like everything in my life, this is completely fucked up."

I think for a minute.

"Hey, who's on the staff of the Daily?" I ask.

Jenny reads the names. There are two people I know.

"Be outside of your apartment in five minutes. I'm picking you up, and we're going to the Daily office."

One of the two people I know is working, and after much bribing he does what he should not: gives me the name of the person who took out the ad.

It's a dancer.

Jenny and I stare at each other. In lockstep, we say, "I thought he was gay."

I feel more vulnerable than I did before.

He puts two more ads in the paper before our big performance. Every time I'm on the stage, he's backstage staring at me.

I want to run. I want to be anonymous.

No one knows how shaken I am. No one really notices that I never go anywhere alone. But by the time VEISHA (ISU's week-long campus celebration in spring) rolls around, my stalker has gotten the message, my dreams aren't as numerous, and I'm enjoying the festivities of my senior year.

I tell Jenny I'll meet her at Thumbs.

"I'm surprised. Where is everyone?" I look around the near-empty bar.

"Yeah, it's a little unusual, but hey, it's VEISHA, things are bound to pick up," she says.

We settle in, eventually more friends join us, and then I turn around. The bar is packed to the four corners. This happened without me noticing. Nighttime has also arrived unnoticed.

"I'm going to the loo," Jenny says.

"Okay," I barely return.

Something has gone very wrong. The crowd circles in front

of me as I do a few 360s, and, like how the air before a tornado changes, something has definitely changed, and it's not for the better.

My instincts say run.

"I'm back," Jenny touches my shoulder.

"I'm leaving," I say. I leave the bar without answering her question why.

I feel a huge resistance as I make my way to the door. This is not normal. Something is off. But what?

It's hard not to think of Dorothy as I open the door and step outside, only because I step into a completely unknown world.

People are everywhere. That's not unusual. It's VEISHA, tons of people come to Ames for the event, and it's a beautiful spring night. Of course, lots of people are about. But what's not usual is that they all have open containers, on campus.

People are sitting on the curb drinking.

People are strolling down the sidewalk drinking.

But they're not just talking and having a good time. They're yelling and screaming. Their gestures are huge and grotesque. Everything and everyone seems completely out of control.

Then, BANG, followed by loud cheers. BANG, again followed by loud cheers. I try identifying the sound. It sounds like crushing metal, but . . .

An imaginary hand turns my head, changing my focus from a guy sitting on the curb, who just poured beer down his shirt when he leaned back in uproarious laughter, to the street.

BANG!

Cheers.

BANG!

Cheers.

Slack-jawed, I stretch to see above the crowd and watch as people try to roll a police car.

People everywhere are going crazy.

Then, a momentary, stunned silence befalls Welch Avenue when something I can't see is set on fire. A celebration full of righteous defiance (over what, I have no idea) explodes.

What has made everybody go nuts?

Violently nuts.

I try to find a frame of reference for what I'm seeing. I can't.

As inconspicuously as possible, I walk to the top of Welch Avenue where I parked my car.

"Whoa, sorry man. Didn't mean to do that," someone says to me. He starts trying to wipe off the beer he just intentionally poured down my shirt. He casually stops, both hands on my breast.

I shove him away. "No worries," I say.

Loud clamors of success drown out whatever he says back to me; all for the better, as he looks pretty pissed.

I turn to see what all the hand pumping and chest pounding is about. A shirtless guy has scaled a flagpole, and is hanging three bras from it.

"What the hell," I say to no one. Other than the turmoil and chaos of my own life, I have nothing to compare this to. It makes absolutely no sense. It defines being unhinged without a purpose.

I slink to my car, luckily unnoticed, and head for home.

Thank God, I live off campus.

I wake up assuming this was all some weird hallucination. It didn't really happen. Somehow it was just my internal chaos externalizing itself. I really believe I am the only one who saw this.

Until I read the *Ames Tribune*.

By the end of the weekend, VEISHA 1988 goes down in history as the first VEISHA riot. There's a large amount of property damage; a huge hole has been left in the asphalt on Welch Avenue where a huge bonfire was set; there are multiple arrests, of which only a small percentage are ISU students; and, ISU is something it was not before: a campus where large-scale violence broke out for no reason at all.

A decades-old campus tradition is forever scarred. I'm only grateful I was able to choreograph the annual musical for Stars Over VEISHA, *The Best Little Whorehouse in Texas*, my junior year before it all blew up.

Joe calls me from Boston, "What the hell happened in Ames?"

"I wish I could tell you," I say. "It was all so unhinged, and very scary. I'm glad I just left campus. The energy was all wrong."

I think, but don't say: *you know, like our lives.*

"All I know is I don't ever want to be in a mob like that again," I add.

Unable to graduate in May, I'm on campus for the summer taking a philosophy class in order to receive the three credits I lost as a result of dropping my class in the fall.

I'm punting my way through this class while trying to figure out where I'm going after I graduate in August. Forked River is not an option. I'm leaning towards going to Boston with Joe and Kathy, but somehow that feels suffocating.

It's July 4th.

The trial is now over and behind everyone. The woman was indeed charged and sentenced to several years in prison in the absence of a weapon and with reasonable doubt. My dad, who originally said he could not identify the shooter because he hadn't seen the person, somehow at the trial knew exactly who it was, "I would recognize that voice anywhere," he said to me on the phone, and I'm assuming in the courtroom, too.

I actually considered going to the trial.

As I sit in my apartment and weigh my options for the evening (stay in, go out with friends), my mind reflects on the day I skipped class, got in my Hawkeye-colored Mustang, and drove south on I-35.

I crossed the city limits of the small town where the trial was being held, and pulled into a parking lot. The sky was a football-day sky: bright blue with large, puffy white clouds billowing through the air. It was one of those spring days that feels more like fall. I thought about campfires, hot dogs, and roasted marshmallows. I didn't want to think about love triangles, murder, and how I had no degree of separation from the whole thing.

I sat staring at a Phillip's 66 sign and recalled the one conversation I had with my dad before the trial. Well, I can't really call it a conversation. It was a monologue from the minute I said hello.

His emphasis was on the persecution he had suffered, "You

know, there were a lot of men in Forked River doing what I was doing."

I laughed. I was about to say, *nice euphemistic phrase for cheating*, but he rolled over me. He went on as if he were now the representative Everyman of adultery. "And who are they to point the finger at me? What hypocrites."

After several minutes of this, I interrupted him, and asked, "Are you at all curious as to how I have been affected by all of this?"

"You know, I'm the victim here, Connie Sue," he spewed.

I ended the conversation.

"What the hell am I doing here?" I reproached myself out loud. A man pumping gas heard me, and turned in my direction.

I exited the parking lot, made a right at the lights, and left town.

I couldn't stomach watching him play the victim. And, of course, the suspected woman would be there. I knew that I'd know by looking at her if she was innocent or not; and regardless, I knew she'd be convicted. Whatever the truth is in all of this, no one knows, but it does seem like something was, is, and has been covered up: the truth protected.

This leads me to conclude that my father is being protected. He's been allowed, on the largest stage of his life, to be the victim: the one everyone is supposed to feel sorry for.

How do I grant compassion and victimhood to someone who has forsaken everything concerning my siblings, my mother, and me, and has blamed us for everything that has gone wrong in his life? Looking back, it seems to me he had it pretty good. I'm still searching for that awful, worthy-of-breaking-a-blood-bond thing we all did.

On my drive back to Ames, I wondered if I would feel differently if he had had a heart attack, or he had been in a car wreck, or he had slipped and fallen off a cliff.

I couldn't go to the trial and feel sympathy for a man whom, the few times I have risked letting him know he was hurting my feelings, either told me he wasn't responsible for how I reacted to things or started crying and accused me of being mean for even suggesting he would do such a thing.

My burning question: what is the purpose of him surviving?

I arrived back at campus in time to make company class.

Jenny looked at me when I entered the studio, waiting for my signal. I gave her a thumbs up, and melted my body down onto the floor to stretch. On that day, more than ever, I needed our visit to Thumbs after class. It had become part of our regular Thursday night routine during the spring semester. Two of the bartenders knew us, and as soon as they saw us coming, two glasses and a free pitcher were placed at the bar for us. A lightweight to begin with, and having just danced for two hours, I was usually quite trashed after this weekly event.

My emotional equilibrium was off and I struggled through class. I was relieved to discover my instability had been concealed, when one of my professors told me that was the best he'd seen me dance in awhile.

Maybe he was just being nice. He let me know privately at the beginning of class that he had been thinking about me, "today," he emphasized, to let me know he knew the trial was taking place.

I left the studio thinking my world was completely upside-down. My father was sitting in a courtroom that day, while a woman he supposedly had a decades-long affair with was on trial for shooting him and murdering another woman.

I stopped.

I wondered if the murdered woman's husband was there.

I couldn't imagine that man's world. I knew my dad was an asshole. The husband claimed in an interview he had never heard of my dad until the day his wife died. I suspect he's completely lost. I'm sad for him because I'm sure when all was said and done, he didn't feel like he knew his wife either. I really wanted him to know that my dad had ruined many people's lives.

I felt exposed in dance class that evening. Everyone, I assumed could tell I was in crisis. Everyone else in the studio was not, or so I assumed. I guess you never really know. It's just that mine was a super-hyped-up-very-public-all-over-the-news kind of crisis. Everyone knew mine, but no one really *knew* mine. No one ever asked. Or if they did, it was not in a sincere do-you-need-to-sit-down-and-talk kind of way. They expected fun, funny, always smiling, full of energy, Connie. Not sad, out of control, fuck all of this, Connie. They used to love all my philosophical meanderings until I had something to really philosophically meander about. At least this is how I felt.

I got lucky and got a parking spot right in front of Thumbs. Jenny was already at the bar.

"Boy, do I need this tonight," I said, and pulled my stool up to the bar.

"You were a little quiet tonight," she said.

"Yeah, the trial started today."

"That's right. Well," she said, and took my glass, "you'll be needing this then."

We both laughed. If one thing defined Jenny and me, it was laughing. We were a comedy show unto ourselves, and it was all very hysterical that night until I turned to face her.

"Oh, Jenny, you are so right. That is so fun . . ." I moved to slap Jenny on the shoulder in a gesture of agreement and I missed. I sailed right by her. My beer went flying in the air, spilling on the floor below me. I landed in a push-up position, and stopped my body right before my face hit the floor. Beer got in my hair and on my shirt. I stayed there for several seconds. My world spun around me and phased out. I didn't hear, see, or smell anything of the bar.

I'm in trouble, I heard. It was my voice, but it wasn't.

I need to stop this now, the I-It continued.

There's no need to overcome alcoholism before being able to deal with all the familial shit.

I wholly agreed with the I-It.

Suddenly, overwhelmed by the smell of beer, I was brought back to Thumbs and Jenny and the two bartenders leaning over the bar in wide-eyed, mouth agape, stunned breathlessness, waiting to see if I was okay.

I stood.

Beer dripped from my hair. My shirt adhered to my stomach.

"Are you okay?" they asked in unison.

"Yeah, but I'm going home," I said, and left.

I got in my car, and drove on autopilot to my apartment.

The night's events made me all too aware of two things. One,

I was officially messed up, and two, I didn't want to become an alcoholic to cover up that fact.

I sigh and let the sting of the memories pass.

Since it is the Fourth, everyone will be partying. This makes me not want to be on campus.

I don't want to be anywhere really, least of all where I am, wherever that is.

I'm now officially acting happy when I am not, so therefore, I'm always acting. My natural disposition of optimism and felicity is now overwhelmed by my reality. I feel like a shadow is always hovering right above me, muting the sun. I am never comfortable in my skin, which is new and foreign to me. I don't like it at all. I have avoided the dance department all summer. Not sure why, but this means I haven't danced now in over a month. That might be part of my problem. Nothing is getting out of me. Nothing is being released. Maybe that's a good thing. Maybe it will make me look at some stuff, but it feels awful. It feels crawly. It feels dark and murky.

I order a pizza.

I eat alone.

It's 8:00, and I decide I'm going home.

Halfway through the drive, darkness overtakes the cornfields. Iowa, a state many people think is flat and part of the plains, is actually very rolling in my corner of the state. I always feel like I've been dropped inside a huge down-filled pillow, its sides billowing up around me.

Tonight, that imagery is freaking me out.

As dusk falls over row after row of cornstalks, green waves

roll over these gentle hills. The stalks create the illusion of an emerald sea stretched out across the acres of regimented fields.

There are no lights on the single-lane country roads, but every small town within my vision is setting off fireworks. Little colorful spirals pop up all around me in the distance. I'm enjoying it all until I relax. Then, my fears surface with ferocious intent. Every pop of the fireworks is a gun. I duck as if they are real and someone is shooting at the car.

I see images darting into the road. I swerve when nothing is there. Then, speeding, I come upon a railroad crossing and throw on the brakes yelling, "Oh, my God. Oh, my God," convinced I'm about to hit someone. My car stops parallel to the railroad tracks. I straddle both lanes of traffic. Thank God, no one else is on the road.

The cool leather of the steering wheel feels good on my forehead. My whole body is shaking as I rest there.

I cry.

I breathe.

I calm myself down.

Now, I can identify that the 'someone' who freaked me out was the railroad-crossing gate.

If I don't collect myself, I fear I'll be dead before I reach Forked River.

I stay where I am until the hills are no longer big monster blobs coming to cover the car, the railroad gate is just a railroad gate, and I can make out other normal things like farmhouses and silos.

I put the car in first, slowly release the clutch, and cross the railroad tracks.

My mom is upstairs when I get home.

"Something just told me you were coming home," she says to me from the landing. "I wish you would've come before dark, though. You know how I worry so."

I tell my mom about my crazy drive, the railroad gate man, and the monster blobs. We're sitting at the top of the stairs. She's stroking my back and my hair. She doesn't speak. She just listens and offers the occasional, "Uh-hum," and adds when I'm finished, "I'm just glad you got here safely."

We fall into a conversation of happier times, like when she and I walked to town in a nice, gentle snow that turned into a blizzard on the way home.

We stopped at a friend's cake shop about five blocks from our house where we enjoyed cupcakes and tea before continuing home.

"The cupcakes will give us the strength to get up the Second Street hill," my mom had said, winking at me as I licked the frosting off my cupcake.

I go to bed not sure how to classify my childhood memories anymore. Good times that I experienced with my mom, and only my mom, remain solid and real, but anything involving my dad just feels like a farce. They couldn't mean anything to him, we can't mean anything to him, or he wouldn't have walked away. And he most certainly walked away from our whole family, not just my mom. No matter what he says, someone who cares doesn't injure and hurt. I just know this to be true. I don't need any more evidence than that tether I still feel to the place before. It's much weaker than when I was a child, but I'm certain that what I feel is love from that source. A person who intentionally injures another doesn't also love that person. And I'm clear that this is not the same thing as parents disciplining their kids. I know the difference.

I'm roused out of sleep. My mom is quietly saying my name and rubbing my shoulder. I open my eyes and find her sitting on my bed.

"What? What is it?" I ask.

"Can I ask you a question?" she says.

Oh God, here it comes. What do I say when she asks? The truth?

"Yes, I've had sex. Not a lot, but I've had it."

Or do I lie?

"Nope. Not yet."

Then she throws me for a loop, "Do you think I'm still sexy?"

First, I feel immense relief. Second, I feel a sticky, icky feeling.

Ask one of your friends, flies through my brain, but "Sure Mom," is what comes out of mouth.

"Really," her face lights up.

Doesn't she know sexy is not my impression of her? Beautiful, okay, my mother was a knockout in her youth. Vivacious, yes, my mother is always full of enthusiasm, optimism, and laughs. But when it comes to sexy, no. That category is replaced with naïve and innocent.

"Thank you," she says, and kisses my cheek.

I close my eyes. I'm immediately walking up to the house from Ash Street. I've been aware of the person following me for some time, and because of the position of the sun, his shadow is elongated beside me. I can see the shadow of the rifle bouncing up and down in his palm.

And then the air changes.

The man's shadow disappears.

I smell the air, and run to the house.

I find my mother first, "There's a tornado coming."

I run to the front door. It's about two miles away.

"What?" my mom asks.

"There's a tornado coming," I say, pointing towards the door.

"Let me see," she says, and right before she can look, Fran distracts her.

"Fran, there's a tornado coming," I yell.

"So what? Mom, I need you to do…"

The sound of the wind muffles the rest of Fran's response.

I begin to panic. Every time my mom is about to look, someone else distracts her. I try, and try, and try, until my dad tells me to leave her alone.

"But there's a tornado coming. We all need to get to the basement. Come, look out the door," which I do. It's now across the street shredding our neighbor's garage.

My dad sits down in his recliner, smiles at me, and shakes open the paper.

"Mom! Mom!" I yell. "We have to get to the basement!"

"Go ahead, Connie Sue. I have to help your siblings. We'll be there in a minute."

In a split second, I'm on the familiar track. I jump the stairs, run down the hall, hide under the stairs, and count to eight.

And then, it's all over.

The house is gone.

No one made it to the basement but me.

I return my cap and gown to the woman assigned to A thru M. She hands me my diploma.

"Good luck," she says.

I find my mom and Fran where I asked them to wait, and off we go to dinner. I don't know how to act really. This is another big moment in life that has gone off rather flat. I'm beginning to expect little from events meant to draw one's family around in love and support and celebration.

The first and last time that happened for me is when I was in the Forked River Jr. Miss Pageant. I had to stay with a host family for the weekend of the pageant, and the day of the competition my host mom gave me a card and a present. My whole family had signed the card wishing me luck. The present was a necklace with three freshwater pearls and a small diamond on a gold chain.

I still have that necklace.

Every time I wear it, I feel what it represents for me: hope, innocence, and what once was. It represents a time when my whole family was there for me, and it's also the announcement of my family's death. It represents joy walking hand in hand with sorrow. It may well be my destiny to always embody these two things simultaneously like lovers dancing around, within, and through one another. I am a Gemini after all.

It's nice of Fran to come with my mom, but I'm uncomfortable. Plus, I have a date with a guy I've been seeing for about a month. It's our good-bye date. I have no feelings for him. We've had some fun. But that's not hard to do.

The only real relationship I had in college was about two years long. Matt was a great guy, but possessive and suicidal.

Not in a depressed way, however. He was just done with this life, and told me often, "I just want to return because it's a lot nicer there. I haven't forgotten what it's like, and I miss it."

I never told him that I knew exactly what he was talking about. I had a feeling he would try for a couple's suicide. But I was, and am, far from done with this life.

Although I have experienced things I could have never imagined, I'm still standing. I'm still walking. I'm still breathing. And while I might just be surviving at the moment, my optimism outweighs the events of the past twenty-one years.

I have yet to discover who I am, and I want to know.

I leave my mom and Fran at the hotel, assuring them I will be back by eleven. I'm not in the mood for a late night, and I don't want to keep them up. Still, I feel like a heel. They made the effort to come up, and I'm ditching them.

Back to the hotel by ten, I explain it truly was just a good-bye date, and we chat about nothing really. Over the course of the last three weeks, I've decided to move to Milwaukee on a whim. I have no job, but I have a place to stay with a friend, and figure I will head straight to Manpower. Having been one of their scholarship winners, and knowing how an office runs, I figure I can get something.

"When are you leaving for Milwaukee?" Fran asks.

"In a couple of weeks. I told Susie I would be there September first," I answer her in the dark.

Soon we all exchange our good nights, and at least pretend to sleep. But I feel it is a long time before any of us actually do. I feel we are all staring into space, into the dark void of all of our futures.

Finally, I fall asleep.

The man with the rifle is immediately following me as I drive out of Ames. He's speeding down the highway behind me, the barrel of his gun sticking out his window. I try everything to ditch him.

I wake up before I know if I eluded him.

Sitting in the dark, staring into the unfamiliar space of my future, I pray my nightmares don't follow me to Milwaukee.

Part III

Clean Up

"When our inner situation is not made conscious,
it appears outside as fate."

– Carl Jung

"I learn by going where I have to go."

– Theodore Roethke

"It's just two simple words."

– My therapist

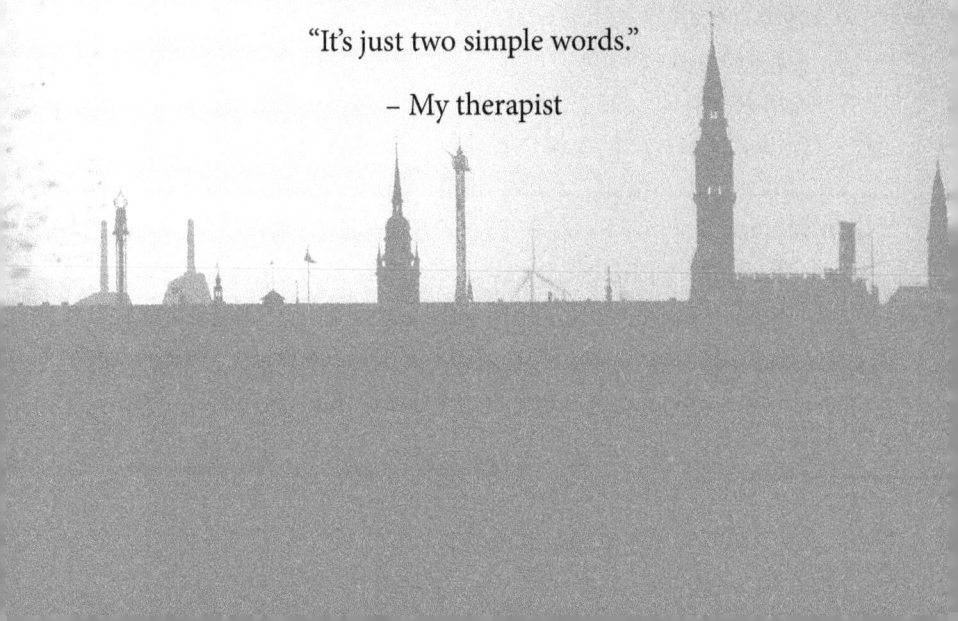

"If we walk far enough," says Dorothy, "we shall sometime come to someplace."

– L. Frank Baum

And she does: the Emerald City of Oz. Dorothy believes upon arriving that her troubles are now behind her. After all, she and her comrades escaped the wicked witch, found their way through the forest, and were unknowingly rescued by Glinda in the poppy field. Now, surely the great and powerful Oz would send her home. Right?

Much like Dorothy, I left Iowa convinced, or at least very hopeful, that my hard times were behind me. At least my father and his actions couldn't touch me in Milwaukee; and my story, as much as it could be, was mine to share. I didn't have to tell anyone anything about my past if I didn't want to. And because of that, I believed I could tuck my past away in the attic trunk of my mind and be shut of it.

I could now be me.

Couldn't I?

When I arrived in Milwaukee, I didn't get my hair done, my dress refreshed, or my make-up reapplied to become presentable for my journey ahead. Rather, I was thrown right into the hunt with scarce resources and no comrades. When the journey on my metaphorical yellow brick road ended, I saw nothing but wide-open space and uncharted territory. I had done something no one in my family had done before me:

moved nearly four hundred miles away from home with only myself to rely on. I had to create everything that was to come next. And what I desired most, to be in full possession of my life and my future, was now available to me.

When I looked around, nothing was recognizable or familiar.

This was a relief. I was electrified. I was frightened. I was energized. I swam in dread.

I watched everything I had known float up into the sky, like Oz in the untethered balloon. Only I was the one who had untethered the balloon of my life.

I now had what I had desired for so many years: me, myself, and I, free of the unpredictability of my father and the disastrous consequences of his lying and betrayal. This fueled my ability to make my own judgments, to call my own shots. For I believed, left to my own devices, I could create a far better future than the one my parents had prepared me for.

It was this simple in my mind: I was either going to find my way home to myself, or I wasn't.

It's a warm late August day.

I feel somewhat settled in as I walk to my car. I arrived in Milwaukee two days ago with everything I own jammed into my hatchback and two hundred dollars in my purse.

It's not much, but at least I'm not in Forked River.

I have an interview at the Manpower headquarters in an hour. Considering the person interviewing me knows my mom, and I am a scholarship winner, I'm confident I will be offered a job.

I turn off Ogden Avenue onto Farwell Avenue. I like the East Side, but in two days time, I've decided parking absolutely sucks. I haven't been able to park on Prospect Avenue near the apartment once in the last two days.

As I wait to cross the street, I realize my car isn't there. Maybe I parked another block up. My car isn't there either. I walk back to where I originally thought my car should be and read the near-by tow away sign. According to the sign, my car was towed within the last half an hour.

I fight crying as I walk back to the apartment. I call Manpower, tell them what has happened, and reschedule my interview.

Buzzz, the intercom goes off.

"Yes," I make a good effort to sound calm.

"We're scheduled to fix two windows in your apartment. Is this a good time for us to do it?" It's a male voice. He seems pleasant.

I vaguely remember my roommate saying something about this. "Sure," I say, and buzz them in.

I try to stop crying, and then . . .

"Whom did I just buzz up?" I ask the four walls.

"Am I nuts?"

I jump when I hear a knock at the door. Now I'm shaken, and scared.

Standing on the other side of the threshold are two men, one not much taller than me, the other at least six feet. They are both in paint-splotched clothes, and look only slightly cleaner than street people.

For a brief moment, I fear for my life. Overwhelmed by this fear, having no idea how to retrieve my car, and not knowing how to get ahold of my roommate for help, I break down in front of these two strange strangers.

"Oh, my goodness," the short man says. "What's happened? Can we help?"

His voice is fatherly and protective.

I'm defeated by his compassion.

Through sobs and slobber, I say, "I just moved here two days ago, I had a job interview this morning, and my car's been towed. I have no idea who to call or where to go to get it back."

"Oh, honey," the tall man says so sweetly. "Don't you have anyone you can call?"

My singularity in the world blows up in my face.

"No," my response hangs in my consciousness for some time, "I don't."

"I'm from Iowa," I try to collect myself, "and I don't know how to get ahold of my roommate. She's in sales, and in her car all day."

I excuse myself and go to the bathroom to blow my nose. Somewhat composed, I return to the doorway.

"Well," the short man says, "don't you worry. We're going to help you."

"How?"

"Well, we'll take you to the courthouse. That's where you'll get your car back."

"Okay," I say, suddenly overtaken by a feeling of trust.

Their grass green station wagon, complete with two ladders on top, and the back end stuffed full of paint and other supplies needed for their profession, is parked right in front of the apartment building. The word "ramshackle" comes to mind as I pause for a moment, doubting my feeling of trust.

There is no room in the back seat for me, so I slide into the front seat and ride down to the Milwaukee County Courthouse between Lennie and George. They told me their names, but all I can think of are the two characters from *Of Mice and Men*.

Once we arrive at the courthouse, George tells Lennie to go in with me, "I'll just be circling around the courthouse. You guys come back to this corner when she's finished, and I'll pick you up."

Lennie explains my situation to the information desk attendant. Kindly, she directs us to the appropriate office.

After twenty minutes, with Lennie waiting patiently at my side, I'm called into the office of Napoleon. He is my height, so he's no more than 5'4", bald, and has a malcontent I-hate-my-job-and-I-hate-you scowl on his face. I come to learn he hates college-educated people the most, even though the letters behind his name on the little plaque sitting squarely in the center of his desk for all to see suggests that he, too, attended college.

"I don't care if you've only lived here two days. You've been to college. Can't you read signs?" his berating has been going on for at least five minutes.

After another twenty minutes of explaining to me city regulations for parking, and re-emphasizing how much my education failed me, he tells me that my car is in the city tow lot under the 794 overpass.

I have no idea where that is.

"Here, you'll need this," he hands me what looks like a ticket. "You can't get your car until you pay seventy-five dollars. You can do that out at the cashier's desk. Good day," he dismisses me.

My whole body is trembling. I struggle to open the heavy, solid-wood door of his office.

Not knowing the location of the 794 overpass is a concern, but not my biggest. My biggest concern: I only have thirty dollars with me, and no credit card.

I'm certain I look ready to faint when I walk up to Lennie because I feel ready to faint.

"Oh dear, what on Earth is wrong?"

Once again, I feel like I'm in the middle of a Flannery O'Connor story. This tall, awkward, slightly-intellectually-slow stranger comes over to me and wraps his arms around me. I fall into his chest.

I'm in the Milwaukee County Courthouse, alone, away from everything and everyone I know, and a complete stranger, someone I would've been told not to trust (solely due to his appearance and mannerisms) is showing me compassion, mercy, and kindness. Someone is hugging *me*. Someone is asking *me* what is wrong. Someone is helping *me*.

I can't stop crying.

How is this stranger able to do for me what I feel like no one else has been able or willing to do? Why is he interested in simply caring about me in a time of need, when the people who are supposed to do so haven't? I know in my mind that this isn't fully true, or fair, but I do know that my whole family is in need, and that makes their support unavailable to me, just as I suppose mine is to them.

And then, shame ravages my being like a flash flood. I'm afraid to tell this person, who has been so kind to me, that it was all for naught because I don't have the money to get my car.

"What is it?" he pushes me away. He stoops over, so we are looking eye to eye.

This alone terrifies me.

"My car is in some tow lot under some overpass somewhere, and I need seventy-five dollars to get it," I look down in complete shame.

It's next to impossible for me to admit I'm incapable of taking care of myself.

"I only have thirty dollars with me, and I don't own a credit card." I'm probably the only person over twenty in 1988 who doesn't.

"Don't you worry, Connie," the statement of my name hits me hard.

It's not like people don't speak my name, but this is different. I feel recognized, seen. In this moment I realize how invisible I've felt.

"We'll help you," he says.

Then, to my astonishment, he takes out his wallet and gives me forty-five dollars. "Here," he says. "Let's go over to the counter so you can pay. Then we'll take you to your car."

"Thank you so much. You are very kind," I say, as we walk down the steps to go outside.

"Oh my gosh!" I gasp. "Your friend. He's been circling the courthouse for at least forty-five minutes. I feel awful," my insides are melting from humiliation.

"Don't worry. He knows I was with you, so he knows you're okay," Lennie says, and pats my shoulder.

How odd. It never crossed my mind that George would be concerned about my well-being. My experience tells me he would be pissed off because, of course, this only took so long just to piss him off.

Lennie tells George the location of my car.

I apologize, apologize, apologize.

"Never mind," George says. "You obviously needed help. And isn't that why we're all here? To help each other when we're in a time of need?"

That's what I've been taught. That's what I believe. That's what I try to do. But it's rarely been my experience when I've been in need.

They take me to my car.

"Thank you both so much. How will I get the money back to you?"

"We'll stop by next Wednesday at nine in the morning. You can pay us back then."

"Absolutely," I say. There is no way I will let them down.

Two days later, my interview goes well. Since I've worked in my mom's office and my learning curve is short, I'm placed in a Manpower office in Grafton, a small town about thirty minutes outside Milwaukee.

Luckily, I don't start for another week, which allows me to be home today, the Wednesday George and Lennie are supposed to pick up their money.

I'm so grateful to these two men. They gave me their time, their money, and ended up rescheduling the work on the apartment. And George was just out in his car, circling the courthouse waiting on us. He never showed me an ounce of frustration. They were two angels delivered to me that day.

I buzz them up. I stand in the open door waiting for them.

Lennie is so kind when he asks, "Do you have our money?"

I'm so happy to say I do. Even though I'm down to sixty dollars, I'm not so panicked, since I start my job on Monday.

I hand him the money, and they both smile at me.

"You know, Connie, everything's going to be okay," Lennie says.

George adds, "You'll be alright."

"Thank you both. For everything. You really are very kind men."

I say good-bye, and close the door.

I'm filled with optimism when I replay their words in my head, 'everything's going to be okay. You'll be alright.'

Yes, I think, I will.

Overcome with joy, and infused with energy, I head out for a walk along the lake.

I'm in a big dilemma. Steve, a really nice guy I met at the gym, asked me out for a date this evening. Jake, who seems nice as well, but is twice as good looking, called me out of the blue two hours ago and asked me out to dinner tonight. I said yes. I'm now in the position of standing one of them up. For some weird reason, I feel a little queasy when I think of going out with Steve. He reminds me of Jeff from my freshman year in college. He sat next to me in my lit class, and we got along great. I asked him to go to a party with me, and when he said yes, I felt off. In reflection, I can say that I didn't expect it. But when a mutual friend told me that he was happy I had asked him, and that he liked me, I had this same queasy feeling that I do now. So, two hours before the party, I told him I had to rush home to see a sick relative (it didn't feel completely like a lie because my great aunt was very sick), cancelled the date, and asked someone else.

Steve makes me queasy; Jake doesn't. I pen a note to Steve, go downstairs, tape it to the door, and wait for Jake. I can't risk him coming up to the building and seeing the note. I intentionally told him to be here half an hour before Steve.

"Why do you keep looking at your watch," Jake asks as we take our seats in the restaurant.

"Oh, no reason really," I shrug. *No more looking at my watch*, I tell myself. In five minutes, Steve will be at the door reading the note. I feel awful inside. It wasn't right of me to do. Steve is a nice guy, and what am I going to say the next time I see him?

Jake and I have a great time, and we start seeing each other regularly. I can't say we're dating. It's more like a developing friendship, although we're viewed as becoming a couple. We kiss now and then, but nothing real serious. But I like him, and I'm having fun, and he's teaching me where everything is in Milwaukee. By the end of 1988, I know all four corners of the city and most of the suburbs.

I spend my days in the Grafton office primarily writing poetry, little stories, and philosophical meanderings. I think of the days in the student union when I would write what I called erotic micro-shorts while my friends at the table studied. Then, while they devoured the stories, I would study; well, I would pretend to study because focusing on anything non-creative was next to impossible for me during my senior year.

The office, quiet since my manager is gone on sales calls, is bothering me today: something is off. I'm all worked up because Jake hasn't called me for two days. He told me he was going to be busy, but still, I wonder that maybe he's not calling because he no longer wants to see me. I'm certain I've done something to make him change his feelings towards me.

I can't take it. I pick up the phone and call his work.

I ask the receptionist, who knows me now, if Jake can come to the phone.

"Let me check," she puts me on hold.

"Hey, what's up?" Jake says.

He sounds happy to hear my voice. I'm flooded with relief.

"Oh, nothing. I was just calling to make sure everything's going okay."

"I don't understand," his tone changes.

Suddenly, I'm not sure why I did call, "Well, you know. You said you were going to be busy, and I was just wondering if it's all going okay."

"Yeah," his tone makes me suspicious. I immediately wonder if he's seeing someone else.

"Do you want to meet for dinner tomorrow night? My treat," I feel I need to add that in order to get him to say yes.

"Let me get back to you. I have to go," he says, and hangs up before I can say goodbye.

I just pissed him off. I'm sure of it.

"Hello," Jake says. It's late, around 9:30.

"Oh, I'm so glad you're home," relief permeates my voice.

"What's wrong?" he asks. I like the way his concern makes me feel.

"Oh, nothing really, but the restaurant I want to go to tomorrow only has one more reservation, and I just wanted to see if you were up for dinner."

They really had two tables left, but I have this weird desperation going on inside. I'm certain he won't go unless I attach some kind of . . . I don't even know what to call what I'm doing. And then I realize all I'm trying to do is have a date. Right? Right?

"Yeah, I guess," he doesn't sound enthused. But he said yes, and that's all that matters.

The next few weeks continue in the same manner. We talk on the phone most nights that we don't get together. At the end of our breezy conversations, he always turns cold and hangs up abruptly. I spend most of the next day wondering what I said to make his mood change. Luckily for me, life presents me with many opportunities to necessitate my calling him to relieve my troubled mind.

My car needs an oil change, "Do you know a good auto mechanic?"

I need to have my teeth cleaned, "Do you know a good dentist?"

I have a craving for nuts, "Where was that great grocery store with the bulk nuts?"

My car needs washing, "The place where I normally wash my car is closed for repairs. Do you know another good car wash?"

And in between all of these is, "Oh, I was just calling to say hi, and I hope your day is going well."

It's a Sunday, mid-December, and the doorbell rings.

"Jake! What a nice surprise."

I invite him in and we sit on the couch.

He doesn't waste much time, "I don't want to see you anymore."

Stunned, I just say, "Oh."

"I think this whole thing with your dad has really messed you up. I mean, you have to agree, your family is really fucked up," he looks at me as if I have the plague. I immediately regret having told him anything about my family.

All that registers is that he is breaking up with me because of my family. What do they have to do with anything? They're nearly 400 miles away. He is confirming for me my greatest fear, which I seldom really allow myself to think about: somehow all this shit is stuck to me.

He reaches into his pants pocket, "Here," he says, and hands me a business card.

I read the name on the card followed by the initials MSW.

"I have a good friend who goes to her. She's doing wonders for my friend. I think maybe you should go to her. You really need help. I think you are a lot of fun, and you're funny as hell, but you're fucked up."

Before I can ask him to explain what about me is messed up, he kisses my cheek and leaves.

Then, I blow.

I pace my apartment, saying out loud, "How can he say I'm messed up. He's the one whose mood changes on a dime. He's the one who thinks it's hilarious to scare me like the time last week when he charged his car down the alley and stopped it inches before we slammed into a brick wall, and then laughed at me because I was, well, a bit shaken up. He's the one stoned half the time. "Fuck you, Jake!" I yell.

I trip over the corner of a rug, and almost hit my head on the arm of the sofa.

"You're the one fucked up, Jake!" I spew as I regain my balance. "I'm done with you!"

But I put the MSW's card in my wallet.

"Hello," I'm groggy from my nap.

"Hi, Babe," my dad says. Will he ever stop calling me that?

I'm not nice, "What do you want?"

"I'm just calling to let you know your mother has about ten thousand dollars of my money hidden in the attic at home," he says this like the information should shock me and make me curse my mother.

"No, Dad. She doesn't."

I'm aware of back alimony still going unpaid, and another potential lawsuit against him by her, so I'm not all that surprised by the call.

"You know, your mother just wants to ruin my life. She doesn't want me to have anything…" I let him ramble on. It's so disgusting to hear him pout about life's inequities. I'm still trying to find his. He and Meg just bought a new house in a nice neighborhood of Forked River, he has another new truck, and he's doing whatever he wants, whenever he wants.

Our struggles are our fault. His struggles are our fault. He's done nothing to us. We've done everything to him. Why can't Mom just be okay with having nothing? Why do I want a father I can depend on? It really cramps his style.

"Dad," I say when he stops, "I've read the deposition."

"What deposition?"

"The one you and Meg had to give. You surely remember. You were in a room with attorneys asking questions and a court reporter typing away your responses."

He's silent.

"So you really feel that you have no obligation to any of us, financially or otherwise? You're okay with the fact that we're all struggling, in a large part because of your lies and your actions. You're okay with that?"

"I don't feel that way," he indignantly replies.

"I read your words under oath. You said you didn't feel that you should have to sacrifice for us. You shouldn't have to work just so you can pay the alimony you agreed to. I love how conveniently you and Meg have put everything in her name so it appears like you have nothing."

"Meg is not responsible for my bills."

"Oh, but she is. You're married. Oh, yeah, and then there's the house mortgage payments that you paid instead of paying

Mom. In other words, the money was there, but you decided to buy a bigger house that would appear to disable you from living up to your obligations. How do you reason that?"

"You know, Connie Sue, this whole divorce was just as traumatic for me as it was for you," he says.

As always, my logic is returned with nonsense and blame, "If you're in a mess, Connie Sue, it's because of your mother," and on he goes about how poorly she managed money.

I let him blather like an eight-year-old trying to defend the indefensible. My mind travels back to a time when I was in middle school. My mother, after years of being blamed for mismanaging the family funds, turned their checkbook and bills over to my father.

His loud and accusatorial contention was that they never had enough money because my mother (a professional bookkeeper for local businesses, including two pharmacies) didn't know how to manage money. After two weeks, he discovered that the situation was exactly as she had told him. And he didn't like it.

He did not want to be responsible for the fact that their income added up to less than he wanted to spend. That it wasn't due to mismanagement, but rather an incoming versus outgoing situation.

At the end of the two weeks, he threw the checkbook back at my mother and refused to take any adult responsibility whatsoever for the management of their finances. Instead of maturely accepting the reality of their limited income, he has continued to attack my mother all the way to this moment. He wants me to believe he cared so much about the well-being of all of us, yet he never worked for the financial betterment of our family and his future with my mother. Instead, he continued to spend and blame.

I realize that all the desperation my father created in my mother around the issue of money caused her to become a master of robbing Peter to pay Paul (like the seemingly countless times she borrowed against the house.) Had her desperation overcome her integrity, she easily could have embezzled money from her clients. I'm proud of her that she never did. And yet I realize she missed another red flag with my father.

A light bulb goes on in my head.

I have tried to explain to people the difference between my mother and my father. Now it's so clear, at least in this situation. My mother's actions were informed by self-preservation and the need to protect her family. She was reacting to my father's bullying, manipulation, incorrigibility, and his refusal to take responsibility for the finances and well-being of his family.

He was destroying.

She was fighting to preserve.

At the end of the conversation, he condescendingly tells me that it's hard for me to understand these things because I've never been married.

Two hours later, the phone rings again, "Hello," I answer.

Why am I picking up?

It's my mom.

She's whining.

It's not that she doesn't have reason, but God, please, can she find some backbone?

"I don't think I'm going to go through with this," she says.

"Why not?"

"Well, the attorney wants half of the money if I win. What's the point of giving him half?"

This conversation continues on, and I listen to her form of nonsense. As I listen, I realize, for the first time, my mother isn't letting this go. She doesn't want to be done with my father. If she did, she wouldn't care about what the attorney wanted.

"I say, take the fifteen thousand, get something nice for yourself, and be done with Dad and Meg."

My mother stands on her principles, "Why would I let him have fifteen thousand dollars of my money? Unless I can get what I'm owed, I'm not doing this."

The next day, I call the MSW.

"Welcome," she says, and gestures towards the seat she wants me to take.

Her office is very inviting, as are her big brown doe-like eyes. She's prematurely grey, which offers her an air of distinction. She is petite, quite pretty, and calm. She inspires calm. That makes me a little crawly.

"Tell me about yourself. What do you do?"

"Well, I'm a dancer. I just moved to Milwaukee this past August. I've been working at a Manpower office in Grafton while taking some classes around town. I'm just getting to know the dance community here. And I want to be a writer. It's my plan to dance until I'm thirty and then start writing."

She smiles, "You're my first artistic client."

She explains that she is recently out of school and is working at this clinic to earn the hours she needs to open her own practice.

"I must let you know," she says earnestly, "that I can't prescribe drugs. Only psychiatrists can do that. And I won't recommend that you see a psychiatrist until after a year. If, after that long, I haven't been able to help you, I will recommend either another MSW or a psychiatrist for you."

"That's actually a big relief to hear. I don't want to be on drugs. I don't believe I need drugs. I know where my problems are coming from, and drugs aren't going to help me."

"Well, then, why are you here?"

I explain my family, all the characters involved, the divorce, the shooting, the ongoingness of it all, and then I say, "I can, from an intellectual standpoint, tell you what a healthy relationship looks like, which is what I want, but I'm certain I have no way of knowing how to achieve it coming out of my parents' home. Healthy role models, they were not," I laugh.

"No," she chuckles, "I would agree, from what you've told me, they weren't."

"I don't want to carry my past into my future."

"I can help you. In order to help you though, you will have to learn some new definitions of words like relationship, honesty, responsibility, trust."

"I can do that," my optimism is restored.

"It's not going to be easy and it will require taking a hard look at yourself."

"I can do that, too," I respond.

Though I pause and wonder, what does she mean? In my opinion, I'm already someone who takes a hard look at myself.

"How long do you think this will take me?" I ask.

"I would plan on five years," she says.

"Okay," I respond. It sounds reasonable to me. I'm still young.

We plan that I will see her every other week for now. I schedule my next appointment and leave.

I feel good.

I feel hopeful.

Hope is something that I hadn't fully realized I had lost.

Three Years Later

Stretching, I recognize that my sleep has been complete and substantial.

The clock reads 7:15, not as late as I expected. I roll onto my back, take a deep breath, and am overcome with an unexpected urgency to attend my therapist's weekend workshop. Without another thought (I've learned to pay attention to these unanticipated insights), I grab the phone receiver, punch in her number, and wait.

"Hi, Kelly, this is Connie. I know it's cutting things close, but I would really like to attend this weekend's workshop. Please give me a call if it's possible. Thanks," I hang up.

She calls back within five minutes, happy to hear that I want to attend, "There's one spot left," she tells me.

This is unusual. Her weekends are always full. My indefinable need to attend swirls inside me coupled with expectation and excitement. All of it makes me anxious in a now known and understood way. Something big is going to happen, but what, I have no idea. One of the reasons I didn't originally sign up for this workshop is that I felt I had nothing impending to work on.

I eat a quick breakfast and shower. Grateful for the block-and-a-half walk to my car (I'm now well acquainted with all the parking regulations in my neighborhood), I breathe in the fresh spring air and toss up a nod to the universe. I feel as if I'm being pulled along, nudged forward by an unseen force saying, "Go. I'm with you."

I chuckle to myself, "I'm going. I'm going," I say telepathically to this unseen voice. "I trust you."

Though for the first time in a long time, this feeling of trust is met with a tinge of apprehension. Well, whatever lies ahead, it is definitely in my best interest. That is something that the last three years has taught me. The apprehension is what tells me I'm going right where I need to go. I've learned this feeling is different than fear. It's taken a lot of work but I'm now able to separate my nervousness to go deep inside and look at myself, from my fear, the mechanism that tells me to get the hell out.

It's a beautiful drive from my east side apartment to the Catholic school on the south side where the workshop is being held.

The lake is a magnificent blue this morning as I cross the Hoan Bridge. The wind is roughing up the water, and small whitecaps appear and disappear over the surface. It's beautiful.

As I turn my focus back to the road, the bridge and time extend out in front of me. Like the coast of Michigan that is out of my sight, suddenly I cannot see the end of the bridge where it gently slopes down and joins land again. Time has taken on a weird effect, and I feel near to motionless as I continue my journey to the south side.

While much has occurred in the last three years, significant scenes play out in front of me.

I'm returned to my third visit to Kelly, and she asks me to close my eyes. While that is not a difficult function for my body to perform, somehow it resists my attempts to do so.

"Just put your feet on the ground straight under your knees, straighten your back, put your hands on your thighs, and close your eyes."

I follow her directions as if she were choreographing a dance for me.

"Now take a deep breath. Just breathe in, and then exhale as if you are taking a huge sigh."

Immediately, gravity is that upward force I encountered so long ago when Joe told me about my father's shooting. But now, I'm not only moving upwards, I'm growing larger than the chair, than the room, and right before my body fills the room, I am seized by panic.

"I can't do this," I shoot open my eyes. Immediately, I fall back down into my correct proportions.

"What happened?" the calm never leaves her voice or her posture.

I, on the other hand, am barely breathing. I keep pushing myself upwards, and my words come out in a rush, "I just kept expanding and growing larger, and I was being forced upward. I felt like a huge elephant in a tiny room, and suddenly, I knew if I breathed any deeper, I would blow up, and like little marbles be scattered all over the floor."

Before she can say anything, I add, "You know. It's so weird. Every time I'm driving I feel like if I don't have my seatbelt on, I'm going to float away. And my hands. My God, they ache from how tightly I grip the steering wheel. It's the only way I feel I'll stay in my seat."

"You're a petite person, with huge feelings that haven't been processed. I need you to know that you don't have to face them all at once. We can deal with the little ones first, and work our way up to the big ones."

I tell her about that moment in Joe's apartment when we ran into each other in the hall, and how I told myself that now was not the time to feel what was going on.

"That's very beneficial in the moment," she says. She explains that it's what people do when they are in crisis and need to survive. "But now it's time to move out of survival mode."

She explains defense mechanisms, and how we need these defenses to survive trauma. "That's why you can have three people experience the same trauma but react differently. We all have different defense mechanisms to help us cope. The problem with defense mechanisms is that while they are beneficial during trauma, they stay with us after the need for them has passed. Unfortunately, we are unaware that we are acting out of those defenses. They skew our ability to accurately interpret our present reality, and we create trauma and crisis where there is none. The question is, Connie, what are your defense mechanisms?"

I don't know Kelly that well yet, but something tells me that if I let her, she'll help me identify all of them.

She explains that I just had a panic attack.

"Oh, is that what that was," I pause.

"I have them a lot, I guess."

She explains that I won't be able to process anything until I can breathe fully through my body, and that panic attacks and hyperventilating occur when our breathing is so shallow that the air bounces between our chest and head.

"All your emotions are stuck in your throat. I can teach you how to move them down, through, and out of your body," she says, as if it's as easy as teaching me how to tie my shoes.

No wonder I've been having a hard time dancing. I can't breathe.

She left me with the words, "The amount of joy you experience and feel is proportional to the amount of sorrow you have experienced and are willing to feel."

Back at home I revisit the feeling of nearly blowing up in Kelly's office. A feeling I accurately reproduce over and over again; a dancer's body is highly trained in kinesthetic awareness. I become intimate with my fear to feel anything. Am I brave enough to go into what feels like a dark, swirling pit of ugliness?

And then it dawns on me. If I believe what she said about joy and sorrow, then great amounts of joy await me, if, indeed, I can process all my sorrow. In my rough estimate, I've experienced more than my fair share of the latter.

"It seems quite clear that you have a fear of abandonment," Kelly says to me, her brown eyes searching to see if I'm ready to hear this.

I'm confused. I know I have been abandoned, but my ability to connect how that manifests itself as a fear of being abandoned is beyond my mental reach. "I don't understand," I say.

"Why do you call Jake all the time?"

This is a strange question, I believe.

"Well," I say slowly and thoughtfully, afraid I'm about to expose something about myself, "sometimes I just want to say hi. Let him know I'm thinking about him. Other times, it's to let him know what's going on." If I'm honest with myself, I'm hoping she's buying this because as I'm saying it, I'm aware that I'm attempting to fool both of us.

"But can't you do both of those things when you're together?"

I get a little pissy with her. I feel she is questioning my actions, and I don't understand how doing something nice for someone is bad.

"Well, sure, but isn't it nice to have someone call you and say hi during the day? I know it would feel good to me if Jake ever did that."

"Does he ever call you during the day?"

"Very seldom. And you know, if we don't have a date, and we're chatting before bed, he always abruptly ends our conversations and nearly hangs up on me."

"How does that make you feel?"

I struggle to answer her question. Again, I feel that somehow I'm going to betray myself.

She doesn't push me. Instead, she says, "I have an assignment for you."

"Okay," I like this idea. I love learning and figure I can ace any task she gives me. I'm naïve enough about therapy, and myself, to dive in headfirst.

"Every time you feel the need to call Jake this week, I want you to stop yourself. I don't want you to call him at all. I want you to just sit with yourself, breathe, and pay attention to how you feel. Same thing if he abruptly ends a conversation with you. But again, let him call you."

I'm overcome with panic before she finishes. I can't sit still.

I can't breathe. I want out of my body. I want out of this room, and as far away from her as I can get.

Instead, I allow her to guide me through my attack. She gets my feet on the ground, and with her ever-present calm voice, instructs me to breathe, "Deep breaths," and like the midwife that she is, she begins modeling the breathing she wants me to perform.

As calm and control is restored to my body, she asks, "Can you do this, Connie?"

I hear a challenge in her voice, and I'm not going to fall short of the challenge.

"Sure," I respond, with some reserve in my tone. I know that I have no idea what accepting this challenge means. I'm more than a little frightened of where it might lead me.

I do as she instructed though. It's not an understatement to say it takes absolutely every ounce of energy I possess to do so.

I pace.

I have panic attack after panic attack.

I feel sure Jake's not calling me is a sign he's leaving me or cheating on me, and my panic surges knowing I can't call him to confirm for myself he's not.

I'm overwhelmed and surprised by how desperate I become.

I need to know. Is he still there? Are we still a couple?

Hourly, sometimes minute by minute, I run through my list of reasons to call him. I fight to find one that is legitimate enough to break the challenge.

I get physically sick. I need a doctor. I don't know one. I can call for that. I hear Kelly say, "You could have called a friend instead." I don't pick up the phone.

My sickness intensifies. I need help.

He calls mid-week: immediate relief followed by same abrupt ending to our phone call.

I'm out of my head all day Thursday.

I can't do my day job.

I can barely teach my dance class, and forget practicing.

I force myself to breathe: I fluctuate between deep and shallow breaths.

And then, over the weekend, something breaks.

I relax.

And in my calm, I find clarity.

I see the debilitating desperation I encounter when faced with my now acknowledged fear of abandonment. All the time, all these excuses I would find to call Jake were only that, excuses. I turned them into something more magnanimous in order to avoid my fear of abandonment.

In my calm, I begin, like a child, to discover something new, to understand on a level that is moving beyond the surface what Kelly meant when she told me I would have to redefine honesty (I'm not calling to be nice or thoughtful), truth (I have a fear of abandonment, and it controls me), responsibility (these are my reactions to abandonment), and relationship (the baggage I bring to our relationship drives Jake nuts), and I come to realize while I'm not the one who put the fear of abandonment in me, I'm the one living with its consequences, and I don't want to live this way.

But there's still the fact that Jake hangs up abruptly, and this puzzles me. Isn't he responsible for his actions too? If I'm responsible for understanding how his actions make me feel and respond due to my baggage, isn't he beholden to the same?

I, however, am not ready to go further with personal discovery at this time. In fact, I believe following this one exercise, I'm cured. So I march into Kelly's office, feeling good, really good, and confident. I explain to her that I now understand my fear of abandonment, and with that, I end my therapy, but not before she points out that my defensive reaction to my fear of abandonment is passive aggression. That's a little too close to home, and a little too much maternal association for my liking, so I tuck my now disclosed passive aggression back into my subconscious for the time being.

Kelly, with well wishes, sends me on my way, letting me know, "There's no shame in deciding to come back."

With a warm smile and a hug, I walk out of her office on top of the world.

This lasts for a couple of months.

Jake and I stop seeing each other, and then start seeing each other again. During this off-again, on-again time, I take a gig as a professional ballroom dancer, where I run into a whirlwind of triggers.

Since I'm a trained dancer, I'm immediately paired with a highly ranked dancer whose partner just quit. We dance really well together. However, I'm often frustrated by his lack of understanding of the basic elements of movement. This is not surprising, since he and most of the other teachers came to dance through ballroom at the age of eighteen or nineteen, first and foremost as sales people. Their primary interest is sales. They are simply learning their product the way a pharmaceutical salesperson learns about drugs. Obviously, they have some predisposed talent, or they wouldn't be succeeding. Luckily, my partner has a lot of it.

The studio owners are a husband-and-wife team obsessed with wealth. In my short tenure at the studio, they have proven to have no moral conflict with shaking down desperate single or widowed women for every dime they have to get the wealth they, the owners, so believe they deserve. During my first week, I was stunned to find them humiliating a client (they had left the office door open for all to hear) because she was refusing to buy ten thousand dollars worth of lessons when she still had five thousand dollars worth of untaught lessons on the books.

The male half of the equation reminds me too much of my dad. His predatory nature and unpredictable outbursts cause my gun dreams to flare up.

Between dealing with the studio owners, my gun dreams, and Jake's unwillingness to take responsibility for his inexplicable, cold dismissal of me from time to time, I feel the need to return to Kelly.

"I know you rejected the idea of group therapy before, but there really is nothing like it for moving one's work along. This group has nine powerful women in it, and I think you would make a great addition," Kelly says on my first session back.

I feel comforted in the familiar surroundings of her office. The colors are soft corals and tans, and the scent of a burnt sage smudge is in the air. I love the smell, marijuanaesque, but not. Sage, I was told, is used to cleanse the energy of a person or a room. In the corner, she has a statue of a mother sitting on the ground holding a child. Maternal is definitely a word I would use to describe Kelly.

"Have they met before?" I ask. This is a big concern of mine. For reasons I can't identify, I don't want to walk into something already established. Maybe, upon reflection, I don't want to feel like an outsider.

Their first group session is the following week. I agree to go, and if all goes well, I will do group once a week, and have an individual session once a month.

I'm overwhelmed the first night.

All five of my family members are represented in the personalities of five of the nine other women. I freak out. I wasn't expecting my family to show up.

When it's time to introduce myself, I don't know how to do it. "I'm Connie. I'm a dancer," I say. I can feel my eyes, wide in a deer-in-the-headlights shocked stare. I start crying.

From my point of view, Kelly looms large, and her body fills the room. Her compassionate eyes lock on me. Her all-encompassing face, with her curly gray hair circling her head like a halo, overwhelms the space in front of me.

"They're all here, aren't they," she says.

"All of them," I feel six years old when I say it.

"I know. But please, please know I can help you. Please come back next week," she beckons.

It's odd to me that she thinks I might not. In my coming back, I decided I'm in until I'm healed, but I didn't share this with her, so…

In my current state, the owner of the studio is triggering too much in me for me to think I'm okay, and strange things are happening with Jake. I'm aware the initial euphoria I received from understanding my abandonment issues has worn off, and I feel like I'm falling into a deeper abyss than before.

"I'll be back," I say through my easing tears.

"Good," she returns. "That's all you need to say tonight."

"Thank you."

Her mercy hits me in the chest. I let it touch my clothes, but that is as far as I can allow it to go.

A couple weeks into group, Kelly talks to us about how ego stops us from doing what we need to do, and about how we judge ourselves.

"In order for therapy to work, you have to be able to let go of your egos. You have to open yourself up to vulnerability, and you can only do that in an environment where you can trust your vulnerability will not be abused."

She talks about us being kind, respectful, and compassionate towards others' work and others' issues. For me, it all clicks. Letting go of my ego was something I did every time I walked into a dance class or performed. I can do this, I tell myself. I also realize that's why I'm struggling at the studio. The owner, like my father, preys on people's vulnerabilities. It's how the studio makes money, for God's sake. I don't feel safe. No wonder I'm going crazy there.

Everything comes to a head one afternoon when the teachers are having a class. Mike, the owner, walks into the room, and just the sight of him makes me throw up all over the dance floor. I excuse myself, say I don't feel well, and go home.

The following week, we're due to fly to Miami for a large Fred Astaire competition. While my partner and I have only been dancing together about a month and half, we have a good chance of winning our division: Rising Star Theater Arts. Think ice dancing without the skates, but with all the lifts.

Back home, lying on my sofa, I try to erase Mike's face, body language, and voice from my memory. I contemplate quitting, but the plane tickets for Miami are booked and paid for by the owners, as are the hotel and all the entry fees. I don't have to pay anything. But I can't go. I can't stand to be in the room with Mike again.

In the push to make me feel like we are one big happy family, they've recently offered to show me how to snort a line of cocaine. (Luckily, there's been no pushback since I decline.) Until this generous offer, I was ignorant of their drug use. But now my partner's twitchiness makes sense. His right arm always nervously beats against his side as we set up lifts. Not so reassuring if you're the one about to be put up in the air balanced on that twitching arm. I've trained myself to look him in the eye and just go for the lift. This has proven to be successful because I stop trying to judge exactly where his unpredictable arm will hit my body at the point of contact.

And then there is the fact that I've been asked to marry him, so he can be in the country legally. He's bisexual, but the marriage would only be a business arrangement.

"It will only last a year, and then we can get a divorce," he said to me, smiling with so much charm and guile.

"And what am I supposed to tell the man I eventually want to marry when he asks if I've ever been married before?"

"Anyone would understand helping out a friend, and that's all you'll be doing."

This request has turned into a drumbeat, to which I receive much pushback every time I refuse.

Of course, I'm at the mercy of the number one rule of sales: make the customer give three no's before standing down. I think I'm up to five over the marriage idea.

Again I find myself in a position of just wanting to run away, and of being unable to talk to anyone.

The phone rings.

"Hello," I answer.

It's Mary, Mike's wife, "Are you okay?"

No space for me to answer.

"We've come to the conclusion you must be pregnant," she says with the utmost confidence.

"What?"

"Well, why did you throw up?"

Because your husband is disgusting, he hits on everybody, he lies, he's manipulative, and he's a cokehead. The sight of him makes me sick, but instead I answer, "I think I have a little food poisoning."

She sighs in relief.

"Well, let us know if there's anything we can do. See you Monday."

Out of desperation, fear, and panic, I pack a bag, write my roommate a note that I'm going to Forked River, and flee. I don't really want to be in Forked River. I have to hide there, too. The idea of running into my dad sends me to the moon in craziness, but it's the one place I know they can't find me.

I walk in the door and my mother almost collapses with relief. "Oh, I'm so glad you made it here okay," she hugs me hard.

"How did you know I was coming?"

"Mike and Mary phoned me. They are very worried about you."

The entire kitchen starts spinning. I run upstairs to the bathroom and dry heave for what seems like an eternity.

My mom follows me.

Rolling on the floor, crying, hyperventilating, and trying desperately to get out of my skin, I'm propelled further into these states listening to her explain, "They know someone from Arizona who used to live nearby, they said. They called him because they couldn't remember what town you were from, but he remembered them saying you're from Forked River, so they called information, got my number, and called me."

This is all a nightmare.

I feel trapped.

I can't stop writhing on the bathroom floor.

My mom sits with me. Rubs me. Calms me down.

Once I'm in possession of myself again, we go down to the living room. The sofa proves more comfortable than the bathroom floor.

"I can't go to Miami with them."

In my mind, this is Pilobolus all over again. Only this time, I know for sure they're drug addicts and unbalanced.

"I think you owe it to them to do this competition. They've paid for everything already, and after that, if you want to quit, so be it."

I try to explain to her how impossible this is without telling her about the coke and the marriage proposal. To my little "internal terrorist," as Kelly calls it, that says something more about me than them, and I'm awfully ashamed.

But my Mom's reasoning prevails.

We arrive in Miami on Thursday. Since I have no students competing, I spend most of the day by the pool. The professionals have access to the ballroom around eleven that night, after the day's competitions have finished.

Everyone in the room, or so it seems, is staring at me. First, I'm a trained dancer, which in ballroom dancing in the late 80s is still rare, at least in America. There are a couple other trained women. One has coached me, and the other, her protégé, whom I will be competing against, is favored to win. Somehow I add some mystery to the whole event.

Secondly, everyone in the room, as I come to learn, knows that I "fled" to my mother's the week before. The rumor: it's my first time competing, and I'm very nervous. This makes me laugh, and gives me an edge; stage fright is something I don't have. I love performing! And competing is just one great big performance.

A momentary hush fills the room when we step on the floor. I allow the time this silence creates to take in the room. All the women are fit, beautiful, and pulsing with energy. No one is in costume, but we're all in fashionable, alluring practice clothes. Everything about being a ballroom dancer is about glamour and sensuality.

I look down at my shoes, like Dorothy I think, only mine are covered in aurora borealis stones. They make my shoes heavy, but they feel solid on my feet.

The energy in the room is intense and magnetic. In an instant, I'm restored to my old, before-the-shooting self. I take a deep breath, look at my partner, and say, "Shall we."

Our practice is clean and understated. We run the full dance twice, execute all our lifts, and call it a night.

I wake up early for my appointment with the hairdresser. He shellacs my hair into a beautiful, unmovable, bobby-pinned French twist. Back in my room, I do my makeup, and secure my false eyelashes and rhinestone earrings with glue. When I emerge from my room with my fire-engine-red nails and wearing a ball gown perfectly tailored to my figure, my inner princess explodes.

As we enter the ballroom and wait for our heat, it's obvious that me and the other trained dancer have an edge: we are imbued with an air of elegance and composure from our training that makes us stand out while we are standing still.

"Are you ready?" my partner asks me while we wait on deck.

I look at him, smile, and say, "This is going to be fun."

"And now, the final for Rising Star Theater Arts," the adjudicator of judges announces.

My partner and I, along with five other couples, take the floor. We take our beginning poses and the music begins. From the moment we start, the crowd is clapping and cheering. The whole room is electric, and I feed off that energy. We are flawless. I forget about everyone else dancing, and perform. I look every judge in the eyes and smile as we waltz past them. We hit every lift, which I have to admit is a relief.

And then, for our signature move, he spins me three times, I stop, extend my inside leg to his hand, lay my head upon my knee, rotate on my supporting leg so my whole body goes towards my partner under the leg he is holding, and I open up facing the other direction in a full arabesque. We waltz a little more and pose. The audience goes wild. I have no idea how the other five couples did, but I'm certain we were great.

We have to wait three heats before getting our results. I decide to sit in the ballroom and watch the competition. My partner sits down beside me and says, "Keep doing what you're doing. The judges absolutely love you."

"What am I doing?" I ask.

"You're sitting here acting so composed. You're innocently watching the competition. They love the act."

"I'm not acting. I'm simply sitting here watching the competition," I try to hide my disgust.

"Well, whatever you're doing, keep doing it. They love it. And, oh, when we get back home we want to talk about you going blond and bleaching your arm hairs," he says.

"Why don't you leave before I start acting in a way the judges won't approve of," I smile, and looked back at the dance floor.

Our coach's words from the day before echo in my head, "I told your partner it's going to take his biggest sales job ever to keep Connie in this business."

As I turn back towards the dance floor I realize that's what I loathe most: it's all one big sales job. This isn't about dancing first, it's about sales first, and that makes it bullshit.

The heat finishes. The adjudicator asks all six couples from the Rising Star Theater Arts final to report to the green room. The response in the room lets me know this is highly unusual.

"Come on," my partner says. He takes my hand and we

walk in together. It's obvious no one knows why we're here, and everyone looks on edge.

"Three of you had disqualifying lifts, and since that's half of the heat, we've decided to allow those three couples to correct their lifts, and then we'll rerun the heat." He walks around the room, and says, "You," to the other dancer; "You," to another couple; and then, comes to us, and says, "You". He turns back to the room and says, "The three of you have five minutes to correct your lift."

"Excuse me," I say. My partner almost faints.

"Yes," the adjudicator turns back towards me.

"We don't have a disqualifying lift."

The whole room freezes.

My partner squeezes my hand and whispers, "Be quiet."

"Yes, you do."

"No, we don't. We don't have an overhead press."

My partner is hurting my hand.

"Just correct your lift."

"But which one sir. We don't have an overhead press."

My partner wants to kill me. Obviously, there is an unwritten rule that you don't question the adjudicator of judges.

Just then, the curtains to the green room part with command and flourish. I don't have to be told who this is, I've watched him and his partner on tape several times, and his tall, well-built frame, and presence are undeniable. He is the Blackpool (a worldwide competition held in England) champion in Theater Arts, and everyone in the ballroom world admires him.

"What's going on here," he asks, still holding the curtains open.

I don't hesitate, "He says we have to correct a lift, but I'm not sure which one, since we don't have an overhead press."

The adjudicator, obviously making it up, tries to explain which lift it is.

Mr. Blackpool steps forward, and with force, shuts the curtains behind him.

"But that's a shoulder sit," I say.

Then, Mr. Blackpool walks across the room. He looks directly at me, smiles, and says, "Let me see the lift."

We dance into the lift the adjudicator declares is wrong. It ends with me sitting on my partner's shoulder.

My partner puts me down.

Mr. Blackpool comes closer to me, and cups my face with his soft, large hands. He looks me directly in the eyes and says, "You're beautiful. Just go do what you did before."

We stand there, him cupping my face, me smiling at him, both of us eye-locked. If this were a movie, the audience would be expecting a deep, romantic kiss.

The entire room stands, mouths agape in disbelief.

And then, the coup de grace, he turns to the adjudicator and demands, "Leave them alone. They're just fine." He leaves with the same flourish and elegance he entered with.

"Five minutes," the adjudicator spits, and leaves.

We rerun the heat. Our performance is not as flawless, but is still very good.

Two heats later, we are standing on the floor waiting to see who won. They call off couple numbers starting in sixth place, not us. Fifth, fourth, not us. Third place, which comes with money and recognition going into United States Ballroom

Competition in September, goes to us. The other dancer takes first, and the other couple with a disqualifying lift, second.

As it turns out, we place in the same order as we did in the first heat; however, because the first-and second-place couples had disqualifying lifts, we would have been awarded first place. Rumor quickly fills the ballroom that they weren't giving first to a new couple, of which one half was competing in the business for the first time.

Luckily for me, I fly out of Miami on Saturday, since my competition is over. Everyone else stays through the weekend. I spend all weekend trying to decide what I'm going to do. We did exceptionally well, and there was a lot of attention on us. USBC was the next big comp for us to prepare for, and as a partnership, we have a lot of potential. But everyone and everything at the studio is messed up. Adding to this, another female dancer calls me Sunday night and tells me about the wild party I missed Saturday night that involved lots of sex and drugs.

Yikes, it's worse than I thought," I want to say, but she genuinely sounds like she enjoyed it. "Yeah, I missed out," is all I offer.

Throughout my life, whenever I'm in situations like this, which feel very dangerous and out of control to me, I just walk away. But this time, I'm being seduced by the dancing. I don't know what to do. As a result of always walking away, I never had to hold my ground in high pressure situations. I actually learned from my father that the pressure won't end until I give or walk. I never dated in high school, so I never found myself in a compromising position; however, college was a different story. All of my issues crawled out of my personal woodwork once I started dating. Being involved with a man in ballroom is a whole different thing. It's dance, for one, but the dancing is all about connecting, and that connecting has such a sensuality attached to it. That's why all the best partners are also lovers.

I have no desire to be my partner's lover.

I go to the studio for my morning practice, listen to my partner tell about all the gossip surrounding us after I left Miami, and all his hopes for USBC.

We run our dance again. I spin into him in a beautiful elongated lunge. He is facing the mirror, and my head rotates toward the mirror. Our line is so proportionally perfect. I am being seduced by my own desires to perform, compete and win, until . . .

He lowers his arm, and with arrogance and ownership, caresses my body down my cheek and neck and across my breast where he pauses before continuing down my torso. The pressure will never end, I think. And he believes I'm like everyone else in this business. In other words, he believes I'm corrupted.

Maybe that's the single, strangest thing about me: I should be, but I'm not. I don't want to be messed up. I mean, currently I am, but not the way people like my dance partner think I am; and, like him, no one understands my drive for therapy. They don't understand what I'm trying to escape, in part because it's people like them I'm running from.

We sit down, talk a little more, and then I say, "I'm leaving right now, and if I come back at one, I will for sure be here through USBC, but if I'm not back by one, I'm not walking through that door again."

I stand up and unceremoniously leave the studio.

At noon, I call a woman from my group who's currently

unemployed and ask her to go on a picnic lunch with me somewhere out of the city. We settle on Kettle Moraine, out by the church on Holy Hill.

"Fine, I'll pick you up," I say.

As we drive out of the city into the beautiful country, I explain to her that she needs to stay with me until three o'clock. I need to fight off the seduction of returning to the studio. I know it's the right thing to do, but that doesn't make it easy.

We have a great afternoon, and I return home feeling victorious. For the first time, I have conquered my internal terrorist.

As my car slowly crosses the Hoan Bridge, I think of the twists and turns my career has taken between that day at Holy Hill and now heading over to my weekend therapy group. While I've had various day jobs, I began teaching tap, ballet, and jazz over the last three years, and have been honing my skills as a teacher.

My therapy has been intense and deep. It has unearthed many issues and brought to light my dysfunction.

As a car passes me, my mind travels back to when I began to learn the difference between my emotional age and my chronological age.

"Our emotional age," Kelly explains, "is often tied to a first trauma."

When Kelly asks about my first trauma, it takes me no time to respond, and I tell her about the night with the Harlem Globetrotters ball.

"How old were you?"

"Six."

She explains that our emotional age dictates how we respond to life as an adult. Through our discussions, it's revealed that I responded to relationship issues like a needy six-year-old. I'm longing for protection, and my six-year-old needs are doing whatever they must do to be met. This, of course, brings up my abandonment issues again. And all of it feels thick, disgusting, and repulsive.

I want out of my skin.

Kelly doesn't allow me an easy out.

"Have you ever asked Jake why he abruptly ends conversations?" Kelly asks.

"No. Because I know what he'll say," I respond.

Kelly's brow lifts, "You do? And how is that?"

"He'll say he doesn't do it, and blame it on me, and the way I take things."

"Oh," says Kelly. "And you know this how?"

"Because that's what he does about everything."

"So instead of asking him directly, you do what?"

I think about this. Kelly again has given my thoughts a new direction. I'm always justifying my behaviors on the basis of someone else's treatment of me.

Then a huge light bulb goes on, "I call him. Over and over and over again, to make sure he's there."

As soon as the words are out I'm flooded with shame. She can see this.

"No ego. No judgment. Just pay attention to how you feel."

I trust her. I put my IT (internal terrorist) aside and pay attention.

But I feel awful.

The recognition of my actions makes me feel childish.

"It seems to me someone else has treated you that way," she hangs this in the air like a three-pointer from one hundred feet away.

I follow the ball to the basket, and in fact it's a slam-dunk.

"My father," I say. My eyes race back and forth, my brain overwhelmed by the epiphany.

This now-so-obvious insight opens the door to so many future insights that require deep personal work.

"So, you are emotionally six. We need to grow your emotions up to match your chronological age of twenty-four."

"How do I do that?"

"Well, put your six-year-old you next to you. What would you like her to know?"

The idea initially frightens me. Terrified to look at her, I hesitate, but then she just appears, sitting in the chair next to me, looking at me with pleading eyes. She's cute. She has a little brown bob because she tried to cut her hair and chopped the back of it all the way to her neck. She's staring at me with big blue eyes that in one moment are pleading, and in the next are full of curiosity and wonder. She looks strong and courageous, but also afraid and hesitant.

How often had I helped a student overcome her fear of demonstrating in front of the class, or gave her belief in her abilities when she didn't believe in herself? I had, in a year, become one of the most sought-after teachers at the studio where I teach.

And now, my six-year-old self sits beside me, looking at me

with the same needs and hopes of my students. I smile at her to let her know she's okay with me. I know what to do, trust me, my smile reflects.

"Take her home, be with her," Kelly says. "Love her."

And I do.

I spend the whole week talking to her and listening to her. I let her tell me all her stories. I let her tell me about her tornado dreams. I take her everywhere I go. I let her know someone older and wiser is in control and cares about her safety. I won't allow anyone to hurt her or scare her.

At night, I lie in bed, and imagine myself rocking her to sleep while holding her and stroking her hair and back. I let her cry in my arms. During the day, I run and play with her. I nourish her.

And then, I break down and cry and cry and cry for her. I tell her how sorry I am that she has been made so afraid. I tell her how sorry I am that she has a father who couldn't, didn't, or wouldn't love her.

I reassure her there is nothing to be afraid of anymore.

I let my six-year-old come home. I create a safe sanctuary for her. Now she can relax and grow up.

"What would you say is the emotion you have the most difficult time feeling?" Kelly asks.

"Probably sadness," I say, unaware she's further opening the door to the black box inside me.

"I disagree with that," she gives me a smile that I've come to both love and hate. That smile tells me she knows I'm ready to go deeper, whether or not I think so.

"Well, then," I respond in a mock-confrontational way, "what do you think?"

"I think you are very angry," again she lofts the one-hundred-foot shot.

(At this point in my therapy, I usually recognize when Kelly hits the nail on the head, but this time I did not. When my throat clenched, I stopped breathing, and wanted to punch her, I didn't realize it was because she had hit me where I lived.)

"I think you're absolutely wrong about that," I hiss.

"Well, let's try something, and we'll find out," she says.

"Okay," I hesitantly reply. Seldom has Kelly been wrong, and it's obvious when she is because it doesn't feel right, and it doesn't disrupt my calm. But in spite of my defensiveness, I think she's wrong about this one. I'm not by nature an angry person. A person has to do a lot to override my optimistic disposition. But she is about to correct my thinking, and guide me to a more accurate understanding of what it means to be honest with myself.

Kelly puts three pillows on top of a chair. She then picks up a padded mallet from behind her chair and hands it to me.

"I want you to stand in front of the chair with your feet hip-distance apart."

I do what she asks.

"Now, I want you to lift the mallet above you head."

I do it.

"Now, I want you, in your mind's eye, to imagine your father's head on the top of the pillows. Then, I want you to swing the mallet down and hit his head. Do this with follow through. Go all the way through the pillows, pull the mallet back up, and swing down again."

I don't understand. I think she's nuts.

I stand there for a couple of minutes while I assimilate her instructions. I lift the mallet above my head. I give myself the go-ahead, and I put my father's bust on top of the pillows.

The next thing I know, a surge of energy overcomes my entire body. A flash of light seems to originate inside my head. A mysterious force pulls the mallet back, slams me into the wall, and I black out.

I open my eyes to see Kelly's face inches from mine, her brown eyes glowing with compassionate victory, "So, do you still think you're not angry?"

I'm busted, but it takes me an entire year, and a lot of other excavating, before I can do the exercise.

I continue working with my inner six-year-old. While doing so, I start hearing everything from everyone as an attack against my character. Everywhere I turn, it seems that I am misunderstood. My motives are questioned, maligned, and explained for me. Time and again this is where I end up with men.

One day Kelly asks me, "Why do you think you are attracted to this kind of man?"

"What do you mean?"

"Well, you're choosing these men. Why do you think that is?"

"What do you mean, I'm choosing them?" She's pissing me off.

"According to you, you are in what I would describe as verbally, emotionally, and mentally abusive relationships. You are with men who emotionally pull you in, and as soon as you relax and decide to trust them, they metaphorically slap you. This kicks in your abandonment issues, and so the cycle goes. My question remains, why are you choosing them?"

I fight very hard to keep from understanding her. As my therapy progresses, I become aware of my resistance, and through her gentle guidance, I've learned that resistance is my indicator that she is taking me where I need to go. On this day, I become more fully attuned to that.

"Let's take for instance the trip you've been trying to plan with your boyfriend. He leaves all the planning up to you. He won't settle on a date. He initially acts excited about your planned destination, but can't go when you can. So you keep planning trips, getting your hopes up, try hard to pick a location he'll like, and wait for him to state a date he can go, but he never does. Oh, and he tells you that part of the problem is you can't afford to go to the places he really wants to go, and that's why he really isn't setting a date."

She pauses to let her rundown of my situation sink in.

"What's does all of that tell you?" she asks.

"That it's because I make less money than he does, we can't go where he wants to go, and he's not real happy with the places I'm choosing. That if I made more money this would all be easier, and he would plan a trip in an instant."

"Oh. That's interesting, because that's not what it tells me."

The familiar constriction in my chest occurs, and with great effort I ask, "What does it tell you?"

"It tells me he doesn't want to go on vacation with you."

And up into the tornado I go.

After getting my feet on the ground, and with the help

of her hands on my knees, I'm able to take conscious, deep breaths. I push the air down and out through my feet. My body shakes. I cry.

We discuss how natural this scenario is to me. I explain to her how difficult it was to get my father to plan or commit to anything. He never talked about the future with my mother because (duh!) he knew he wasn't going to be in her future.

"Sometimes, he wouldn't even commit to something the following week," I tell Kelly.

"And the idea of saving money for something in the future, forget that too."

We talk about how things like this had become my familiar, and then she asks me, "So, what are you getting from this?"

"Nothing. Absolutely nothing."

"That's not true," Kelly says, and then she advanced my understanding of truth, which leads to furthering my understanding of honesty, and then my understanding of responsibility.

"What do you mean?"

"It's not true that you aren't getting something from this. I'm not saying it's a good something. In fact, it's toxic to your system. But you are getting something you want, or you would stop."

And outside went my insides. Not literally. The exposure, though, is total. I feel revealed in a way that I haven't before.

I think of a book that I'm currently reading, *The Seat of the Soul*, by Gary Zukav. I think about what he says about intention and splintered personalities. About how splintered personalities may have a conscious intention to improve something, say a relationship, but a stronger subconscious intention to destroy it. The splintered personality, when things don't work out, will tell itself the outcomes were unintended, when in fact they turned out exactly as intended. He goes on to discuss the importance of bringing our subconscious intentions into our consciousness in order to live with honesty, in our light, and with true intention.

Through many group and individual sessions, Kelly leads me to understand that I have not processed the feelings around my father's abandonment and his betrayal, no matter how much I might intellectually understand those issues. As a result I continue to enter into situations that recreate these feelings, and until I fully own them, feel them, and process them through my body, I will continue to do so.

Until I understand and own that it is actually my intention to recreate abandonment, I will not stop creating it.

By this point in my therapy, I'm ready to dive in. I completely trust Kelly to take me where I need to go, to watch over me and protect me while I'm there, and to gently help me find my way back. The abyss still feels dark and deep, but I have a lifeline in Kelly, and I'm ready to discover what lives in my most forbidding caverns.

This finds me back at the pillows with the mallet.

"Remember, swing all the way through, and take the mallet all the way back up."

"Okay," I say.

I hold the mallet over my head. I stare at the pillow, and place my father's head on top. At first there is nothing, just his disembodied head staring at me, lifeless. Then, his expression mocks me, and he challenges me.

I hear him say, "You can't do this."

And all hell breaks loose.

"Fuck you!" I yell. "Watch me!"

I slam the mallet on the pillow. I don't stop my downward thrust until it hits the floor.

All the way up!

All the way down!

Up, down, up down, over and over and over.

I scream and curse. I blame and rage. Halfway through, I almost stop, but I tell myself no, get it all out. Go all in, and bring it all out.

And I do.

I beat the pillow into submission. I don't stop until I'm completely spent.

The mallet falls out of my hands. My body is weak, and I allow myself to fall to my knees. I cry an exhausted, spent cry as Kelly holds me, reassuring me and comforting me. I finally, and fully, understand what she has been trying to teach me about holding things inside.

She warns me that I might get sick, "You've released a lot of toxins, and it's common for people to get a cold after such deep work."

I do, but it doesn't last long. Long enough, however, for me to be quiet with myself, and not go to work for a couple of days. I stay wrapped in a blanket and allow healing to begin.

In that healing space, I own my truth: I am very angry with my father for abandoning me.

I become more honest with myself. I have been denying my truth, and playacting my abandonment with other men.

I take responsibility for the fact that in denying my truth, and in being dishonest with myself, I play the victim in order to fulfill my belief that I will be abandoned again.

At a group session shortly after this, Kelly gives me an assignment, "Make a list of the qualities your ideal father would have."

It's a simple exercise, but it proves to be painful.

He would protect me.

He wouldn't lie.

He would love my family and me.

He would put us first.

He would show compassion.

I would be the most important thing in his life. Nothing and no one could take him away from me.

He wouldn't manipulate me.

He wouldn't try to taint my feelings about my siblings and mother.

He would be sorry and show remorse.

"But that's not the father you got, is it?" she says, after I finish reading the list.

Feet on the ground, deep breaths, feel the disappointment, and move it through.

"No."

"Do you realize your searching for someone to be those things?"

This almost hurts more then accepting that I didn't get the father I needed or wanted. I feel pathetic and ashamed. I feel my neediness hovering over the room. I become aware of my passive aggressiveness, my justification of other's behaviors, and my need to find a way to make them love me.

With my feet on the ground, I take several deep breaths. As my shame and neediness pulse through my body, moving down and out my feet, I feel a kinship to my mother.

"Is there anything your father has given you? Bad people aren't all bad, and surely there is something there that is positive for you."

I don't have to think long, "Once when I was six or seven, I was home alone with him and he was taking a nap. I decided to go play in the yard, and when I stepped on the sidewalk a dinosaur-sized cockroach (or at least it seemed that big at the time) ran across my bare foot. I absolutely hated cockroaches and was terrified of them. I screamed what my siblings would call bloody murder. My father came running out of the house in a fog from his nap. It is the one time I saw my father sincerely scared and concerned. He asked me what had happened. When I told him about the cockroach, he spanked me and told me never to scream like that again."

"After we both calmed down, he told me that I should never do that unless someone was hurting me, trying to take me, or if I was seriously injured. He explained to me the story of crying wolf."

"I knew I had scared him. I wasn't mad at him for spanking me, and I have always held on to that lesson. I don't manipulate people in order to get them to do something I want and I think very carefully about when I need help."

I stop and roll my eyes at myself, "Well, except when I'm in a relationship having my dysfunctions triggered."

We both laugh.

"And he always told me I never had to wait for any man to tell me what I could or could not do in this life. I now know that was because he knew he was going to abandon me, and therefore didn't want me counting on him, but nevertheless, it was a good message that has stuck with me. Again, when I'm not in a dysfunctional relationship."

"Those are great lessons, and you are not condemned to dysfunctional relationships. But until you fully understand what triggers you, why you're triggered, and how you react to those triggers, you won't be able to have a healthy, mature relationship. The beautiful thing is, everything you're dealing with is learned behavior, so all you have to do is learn new behaviors, and acquire new tools, and those are things I can teach you and give you."

I laugh.

She asks me why I'm laughing, and I tell her, "When I was twelve, my ballet teacher retired, and my tap and jazz teacher bought the studio. She was actually a trained classical dancer, and couldn't wait to start teaching us ballet. She explained to us that my old teacher had been losing her eyesight, and so while she was giving us good general directions, she was never actually correcting any one of us specifically. This led to my new teacher repositioning my body in plié, which threw me off my balance, and everything felt wrong. I got all huffy with her and told her she didn't know what she was doing. And that I could dance before she started teaching ballet."

"She looked me in the eye and said, 'If you want to learn how to dance, you will do what I'm telling you, otherwise there is the door. You may leave, and you will not be welcomed back.'"

"She'd never lied to me. I knew she meant what she said, and I knew I wanted to dance. I choked back tears, took a breath, and said, "'What was it you wanted me to do?'"

"I have to say relearning new tools, or in that case new technique, worked out pretty well for me," I smile at Kelly.

I have grown so fond of her; I know I will follow wherever she leads me.

My gun dreams start to haunt my sleep again. It's the same three replayed over and over again: I'm being stalked, Lily Tomlin's countdown as my father shoots my family, and BAM! I'm shot between the eyes.

We start talking about what it means to be out of control, and how I've lived in crisis mode since the shooting, but probably also since the divorce. I come to accept, though not without a good fight first, that I will never know the truth concerning my father's shooting, and that I have to come to peace with that if I desire to move on.

I tell Kelly about a phone call with my dad sometime after the anger exercise.

"He didn't ask me how I was doing. He didn't ask me what I was doing. He just wanted to make sure I knew he was the victim of the shooting. I asked him how he knew the woman convicted was the one who shot him, and he said, 'I'd know that voice anywhere.'"

"When I brought up the woman who was murdered, he simply said, 'She just happened to be in the wrong place at the wrong time.' I told him that sounded a little cold considering she wouldn't have been shot if she weren't in the park with him, and then he whined more about his victimhood. I replied that he was the one having all the affairs, and he said to me, 'I wouldn't walk across the street for a piece of ass, Connie Sue.'"

I slump after I say this.

"What," Kelly asks.

"Right before the last time I was in court with my parents, my dad and his wife were deposed to see if my dad was in contempt of court for not paying my mom's alimony. I read the deposition again recently, and it's astounding to me for a few reasons. First, he talks about the divorce as if my mother initiated it. He told me he would make sure Mom was okay and he was going to let her keep the house, and then he complains about how she got the house and all he had was an old car and his clothes. He talks about the trauma the divorce put him through," I laugh.

"It's a little hard to be traumatized when you're calling all the shots, and the other party isn't contesting a thing."

"Then, it's very disturbing when he refers to 'that lady who got killed.' He knew her, obviously rather well, and this is how he refers to her. And the complaining about how he's worked thirty-one years, and he doesn't want to work anymore, and doesn't think he should have to, even though he agreed to pay my mom alimony."

I look out the window and inhale some of the remaining aroma of the sage smudge Kelly burned at the beginning of my session. I want to stop talking, but I can't.

"He referred to our situation as a 'father-daughter little scuffle,' but the part that is really astounding to me is whenever he's pressed to own up to anything, especially when the attorney is trying to figure out when his and Meg's relationship began, he won't answer, he gets all defensive, and I can hear the anger in his tone. I can see him sitting in that chair, his back up against the wall, and for the first time in his adult life, he's being held accountable, and he can't just say, 'Kiss my ass,' and walk out."

Shame is spilling from me like an overflowing bucket. This is the legacy my father left me. My nature disallows any romanticizing of it. I can't tell myself it was all really something else. I've seen the destruction denial has leveled upon my mother.

"Then, not because he asked, but I told him I was in therapy," I say, returning to my phone conversation with him.

"What did he say?" Kelly asks.

I chuckle, "He said that was probably good for me. I needed it to help me get past the divorce, and all the brainwashing my mother had done to me."

"Wow."

This authentically stuns her.

"He then proceeded to tell me that he went to a therapist for a week once he recovered from the shooting. He asked me, quite smugly, if I knew what his therapist told him, 'He said all I have to do is give you kids time, and you'll come back around.' I asked him if he told the therapist everything he had done to us because I'm quite certain the therapist wasn't suggesting we would do so without him taking some steps towards atonement. He then yelled at me again that he was the victim, told me I could kiss his ass, and hung up."

"I'm beginning to believe your father might be borderline

psychopathic," she says. "He's definitely narcissistic, he shows no remorse for his actions, he blames others for his misfortune, he believes everyone is out to get him, and, from the way you described it, he projected an image of a family man publicly."

I hear Kelly saying these words as I finish my drive across the Hoan Bridge. It slowed me down at the time, but now as I'm driving along the lake, I think there must be something very profound in the idea of not being psychopathic yourself, but being raised by someone with those tendencies, and having them shape your worldview.

Back in her office that day, I tell her that I'm thinking of ending all contact with him. While she says she'll support my wishes, if that's what I choose to do, she feels that I should confront him in person, so that I can be absolutely sure I want to do that.

"Estranging oneself from one's parent is a very dramatic step, and while I can't disagree with your decision, I think you want to be absolutely sure that's what you want."

Two weeks later, I'm in Forked River with my dad, sitting on a picnic tabletop in a park. Not the one where he was shot.

Before I left my mom's house, I drew an angel card to have something to focus on for this meeting. The card features an open armed angel and the word "Release." I carry it in my pocket during the meeting.

As I sit next to him, I'm very thankful for all the breath work I've done. After a group session where I moved from hysterical laughter, as all my energy went up through the top of my head, to hysterical sobbing as all my energy went down through my feet, I was finally able to break through the separation in my hips and move all my energy downward and out through my feet. Not an easy thing for a dancer, who is taught that while your body moves downward all your energy moves upward.

I have not been in my father's presence for over two years, so it takes everything I have to keep the energy in my body going downward. But in so doing, I avoid a panic attack. I'm grounded and focused on the present. I'm able to be clear-headed and function in a healthy way.

I rotate my rose quartz sphere pendant. The stone's smoothness aids in calming me.

"I called you here because I'm very bothered by our relationship, and I need to talk to you about that," I say.

"Well, I'm always here for you, Connie Sue, you know that. I want to help you in any way I can," he returns.

We are both sitting on the picnic table with our feet on the bench. He's leaning forward with his elbows on his knees, his hands clasped together.

"I'm very troubled by some of the things you've said to me over the years, and definitely by some of the things you've done. You've lied to me. You've manipulated me. To be honest with you, I watched you do those things to all of us, but right now I'm not concerned about the relationship you continue with them. I'm concerned about ours. I don't want to be lied to. I don't want to be manipulated, and I would deeply appreciate some kind of accountability on your part for all the things you've done that have deeply hurt me, and driven a wedge between us," I end.

I have more I want to say, but I'm growing nervous, and I

don't want to slip into my defensive dysfunctional self. I force myself to sit silently and wait. I roll the stone.

He proves to me why it is so difficult for people to confront their abuser. You know before you go in what you'll get, and it's the proof of that that you don't want to accept, feel, or be responsible for. The sense of futility is overwhelming.

"You know, Connie Sue," he opens and closes his hands. His toupee blows in the gentle breeze, and his yellow jacket billows at the back. He looks right at me, his eyes full of scorn and retribution. He is finished playing Mr. Nice Guy.

"I've been nothing but a good father to you. Did you ever want for anything? Did you ever starve or not have a roof over your head?"

I can't let this stand as proof for good fathering, "Dad, Mom worked just as hard as you did, and paid for just as much as you did." In fact, my mother had become a workaholic in order to help her delusions along.

"Goddammit, Connie Sue, you can say what you want to about me. Call me an asshole if you want, but I don't owe you an apology for a goddamn thing," he goes on. I tune him out, and force myself to breathe. I force myself to feel right then in that moment every emotion that is present. And in the end, there are only two: profound sadness and disappointment.

When he finishes, I root my feet to the ground, breathe, stand up, and say, "Dad, I don't want to have a relationship with you, if it's your desire to continue treating me the way you have."

Then, he says the thing that drives home the pain, "Well, we all have to do what we have to do," and proves he's willing to let me go if indeed it means changing.

"I don't know why you can't get over the past. I know I have," he adds a little salt.

I stare at him for a moment. I want to explain how this isn't about the past. It's about moving forward into our shared future in a more loving, healthy way.

"I really do wish you could get over the divorce, Connie Sue. This isn't good for you, Babe."

I look at him and sigh-smile. "You're right Dad," I say. "It's not."

I turn and walk away.

To my back, he says, "You know, you're welcome at my house any time."

I realize as I walk past a familiar elm tree (I came to this park often as a child, but in this moment I doubt I will ever return), this is how he always puts the onus on me. I can hear him now, "I told her she was welcome. I haven't closed my door to her."

He sets it up so it appears that I'm the one abandoning him. I'm the one who doesn't care about our relationship.

When I get back home, I allow myself to cry, and I allow myself to accept my mother's passive-aggressive apologies. She's relieved for so many reasons of her own, but somewhere inside of them, she's sad for me, but also glad that I'm protecting myself. She tells me over and over again that this isn't how she thought her life was going to turn out. How can she think this? What about my father ever led her to believe things were going to be different?

I recount the events to Kelly at my next individual session. I tell Kelly that I no longer want a relationship with my father. I want to be free of his sick, toxic energy. She takes me through a death ritual, and I visually and emotionally bury my father that day. I walk out of her office grieving the loss of my father's love and concern; two things his actions have forced me to accept that I never really had. However, I'm ready to move on, and I allow myself to feel both my loss and my liberation.

It's a stunning Saturday as I park my car. The trees are vibrant green and swaying against a cloudless blue sky. I can smell the lake.

I sit for a moment, wrapping up my thoughts of the past three years. So much more has gone on than I can recall in this drive. I'm amazed at how far I have come, and while I'm sure there's more to go, I'm confident that the worst is behind me. I get out of my car and enter the building with a skip in my step and joy in my heart.

The room is calm when I walk in. People are talking in soft voices, and the scent of burning sage fills the room. Twenty red meditation chairs circle the floor. The expanse of Lake Michigan is picture perfect. The lake and the treetops are the only view out the east side windows. The stage is set for something big, but what I can only imagine.

A few people address me with surprise, "I thought you said you weren't coming."

"I woke up this morning and wanted to. Luckily, there was one spot left, and Kelly said it was fine to come."

We begin by passing around the Voyager Tarot deck, and we each draw a card to give us focus for the weekend. I draw the

Moon card. Number eighteen in the major arcana. It speaks to many things, but two catch my attention most. One, it speaks to evolutionary changes and says, "a continuity-transformation in which natural completions create inherent new beginnings." And two, "complete old relationships and/or old patterns of relationships, and move them into a new phase. And then it encourages the drawer to be "like the dolphin, intuit and feel out the truth."

The weekend progresses along a natural, organic track. It seems no one has anything big to unearth. I don't do any individual work. I simply enjoy the group exercises and meditations Kelly leads us through.

"Well, we have half an hour left," Kelly says. It's Sunday, and the workshop is about to end.

"Does anyone have a need to work," she asks.

"I do," I surprise myself when I say this.

She asks me what I need to work on.

"I really don't know. I just suddenly feel there is something I must do."

"Well, then, why don't you come over here and lie down on the floor."

I do as she asks. I lie on my back, arms at my sides, with my knees bent and my feet flat on the floor.

"Just close your eyes, breathe, and see what comes up."

Nothing happens for a minute or two, and then in my mind's eye, I start tumbling down a dark tunnel. Visually, it's more like a wormhole in deep space. And the deeper I go, the faster I go. I can tell that I'm squirming.

Kelly instructs people to come and put their hands along

the sides of my body. I start to crawl. I don't like the feeling: trapped with nowhere to run/hide/escape from whatever is about to name itself.

"Make them go away," I say, knowing she won't do it. It never hurts to try though, right?

Kelly laughs, and says she won't. She places her hands on my feet. Now I'm going out of my head. She instructs someone to put his hands on my knees and push downward.

I can't take it. I'm going insane.

Then she says to a woman, "Go and put both of your hands on top of her head. Cover her whole head."

With that, the only exit available to my energy is through the bottom of my feet. As soon as the hands cover my head, all energy is forced downward, and as it passes my throat, I open my mouth and scream and scream and scream and scream.

I fight to get away, but Kelly won't let anyone let me go.

"Keep her down. Keep her head covered," I hear her call out above my screaming.

My scream, long and continuous, is deep, ancient, and loud. I can't stop. The scream has a life of its own, and it won't stop until it is dead.

But Kelly stops me.

She has everyone ease away from me. She rubs my legs, and comes up to my side, calming me and bringing me back to the room with melodic shushes.

"I need you to stop, Connie. I'm afraid you are going to hurt your throat."

I look at her, and I plead, "But I'm not done. There's more."

"I know," she says. Her compassion overwhelms me.

"It's the first thing we'll do in group on Tuesday," she rubs my shoulder.

"Okay," I stand up. I'm a changed person. I feel like I'm in limbo. I'm in half-scream limbo, if that's possible. How can there be more?

On Tuesday, Kelly explains to the group that I started some pretty big work that I need to finish. She asks them to understand that it might take up most of the time.

Everyone is happy to do what she can to help.

Again I lie on the floor. Slowly, hands are placed on my sides, Kelly places her hands on my feet, someone places her hands on my knees, and then my head is covered. In less than a second I'm racing head over heels down the wormhole and I am screaming, deeper and more violently than before.

"Please, someone go upstairs, and tell my daughter everything is okay down here," I hear Kelly say. It frightens me to think that I sound so frightening that I might scare her daughter.

My screams last longer than they did on Sunday, but Kelly doesn't stop me. This time she lets me scream myself out. When I finish, my body is shaking, and I'm crying. Everyone is gently, lovingly rubbing my body.

Kelly moves the women who are on my right side. Kneeling beside me, she brushes my hair back from my forehead, and asks, "What has terrified you so badly?"

I'm aware that it's a rhetorical question, but I respond in my head, and with my eyes, *Everything*.

It takes a few moments, but I'm able to sit up. We all return to our red meditation chairs, and I'm comforted by comments of how brave I was to do what I did.

"My heart weeps for you," a nun says. I have three nuns in my group, and they're awesome. Talk about having father issues. And I don't just mean their biological dads.

After more comforting and supportive comments, Kelly asks me to sit in front of the woman to her left. I do so and say, "Now what?" as I try to process and absorb everything that has just happened and the love and support that I am surrounded by.

"I want you to say something for me, Connie. It's just two simple words."

I look at the woman in front of me and we smile. How hard can two simple words be?

"Okay," I sit up tall, breathe, and look at Kelly. "I'm ready."

"I want you to go around the room, look each person in the eye, and say," she lofts the basketball again, "I'm alive."

I'm circling the rim. My blood stops flowing, my eyes bulge, and I'm terrified. I sit frozen in front of the first woman, one of the nuns. I don't know how long I sit here debating with myself whether or not I can say it, whether or not I can accept it.

The entire room is silent and waits patiently without judgment or contempt for the amount of time I'm taking. Instead, all I feel is love, compassion, and hope.

I swallow hard, open my mouth, and close it. I look up at the nun, who has suddenly become very angelic.

I straighten my back, look her in the eyes, and quietly, almost in a whisper, say, "I'm alive."

The words jolt my system.

"Move on," Kelly says.

I scoot over, look the next woman in the eyes, and say quietly, but not in a whisper, "I'm alive."

Electricity surges through my body.

I move on. Each time it gets easier, and I indeed begin to feel alive. By the time I come to Kelly, I'm jubilant. With celebration, certainty, and a strong, grounded voice, I look her straight in the eyes and proclaim, "I am alive!"

"Yes, Connie. You are," she smiles. We exchange a huge, warm hug.

I stand up and dance around the room. Everyone's laughing and cheering and celebrating with me.

"I'm alive," I say it over and over again.

"I have an announcement," I say. It's two weeks after I reclaimed my life.

"I have decided to end my therapy. I feel ready to go out into the world. I feel I am well equipped with new tools, and I'm ready to go test them out."

"I agree with you," Kelly says.

This gives me even more confidence in my decision.

"Next week, we will have a closure ceremony for Connie," she says. We all know what this means, as I will be the fourth of the original ten to leave.

Many members take me out to dinner after my last session. I know it's not the last time I will see most of them. Some, I have become very close to.

Once home, I put on my pajamas, crawl under my blankets, and reread the cards of well wishes I received during my closure. While they are all beautiful and offer me so many blessings, one by the nun to whom I first whispered, "I'm alive," is especially touching.

The card's message is simple. It reads "Stay Connected." She writes, "Connie…Lovable one, young and wonderful treasure that you are! I am so glad to have had the time to experience your deep desire to grow. Continue to exude your compassion to others…blessings on you, and may you dance into forever."

I press the card to my heart. I've come to know what it means to be supported, loved, and heard. The most wonderful thing for me is that my compassion and love and support have all been received and appreciated, and I, too, have helped others in their time of need.

I truly feel that something is ending, while something else is beginning.

I've closed a chapter.

I survived.

And now, I am alive again.

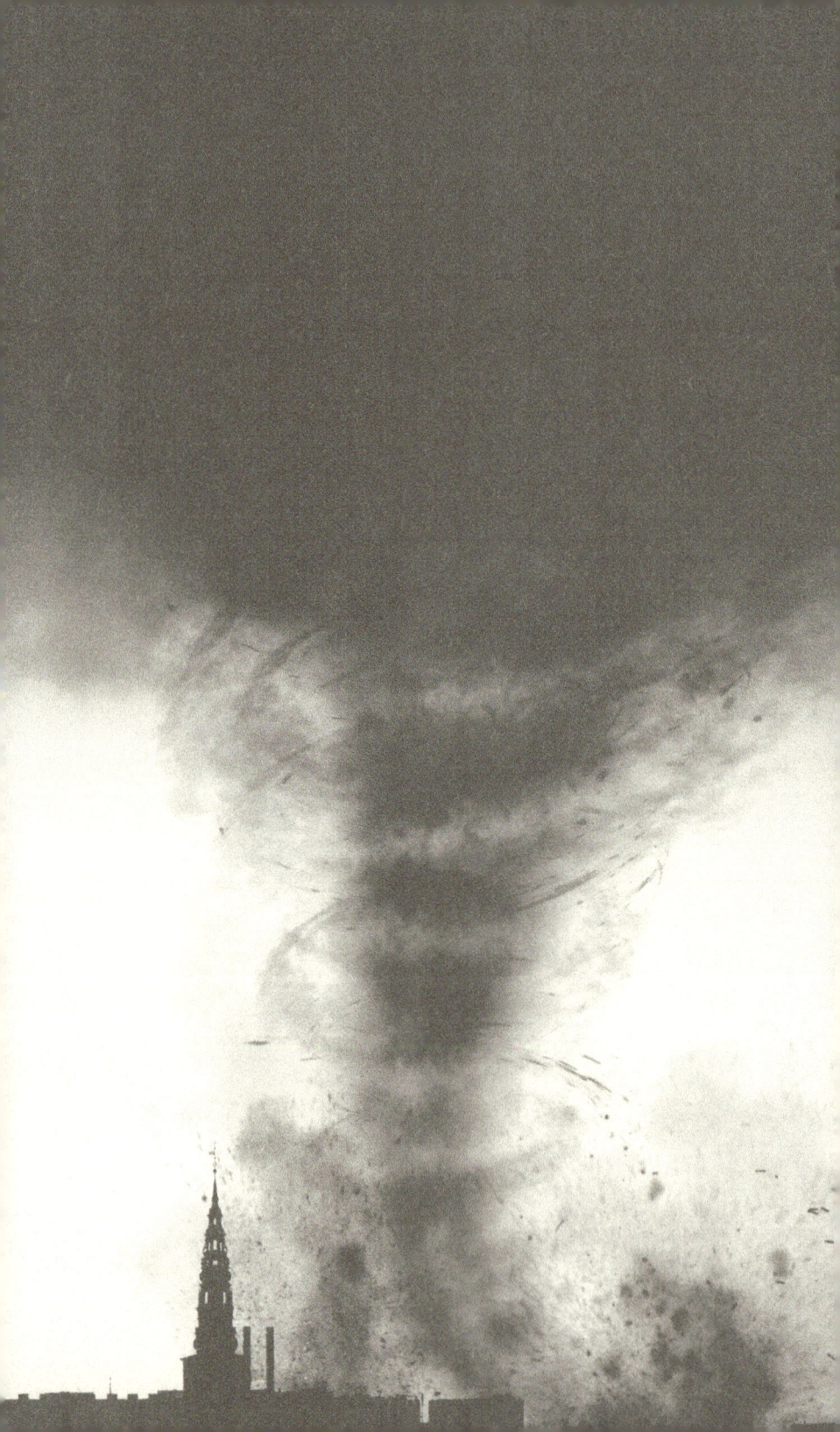

PART IV

REBUILDING

"Pain wanders through my bones like a lost fire."

– Theodore Roethke

"Dance, dance, dance, little lady!
Leave tomorrow behind."

– Noel Coward

"Tomorrow
The moon will melt
The snow will melt
And we'll have a
brand
new
day."

– My daughter

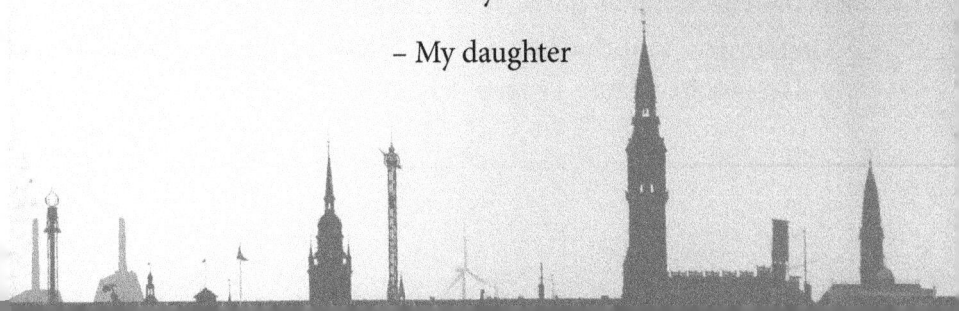

"If I ever go looking for my heart's desire again, I won't look any further than my own back yard. Because if it isn't there, I never really lost it to begin with."

– L. Frank Baum

When Dorothy wakes up after her journey to Oz, she finds Uncle Henry, Auntie Em, Hickory, Zeke, Hunk, and Professor Marvel all at her side, grateful that she is okay. She tells her story and finds herself confused by the likelihood of its reality. But the reality of her journey is secondary to the reality of what she comes to realize, which is the deceptively simple "there's no place like home."

I have a vision of waking up in the aftermath of the destruction that my father, like the tornado of my dreams, wrought in my life. I'm spread eagle over the debris in my yard, looking through the ravaged limbs of the maple tree into a clear blue sky above. I begin to spin as if I'm lying flat on a merry-go-round, slowly and smoothly I go round and round. As I spin, the tree and my home are restored, the tree begins to shrink, the fence goes away, both the white stone path and fishpond return, and the shed is gone. It is once again the yard of my childhood.

The sky is a beautiful, crisp autumnal blue, the air is warm, and the late summer bugs are in full chorus. I can hear Joe asking my dad to throw him a pitch. These are the days when my dad coached Little League. I hear Sam and me running about, laughing and playing together. Fran is painting a large daisy on the seat of her desk chair. And my mother is clipping zinnias to make a bouquet for the kitchen table.

I am able to hear the laughter. I'm able to remember that there were good, simple times when my life and my family were as normal as a life and a family can be. I remember that I loved my home. The way the early morning sun lit my bedroom and the kitchen, and the way the late afternoon sun, more orange than yellow in its color, created a pastoral atmosphere in our living room.

And I know without a doubt that everything I ever needed to live this life to the fullest was in my own backyard. My parents, through their own imperfections, their own self-abandonment, and their inability to care for me in a healthy way, gave me everything I needed to live an adult life full of love and grace, as long as I was willing to go in search of it.

Spring 2017

It's a rainy, dismal day. I'm watching my husband and daughter walk down the sidewalk to the corner, where a small pond has been formed by a storm sewer clogged with pollen, mud, and other various items of spring detritus. I understand its beckoning call to my daughter to jump and splash, and I'm delighted my husband is the one who suggested they go.

They look, to me, like Christopher Robin and Pooh headed out on an adventure. They are both carrying umbrellas. My daughter, in her favorite pink wellies, skip-walks next to my husband. An aura of happiness encircles them. My heart is overcome with joy.

There are times I am surprised I had the courage to have a child at all. It didn't come easy for us. I suffered two miscarriages and a blighted ovum pregnancy to get here. After all of that, at the age of 41, I became pregnant with our now eight-year-old daughter.

It is only very recently that I have stopped envisioning a disastrous end for her around every corner. At the family picnic last fall to kick off the school year, she and my husband took off for the playground. She was slightly in front of him. She came to the parking lot first, and as if it were real, I heard the brakes screech, the thud of her body against the car, the people screaming. I ran up the stairs to find my husband standing over our daughter's dead body.

A poorly thrown Nerf ball hit my leg, mercifully jolting me back to the present. Still, I traced their steps to make sure they made it to the playground intact.

While all parents worry about their child's safety, my history has left me in a life long struggle between relaxing into the good, healthy life I now have and seeing crisis and disaster around every turn. Life can change on a dime, and in my experience that has been with dire consequences. I direct a large amount of conscious, concerted energy towards my heart in order to keep it open, allowing myself to embrace the bounty I now know.

While I spent my childhood telling myself this isn't my life, this isn't real, I have spent my adult life telling myself this is my life, this is real. And my life is grand. Kelly was right, you can only experience joy to the degree you have experienced pain. And today, in my world, in the sanctuary of my home, with my husband and daughter, I experience much love and an abundance of joy.

I feel like I spend most of my day giving thanks. Thank you, dear God, for giving me the courage to discover my truth and to open my heart, for the gift of Kelly, for the love and support I can now embrace from my husband and closest friends, and for the sweetness of my daughter. For, in her, I see what I would have been as a child, had I known the love from my father she experiences from hers. She has proven to me that love does make a difference.

And my life has proven to me that getting help at a young age made all of this possible for me.

Spring 1996

"Are you ready?" he calls from the living room.

"Yes," I sigh, deep and heavy.

This has been going on since we moved in together, and I'm sick of it. I fight him all the way, but he won't stop doing it. I feel belittled and disgusted inside. I know I'm being manipulated by him, but to what end? And again, I ask, why does he keep doing it?

I sit down on the floor. I lean over the glass-topped coffee table and say, "Well, here I am."

"Do you have *my* money?" he asks.

My money! The way he says it makes my skin crawl.

"It's not *your* money. It's *my* money to cover *my* half of *our* rent."

"Well, I'm the one who writes the rent check, so it's *my* money."

He smiles, and I recognize that smile. It's like my dad's, and everyone I've dated like him. It's a smile that suggests he has me where he wants me.

I count out $350. He demands that I give him cash, which makes me go to my employer's bank on payday and cash my check because of the three-day wait for available funds at my bank.

"You only write the check because the landlord will only

accept one check. But you are not paying all the rent," I say, and slam the money on the table.

My defensiveness begins to crawl up my spine like a centipede, every leg digging in with every step.

I write out my checks for half of the phone, electric, and gas bills and put them in the envelopes. I then pay my credit card bill, stamp the envelope, and stand up.

"Where are you going?" he demands.

"I'm done paying my bills and I have other things to do."

"I want you to stay here with me while I pay mine."

He does this every month. He's done it every month for the three-plus years we've lived together. He makes me ill, and yet, I sit down. And instead of questioning why I sit back down, I wonder how I can reason with him. How do I make him understand what he's doing? He's belittling me, controlling me, and I'm a grown-up. Grown-ups don't take too kindly to these kinds of behaviors. And, as a grown-up, I have more agency than I did as a child. Right? And I'm certain he wouldn't tolerate it if I did this to him.

"I'm finished paying my bills. Like I said, I have other things to do. Why do you want me to sit here with you?"

I ask the same question every month, and perhaps I'm hoping he will say it's because he likes my company, which I think he does, but my company has nothing to do with this scenario.

"Well, I think you need to know how much money I have to pay out each month."

"Why? I don't think you need to know how much my credit card bill is."

We're not married and our money is not commingled.

"Well, look at how much money I'm spending. I'm covering more than you are," he says this as if I will not trust my own judgment.

"None of my personal expenses are on your five credit cards. You are not covering anything for me. So if you don't like the amount of bills you have to pay, stop using your credit cards and spending money you don't have."

He launches into the same old conversation about how he wouldn't be in this position if I covered more of my fair share of the bills. Translation, if I paid part of his bills.

Like every other month, I exhaust myself trying to reason out his thinking. I painstakingly, and futilely, try to get him to understand how he is misguided in his thinking.

Why am I doing this?

I leave the table frustrated. This futility, this argument, is so familiar and old, I feel like it's inscribed on my bones.

I turn and look back at him. The smug smile on his face sickens me.

Two weeks later.

It's Saturday, and I'm feeling good. I just finished teaching three private lessons at the Pettit Center, and I don't have to work at the bookstore tomorrow: my first Sunday off in five weeks. I can go out tonight and enjoy myself, knowing I can relax all day tomorrow. I don't like going out the night before I have to work, especially if I'm teaching the next morning. I'm not sharp, and I don't like that feeling when I'm facing twenty students expecting my best. Plus, with my high-school-age students, I need credibility when I point out that they're hung over and I'm not.

I park the car.

I breathe in the warm, late-spring air as I walk across the lot to our door. It's perfect weather for the capped sleeve dress I bought the day before.

We have dinner and I shower. I'm already tan, so I can forget dealing with makeup. I do my hair, and when I reach the top of the stairs, he says from the bottom, "I'm going out alone tonight."

Fury rages through me. He knows I've been up here getting ready to go out.

"What?"

"I need to try and get some new clients, and that's a little hard to do if you're with me."

He's a ballroom-dance teacher, and my now ex-partner. This is how we ended up living together. I'm wondering why we stayed together after the partnership ended.

"I won't be able to work the room with you there," he says.

I keep buying this excuse, but tonight it smacks me hard.

"You're kidding me, right? You knew I was up here getting ready to go out. You probably knew at dinner you wanted to go alone, and you strung me along."

Like my father, he throws it back on me.

"Well, look at you. You're not even fully put together."

Oh, not this again. "Fully put together," I practically spit.

"Well, you don't have any makeup on. You look like you don't care about yourself. In fact, when you don't wear makeup, you make me feel like you don't care about me."

This was one of the reasons our professional partnership ended. Somehow, when I was going to practice and sweat for three hours, I didn't have any self-respect because I wouldn't wear makeup.

"It's called vanity! What you're talking about is vanity! Not self-respect," I yelled at him one day in the studio during practice.

I'm about to repeat these words from the landing when he turns and walks out the door.

I undress and put on my pajamas. My mood is not conducive to pleasant interactions with others.

I make a cup of tea and settle into a chair.

I'm glad to be alone. He's a big TV watcher. I'm not. So I am peacefully left to sit in the silence with my thoughts.

In reflection, our whole relationship has been like tonight. It's all the same thing, the situations might vary in their content, but in the end, it's all the same. He is constantly making me feel like I don't care. He questions my motives, which makes me overanalyze them, and conjure a way to make them more clear than they already are. I become defensive regarding this because I'm very concerned about him, all the while being told how selfish I am, especially when I get upset because he wants to go out without me. I'm obviously more concerned, he tells me in these moments, about my wants than his needs. This leads to threats of breaking up with me, which leads to my fears of abandonment blowing up in my face, and then I begin an embarrassing display of atonement for anything I may or may not have done to make him feel the way he claims to feel.

But I also deal with his constant feigning (as I believe them to be) of his fears that I will leave him. He is always accusing me of this. Until now, I haven't fully allowed myself to look at this little piece of our relationship. He is always accusing me of wanting to date other people. No matter how much I affirm and reaffirm this is not the case, he constantly accuses me of having nefarious motives. This keeps my attention on my behaviors and me, rather than his behaviors and him, which I justify for him. Somehow, I always give him a more honorable excuse for his actions than he would give himself.

Just like my mother, a little voice whispers.

That little voice makes me feel ugly and sick.

As I watch the day wane, I wonder why I'm here. A question stuck in repetition.

A sense of futility invades my body. It slowly begins to overcome my desires, my needs really, to rationalize my actions to him, to get him to explain his actions to me, to get him to understand I'm not the person he keeps accusing me of being, to get him to care for me by overstating how much I care for him.

I know he's cheating on me. I haven't caught him in the act, but I know. Unlike my mother, I don't need to wait until I have the visual proof to act. I'm certain I'll never get it.

She often justified her inaction by saying, "If I'd only seen them in the act, I would have done something." I've always viewed this reasoning as a way of escaping responsibility because I believe, deep inside of herself she knew. I think of Kelly telling me, "Inaction does not remove us from responsibility. We are responsible for the consequences our inaction breeds as well."

Just last week, I interrupted a little rendezvous he had planned with a new, married dance instructor at the studio. I came home from work early and caught him on the phone. He didn't know I heard him say, "Yeah, don't come over now, she came home for some reason. I'll come by you."

"What was that all about?" I asked him.

"Oh, nothing. Shelly was just needing to talk, but now that you're home," he put on a winsome smile, "I told her I wanted to be with you."

I chuckled, "Yeah, I don't buy it."

He got mad and defensive, accused of me of not understanding him, and stormed out. His version of "Kiss my ass. I don't have to answer to you."

I have no doubt he went to Shelly's. In fact, I wouldn't be surprised if he's meeting her tonight.

The phone rings right as I ask myself out loud, "What am I doing here?"

I consider for a moment not answering it, but then, "Hello."

"Hi, Babe. It's Dad," he says this like I wouldn't know.

Oh, God. I'm so not in the mood for this right now, and I'm still regretting having gone to his house this past Christmas with Joe. I had not seen my father since the day in the park. He'd phoned a few times here and there, only to remind me how awful everyone was and how difficult the divorce had been for him. Whenever I asked him what had been difficult for him, he would stumble over his words and end by accusing me of not understanding him, generally with something like, "You couldn't understand Connie Sue, you've never been married or had kids."

This would inevitably be followed by "I don't owe you, or anyone, any god…damn…explanation!"

When I would ask if he was interested in what was going on with me, since he never asked, I would be reminded that, "It's just all about you, isn't it, Connie Sue."

These conversations only confirmed for me that my decision had been correct, but my boyfriend often accused me of being mistaken in this action. It was due to his prodding that I agreed to go to my father's with Joe last Christmas.

It proved to be a colossal mistake.

During our visit, he and Meg sat so proudly side by side after giving me a royal tour of their home, with the expectation I would be joyful for all that they had. The underlying message: I wouldn't have any of this if I were still burdened by you kids and your mom, and I'm sure it's better than anything you have. He liked it that none of us owned a house yet. I'd never really felt this sense of competition from him. I'd watched him be competitive with my siblings, but never me, but then for most of that time, I wasn't an adult yet.

As we sat in the chairs, I felt like we were paying court to the king and queen, while they informed us of what a hard morning they had had.

"Our neighbor is a man in his mid-thirties with two young children," my dad said. His voice oozed with compassion. Embedded in his tone was, "See, people turn to me for advice. People look up to me."

"Early in the week, his wife just up and left him and the kids. He's been over here every day since, asking us for advice. As we told him, we know just how he feels," my dad looked at Joe and me like an eight-year-old who just scored a goal and wants to make sure everyone saw him.

I could only stare in disbelief. For whatever reason, I couldn't speak the words on my mind, which isn't a situation I often find myself in.

What do you mean offer advice? What have you told him? He knows you're the ones who left, right? You're the ones who made your spouses feel like he feels. You are not the ones who had the burden of dealing with "the kids." You're not the ones who were left. You left!

All this I wanted to say, but instead I sat in stunned silence. I recalled a time from some years ago when my mom called me and said, "Can you believe I ran into Chet Napier, and he told me that your father had told him that I'm the one who left? Your dad is spreading it around that I left."

When we returned to my mom's house later that day, she collapsed in my arms crying. She was convinced that we'd all rather be with my father and Meg than her. Being gone longer than we had anticipated only exacerbated her condition. Knowing her as I do, I'm certain she believed we were all sitting over there talking about her. It's reasonable for her to think this, since my father never misses an opportunity to vilify her character.

For some reason, after we returned to Milwaukee, I called my father and wished him a happy birthday. There was absolutely no recognition that this was a rather monumental act on my part. Instead, he said, "Meg wants to talk to you," and handed off the phone.

Like a teenager crushed out on the new kid at school, she went on about how gorgeous my boyfriend was. She was totally aroused. It was repulsive, disturbing to say the least, and proof my father had managed to marry someone just like himself.

All these memories race through me before I ask, "What's up, Dad?"

Without skipping a beat, he launches into his victimhood. This time, though, he's trying to sell it to a 28-year-old who's been out in the world.

"Do you know I used to get up and go to work every day, even in the summer while you got to stay home, or go to the pool, or play golf?" he pauses. I'm certain he's holding out for a sympathetic comment from me.

Like I'm going to say, *Gosh, Dad. That's just awful. I mean, as an adult, and a parent, you were being forced to go work. No wonder you left us all. I can totally see now, and gee, I'm really sorry.*

"I don't understand your point, Dad," is what I say.

"I worked my ass off for all you, and what thanks do I get!" his shout causes me to pull the receiver away from my ear.

This time, *I* don't skip a beat, "Dad, why do you talk and act like you are the only one who worked? Do you forget that I was in the house? You might have worked from 9 to 5, but Mom did that, plus worked most nights doing books, and during tax season, she never stopped. In fact, during those nights, you were off doing…well, I think we're all clear now on what you were doing while she worked. I think she has you on number of hours worked. And she's never made me feel guilty for being an adult or my parent."

"God damn it, Connie Sue. You're just like talking to your mother. You don't understand anything I'm trying to say. I worked my ass off."

"I'm not saying you didn't. I'm just saying she did, too. And while we're on the subject, Dad, you need to explain to me what you did that is different from every other adult I know in the world. Do you know, oh, sorry you wouldn't because you've never asked, that right now, I'm working four jobs? I work part-time at a bookstore, I teach part-time at two studios, and I privately cross-train skaters at the Pettit center. You know in all the time I was around Sarah's house, I never once heard her dad blame her or her siblings for having to go to work. It's what adults are supposed to do!"

The man's persecution complex did me in.

After he reassures me again that I'm just as stubborn as my mother, I end our conversation, and go upstairs.

I collapse on my bed.

I'm lulled as I stare out the window at the violet-pink sunset.

I fall into a deep cavern. I'm conscious, but no longer in my room.

I'm no longer anywhere.

I'm simply in the universe, engulfed in darkness full of twinkling specks of light.

Suddenly, metaphorical punches start to land: first my right cheek, then my left eye. Over and over and over, my face is pummeled. Yet I feel no pain. But I feel the bumps begin to emerge. I have swollen hills across the entirety of my face and head. I open my eyes, allowing them to adjust to the waning daylight in the room. There is a mirror about ten feet in front of my bed, and I know, if I sit up right now, I'll see the face of an abused woman looking back at me.

Over the course of several minutes, the swollen hills recede, and my face returns to normal.

I sit up.

I'm overcome with an awareness that is both familiar and new at the same time. It originates from a depth in my bones that I've not journeyed to yet.

At that depth, I fully grasp the meaning of this awareness. It is ancient, buried in the time of my being, but no longer. It's been a whisper for years, but now it has strength, power, and volume. This voice lets me know that I no longer need to be afraid. I have everything I need.

"Why do I continue to care so much about my father when he so obviously, blood or not, cares absolutely nothing about me? Or, in the least, is comfortable with leading me to believe he doesn't. Why do I spend any time at all thinking about how my actions affect him when he has never once in my life considered how his actions, which have been mean and cruel, have impacted me? Why am I trying to make him love me when he has shown me time and time again he has absolutely no interest in doing so?"

And then, like water cascading over a mountain, things are set in motion inside me. I allow the water to fall and fall and fall, and as it descends over the rocky edges of my soul, I am flushed out at the bottom, floating, swirling, and spreading out wide in waters that are new. After the fall, my life is changed forever.

Two Months Later

He has a new dance partner. She's a married woman who lives and teaches in another state. This now leaves me, like today, home alone every other weekend, as he travels to practice and get coaching.

My fall, and transcendence, has been happening without my awareness. I'm simply allowing it to guide me where I need to go. On the outside, I'm all fumblebumble.

I drop things.

I bump into things.

My words are sometimes disconnected from my thoughts.

Like a newborn foal, I try to put my feet under me and I slip. I have new legs, and my muscles are not yet toned.

Without understanding why, but not questioning my desire, I'm drawn to an old bin buried in a closet in the spare bedroom. I dig it out and carry it down to the living room. Inside are a bunch of journals, the cards my group gave me when I left therapy, and a piece of paper folded in half lengthwise.

I know before I unfold it that this is what I came looking for.

I unfold the paper, and immediately remember drawing the line down the middle of the page and writing MOM above the left column and DAD above the right.

This was an exercise I had a difficult time doing, and I never fully let myself hear what Kelly was trying to tell me about its significance.

"I want you to make a list of all the qualities you dislike in your parents," she assigned. Like a good student, I went home that evening and did so. At the time, I chafed against her suggestion that I possessed some of the same qualities.

Before reading the list, I'm compelled to draw a tarot card. I get a candle, my sage smudge, and some matches. Along with my favorite blanket, I take all these things and the Voyager Tarot deck downstairs.

I light the candle first, and then the smudge. I inhale its

pleasant scent while taking deep meditative breaths. I place it in a shell bowl letting it slowly extinguish itself. I pick up the oversized cards, wrapping my small hands around them.

I shuffle them and ask, "What do I need to focus on while reading these lists?"

I place the cards on the floor, break them, ask the question again, and spread them in a long arc. I close my eyes, and skim my hand back and forth along the arc. I do this until I feel heat. I stop, and with my eyes still closed, I reach down and draw a card. I place it face down while I collect the rest of the cards and put them aside. I straighten my back, breathe again, and turn the card over to reveal the Seeker/Child of Wands card. There are children of different races on the card. One is in a meditative posture. Another, a beautiful aboriginal child, is staring up at the sky with an expression of questioning and hope on his face. There are various nocturnal animals peering into the darkening sky.

I open my guidebook to the appropriate page and read:

"You are a seeker, symbolized by your wands, the walking stick and arrows you use to hunt down the truth. Like the meditator, seek to know who you are; and as a journeyer, seek to understand where you have come from and where you are going. Be a student seeking to learn the whys and hows of life."

"Oh, God, I want to so much," I say out loud, in reflex to the card's words.

So, here I sit on my living room floor, the Seeker/Child of Wands. After several years of living with a man who verbally, emotionally, and mentally abuses me, I'm ready to tackle my human existence and to learn what I can learn. My faith in love and grace, which comes to me not from this earthly place, and has been with me since my earliest memories, and extends far beyond any boundaries that I know, gives me the strength and courage to dive into my truth. I trust that if I can look deeply and uncover what my fears have prevented me from knowing, I will then be free of the power that these hidden truths have over me.

In other words, I'm ready to discover my deeper darkness.

I want to be light. I want to live in light. That can't happen without going where I'm headed. I can't go where I'm headed without my faith.

Of both, I am certain.

"Hmm," a big smile graces my face.

"I'm ready. I trust you will take me where I need to go," I give a nod upwards, and hold the list in front of me.

I begin with my mom's list. As I do, my internal room grows dark. I fear it will become a lot darker before it becomes lighter. But something has changed in me, and in that change I reconnect to a truth, and that truth is that I no longer need to fear anything.

I feel this truth.

I know this truth.

I trust this truth.

My faith to the process I have learned informs me that I don't get to the light without going through the dark. I thought my Phoenix had come up out of the ashes the day I screamed myself to life, but perhaps, unbeknownst to me, it had only crashed.

Mom
- Passive aggressive
- Never stands up for herself
- Workaholic
- Always justifies Dad's behavior
- Allows her good nature to be taken advantage of
- Unable to follow through when she does take a stand
- Always justifies her own actions or lack thereof through martyrdom (this makes her sound very self-righteous)
- Has a delusional sense of her life, believes it is better than it is and nothing bad will come of it
- She steadfastly believed if he changed, all would be fine

I take a deep breath, and move onto my dad's list.

Dad
- Pathological liar
- Persecution complex
- Narcissist
- Remorseless
- Actions never match words
- Manipulative
- Willing to throw his family under the bus to save his own ass
- Unpredictable
- Held his love for ransom
- If I tried to establish a boundary, he would accuse me of being an ingrate and selfish
- When my mother tried to establish boundaries, he accused her of being controlling

I sit with the list in my lap.

Tears roll down my cheeks as a familiar, yet before this moment, disallowed awareness crawls up out of my darkness and slaps my consciousness awake.

These are my parents, with all their flaws.

I choke when I allow myself to say, "I wanted better."

Through my therapy, I learned my father was an emotional, verbal, and mental abuser. I left therapy with the tools to identify the same in a potential mate; and yet, here I am, in a relationship with someone just like him. And in this relationship, I have fully become my mother.

Something knocks hard on the door of my consciousness. I feel my hesitation to let it in, knowing as I do, that once it is in, I will be responsible to the truth it unfolds.

I close my eyes, take a few deep breaths, and ask, "What are you asking me to see?"

I ask God, the Universe, whoever is listening and assigned to help me discover all I need to know in this moment. Spirit guides, angels perhaps.

"What have I been unwilling or unable to see?"

I sit quietly, my eyes darting back and forth, as they search internally for the answer.

My thoughts travel to Kelly saying, "As a child, we don't allow our parents to abuse us, we are in that moment truly a victim, but as an adult…"

She stopped speaking.

"As an adult what," I ask out loud.

My body starts to tremble.

Quiet, I tell myself. Listen. She'll tell you.

In reality, Kelly had told me this many times in therapy, but I always fought her. I always felt she was letting my current partner off the hook for his behaviors, all the while making me responsible for everything going on. Especially when she would point out how my passive aggressive behavior affected others.

I'm quiet.

I breathe.

I wait.

"As an adult, we allow ourselves to be abused."

I scream out in rage, "No, I don't."

This outcry is immediately met with, "Oh, but you do."

My work with Kelly has also taught me that when I fight this hard it generally means the proverbial nail has been hit on its proverbial head.

I cry.

I shudder.

I fight.

But I want to know the truth.

All of it.

I want to be done with this cycle.

And, so, on my knees, I surrender, and what comes is the rebirth of my Phoenix.

Kelly's words come at me, "This is not about him. This is about you. Why do you allow yourself to be treated this way? Why are you with him? Yes, he may be a jerk, but you are deciding to stay with a jerk. Why?"

And then, from the deepest recess of my memory, to be brought forward when I was ready to hear it, she says, "You are still searching for your dad's love. You are still searching for the perfect daddy. So you date your father, and try to turn that person into the man you desire."

And then, again like Dorothy on her bed, when the house comes to rest in Munchkin Land, I am stopped, and reflexively say a surprised, "Oh."

I'm surprised because all my fear has vanished in what feels like a millisecond. I know it has been dissipating over time, since releasing my father, metaphorically burying him, and recognizing in our last phone conversation that I was fighting for something he didn't even care about. But I can now finally and fully surrender to the truth and the power of Kelly's words. After years of having one foot in and one foot out of my relationship with my father, I have now placed both feet out, and by doing so I have put an end to my self-abandonment. And by stopping self-abandonment, I no longer need to be with men like my father. They no longer serve a purpose.

But certain that this isn't all this moment is bringing to me, I refocus on the quiet.

I look back at the list.

I read it over three times, and each time, clarity comes nearer.

My subconscious and conscious selves are uniting.

I feel a wave of nausea wash over me. In the beginning of my therapy, this nausea would cause me to disengage. I was certain it indicated that things were wrong. I now know that it is, paradoxically, the indication of how right things are.

I breathe through the nausea, allow it to flow before ebbing, as I know it will, and wait.

I find disgust wash over my body like a flood of sewer-tainted water. I have become my mother over the last few years. Willingly, I have allowed myself to be manipulated, used, abused, and belittled, while granting excuses. I have been passive-aggressive while trying to get his attention and affection. I have been unable to follow through on my threats, and have, with a sickening self-righteousness, gone about trying to change his behavior, instead of...

Instead of...

Instead of accepting it, and realizing it is not about me changing him, but deciding whether or not I can live with someone like him. "It's not about what he's doing, Connie. It's not about trying to change him. It's about you. It's about why you are with him. What attracts you to people like him? It's about honestly looking at him, and deciding whether or not you can live with who he is," Kelly's voice booms inside me.

I get it.

I finally get it.

This is how the cycle is broken.

I can't live with a person like my father without becoming my mother. It is impossible for me. I have absolutely no respect for this man, just like I have none for my dad. I don't have to be with him. I don't have to take it anymore.

And then, out loud to the heavens above, I say three very powerful words, "I deserve better."

This is how this isn't about him.

And then the sick, disgusting feeling engulfs me again. I roll back and forth on the floor. Yuck. I have allowed intimacy with someone who mocks me. Who uses me. Who cheats on me. I feel absolutely wretched inside.

And yet, I have stayed.

Why?

Kelly fills my presence and asks the questions again. "Why have you been tolerating this behavior? What have you been getting out of it?

The same questions repeat and tumble through my brain until I breathe them down and through my body.

A shuddering, like a million butterflies in a single tree, cascades through me, awakening me to a truth that lives in me at my deepest core level. I hear voices reminding me that I am the descendent of all that has come before me. They try to tell me that I am bound to a code, and that code dictates that my life, my adult life, must reflect the toxic dynamics in which I was raised. That in order to honor my father and honor my mother, I must repeat their lives in order to prove I don't hold them accountable for what has been passed on to me. That code dictates that I remain unconscious and abandon myself.

I refuse to accept that.

I'm here, so that I might meet my mother, the woman whose destiny I so long to escape. I'm here, so that I can embrace her dysfunction, which also lives inside of me, so that I might comfort and console and show a lifetime of compassion to her, and then give myself permission to live a different life. I'm here to embrace all that is wonderful and beautiful about her, so that I can allow myself these things as well.

I'm also here to put to rest the need for my father's love, which he has proven I will never get. I'm here to understand that the reason I chose this relationship with this person is to work through all of this. It doesn't excuse his behavior by any means, which is why I always chafed against this message. It always felt like Kelly was asking me to take responsibility for my actions while excusing my partner's actions.

The fact is, she was.

Yes, he triggers all my dysfunction, but he is not the cause of my dysfunction. So I'm left to answer the question, why do I choose abuse over love?

Again Kelly speaks to me, "So that you can become responsible for your actions in a relationship. You can't have a healthy relationship until you own your part in unhealthy relationships. What makes you passive-aggressive? What makes you manipulative? What makes you take on responsibilities that are not yours? Are you truly honest with yourself about the part you play in a relationship and the dynamic you bring to it? What's your baggage, because we all have some? Are you capable of owning your truth, no matter how dark it might seem? Can you, will you, bring that truth into the light and embrace it?"

Then her voice stops. I sit in a calm quiet, and I listen.

I realize that part of my struggle to come to this place is that it requires the leaving behind of my familial dynamic. It's possible that all my tornado dreams prepared me for this as much as they forecast my father's destruction of our family. My dreams were so lucid, so visceral. How many times did I choose to run down to the basement, crawl under the stairs, and ride out a storm that was wrecking my home and killing my family? How many times had I emerged in the aftermath, alone? How many times had I put my feet on the ground and began a journey into the unknown?

And now, here I sit, aware I am about to break an ancient cycle in my family's shared DNA by opening up my consciousness to something new and different in my understanding of my life and my self.

I want something different.

I believe I deserve something different.

And it doesn't matter whether or not anyone else in my family seeks what I seek, because in order to have what I desire, I must walk into the unknown by myself, no matter how many others might be going with me.

Kelly's voice comes to me again, "All traits have a light and a dark aspect to them." She had said this to me when I worked on my parents' list.

Something I also chafed against at the time.

"I'm sure, as a dance teacher, you know how to manipulate your students to get them to do something they don't yet think they can do, but you are aware it's only confidence standing in their way."

"That's true."

"Your mother appears to be a very generous and kind person. Great virtues, unless we are extending them to someone who is neither receiving nor returning our generosity and kindness, but rather taking advantage of our generosity and using our kindness against us. Of course, if we allow that to happen, we are choosing to abandon ourselves."

The butterflies return again, and with them, they bring something unexpected. Again something Kelly made me aware of, but I was only aware of it intellectually until this moment. As much as I need to embrace the dark side of my mother who lives in me, I need to embrace the light side of my father that lives in me. And I have to accept, and not hold suspect, those qualities I share with my mother that my father vilified in her, and by association, vilified in me.

I feel their history raging through me.

I have been to the continental divide at Loveland Pass in Colorado many times, and I am reminded of the meeting of the east/west currents of the river at the divide. They meet, collide, swirl around one another, and move off in opposite directions.

I spread eagle on the floor, close my eyes, and breathe. Soon, I can hear the rushing and pounding of the Mom River as it collides against the Dad River inside me. From crown to crotch, they meet, collide, swirl around one another and move off in opposite directions, each claiming a side of my body as their own.

These two rivers running down my body have been bumping up against a wall that divides me in half, thus leaving my heart splintered and my soul incomplete.

I force my breath deeper into my core, sending it down my legs and out the soles of my feet.

I know what I must do, and I refuse to stop until I'm finished.

I beckon the waters towards one another. They clash violently, refusing to go where I am pushing them, but then like a dam released, the two rivers ford the opposite half of my body, overcoming my own internal continental divide, until they merge and are no longer one river representing her, one river representing him, but now a single, gently flowing river, representing me.

Although I am drained of my energy, I am brought to life as the Me River begins to flow, united, whole, and complete from mouth to delta. I am shattered and restored simultaneously. In this moment *I* am born.

Now my Phoenix can fly.

Summer 2017

I have found it so interesting to write about my past from the first-person present point of view. It has required me to fully step back inside the person I was, and temporarily step outside of the person I've become. But I do believe dancers have a heightened sense of kinesthetic awareness (muscle memory), or at least this dancer does. In fact, all of my senses have always been hyper-alert. It's a chicken-in-the-egg quandary for me. Am I hyper-aware of my surroundings because of my history and the need to protect myself when I was young, or did I come into the world hyper-aware and, as a result, was highly tuned to my surroundings?

Who can know?

All I know is my observant eye, my ever-questioning mind, my ability to roll things out to their natural end, and the ability to transform my trauma into a narrative, have helped me to sort through an otherwise inexplicable, soul-damaging childhood.

I was destined to go out into this world and replicate the relationship dynamics of my family of origin. Those dynamics were and are toxic and dysfunctional, and they set me up to enter adulthood bound to self-sabotage, and the more time I handed over to self-sabotage and what it manifests, the more shame I would have accrued. The more shame I accrued, the more frightened I would become of looking at the things I needed to see in order to heal and move on. All of this adds up to a consciousness suffering from atrophy, and an arrested emotional intelligence. The longer I would have allowed those two things to fall into atrophy and arrest, the harder it would have been to heal and recover them.

This is why I believe getting help young is paramount for someone like me. I interrupted my self-sabotage, which allowed me to use those qualities I described above to change the direction of my future and rewrite my narrative. In my youth, I knew there would be plenty of life out on the other side, and I had very few major life decisions to reconcile at the age of twenty-three. I could just as easily have used them to confirm my self-sabotage, and to continue to recreate my past in my future, living the adulthood my childhood prescribed for me. I believe that past a certain age, living that way seems easier than facing the shame created by all that has come before.

Shortly after the day I merged my parents' DNA rivers into one steady body of water that became Me, I ended my relationship with the ballroom dancer, but not before arriving unannounced to support him and his partner in their first competition. I knew his reaction would tell me all I needed to know, and it did.

As I sat in the front row of spectators on the third corner he would pass, he spied me before he came to the second corner, and to say he looked angry is an understatement.

Ours, now that I was honest with myself, was not the kind of relationship I desired, and I was done.

I was done with ever being with men like him again.

Thank you, dear God.

I was free.

Leaving him and taking control over whom I would allow or disallow in my life was the first thing I did once I was out of the ashes.

Once our lives were separated, I decided to move to Colorado after finishing up my teaching obligations in the spring.

While wrapping things up, I gave heavy consideration to what I wanted to do, workwise and with my life overall. At the age of thirteen, I committed to dancing until I was thirty followed by a writing career after that. Now I was 31, already a year past my self-imposed deadline, and going back out into the world on my own. I had not considered the money factor at thirteen, but now in light of adult responsibilities, I put my writing career on hold and evaluated my situation honestly.

Between the ages of 22 and 31, I held many full-time and part-time jobs, all while teaching and performing dance. None of my "day jobs" were rewarding except for the bookshop and teaching, but I was never going to make enough money being a bookseller, so, in order to support myself, I turned to teaching.

It's difficult to explain my long, meandering path as a teacher. Teaching was something I never wanted to do as a young dancer (at the time, I was convinced my college professors recommended teaching because they didn't believe I was good enough to be a professional dancer). And yet, I would be lying if I said I didn't enjoy it. At 31, with over ten years of teaching behind me, I had come to understand why my professors thought I should teach. I was really good at it.

What had begun as a way to supplement my income and to make my way into the performing community had turned into a viable career. I was known all over the city for teaching and cross training. At that point, I had choreographed floor-exercise routines for competitive gymnasts that were routinely taking firsts at competitions, I was cross-training figure skaters and coaching them on their choreography, and carrying ten hours of teaching dance at the gym. In short, I had, without even paying attention, established a very solid teaching reputation over the course of several years.

I decided I would go to Denver, stay with my best friend from college, make every attempt to recreate what I had built in Milwaukee, and become a career teacher. This task, however, carried one very large self-imposed obligation: personal integrity.

When I was in sixth grade, The American Lung Association visited my class. The presenter had a pair of transparent lungs. She lit a cigarette, took a drag for the purpose of the demonstration, and blew the smoke into a hole meant to be the esophagus.

I watched as the lungs filled with black smoke. I don't know about the rest of the class, but I was astonished. I absolutely could not think of ever doing that to my lungs. She ended her presentation by telling us that if we did not smoke before the age of 18, the likelihood of us becoming lifelong smokers was diminished by some grand percentage. My teacher (I don't remember her name but I'll call her Maude -- she was Bea Arthur's doppelganger) then gave a brief speech on the importance of never smoking.

End of presentation.

That afternoon, my mother and I were in the grocery store. I looked towards the produce and saw Maude inspecting the lettuce. Always excited to see my teachers outside of school, I went up to her and said hello.

When she turned around, we both stared at each other in shock.

She was smoking!

I was devastated.

How could she stand in front of the class and say what she did and be a smoker? I could have respected her if she would have made her speech about the fact that she smokes, and the presenter was correct that once you start it is very hard to stop, and so the best piece of advice is to never start.

Instead, she pretended to be something she wasn't.

Just like my dad.

On that day, when I was contemplating my work future, I realized I didn't want any of my students to experience a similar situation with me. I wanted them to know me as a person of deep integrity. No matter where they might see me, I would be the same Miss Connie they knew in the dance studio. I never really bought into the idea of wearing different hats. I'm not a different person when I teach, or when I'm with my friends, or as a wife, or now as a mother. Connie is consistent. My full name is Constance after all. I only wear one hat, and that is my Connie hat.

Home alone, I got down on my knees that day, rested my forehead on my closed hands, and prayed to God and the Universe.

I made a pact.

And that pact was simple: Bring me students, and I will teach them to the best of my ability, but most importantly, I will be 100% me with all my students, all the time, everywhere.

I vowed not to take advantage of them when they were vulnerable, to always be a role model of good character, and to guide them safely from childhood into adulthood. And, no matter where they might run into me, they would always get the same me. If, at any time I could not do this for my students I would stop teaching.

I knew then, and I know now so completely, that we all have within us the ability to damage another person, and none more easily than a child. It has always been my goal to be a mentor, a guide and a light for kids. I will not be a fraud or untrustworthy for the most vulnerable among us.

When I think back on my childhood, what bothers me most is that the adults around me were protecting other dysfunctional adults' un-evolved emotions at my expense. My ability to form an accurate picture of people, relationships, and love was skewed. Children trust because it is natural, and their survival is dependent upon the people who sustain their lives, and when those sustainers abuse, exploit, and mock the children, who because of biology inherently trust them, those children grow into damaged adults.

Nothing bothers me more than when I hear parents who have been abusive on some level, or who are simply unconscious of the baggage they have brought along and unpacked on their children, say, "Well, you're 18 now. You can't blame me for your bad decisions."

My mother has never said that, but not surprisingly, my father has. I believe that is because my mother has never stopped being there for me. She's not been afraid of difficult conversations, and she doesn't disagree that her shock, naivete, and her unwillingness to look at reality have greatly affected her children's lives. My father, on the other hand, does none of that. My mother views parenting as a life-long job.

Choosing to become conscious is scary and difficult work. I know. I've done it. And I continue to do it daily. It requires a person to be in a safe, loving, supportive environment. Having come from a dysfunctional family, I had to find a healthier, truly supportive environment. This feels, especially since I was fed so much rhetoric about family loyalty, like I have betrayed and abandoned my family by reaching out and forming new bonds with new people. If a family is broken, unconscious of this brokenness, and in denial that things need to be fixed, it is unsafe to seek healing there. In fact, it is impossible to mend within the dysfunctional environment that dynamic creates.

I believe there are people who can be damaged beyond a state of repair. That because of their nature, all they can do is survive their circumstances, leaving them fated to a life of one detrimental decision after another. At the same time, I believe health and healing are available to us all if we are open to it. I am so grateful I got help young. There was a lot of life in front of me. There was plenty of time to acclimate to the new me: to grow accustomed to my new skin. I wanted to live consciously and intentionally, and I had time to begin at the bottom of a different hill, climb it, and send a whole new momentum rolling down the other side into uncharted territory.

After making my vow to whomever was listening, I stood up and said, "You bring them, and I'll teach them, and now I let it go and move on."

And I did.

All it took was a month in Colorado to realize I was already too old to recreate the reputation in Denver that I enjoyed in Milwaukee. As fate would have it, the director of the dance department back in Milwaukee had seriously injured her ankle and was leaving her position.

She informed me of this on the July day in 1997 when I called to see if I could get some hours for the fall.

"If you like, I can recommend you as my replacement," she said.

"Yes, please do," I returned.

And then, with a tone that suggested this might have more to do with her leaving then her ankle, she said, "Given all the sadness around your departure, all the tears, presents, and well wishes, God knows I don't even think they'll notice when I'm gone. I'm sure the owners will see it as a coup to get you back."

The bookshop was happy to take me back part-time, understanding that my hours would be even fewer now that I was directing the dance department.

As I drove out of Denver that July, I watched as the front range slowly shrank and fell away over the horizon. I was sad and joyful all at once. Living in Colorado had been a lifelong dream of mine. Now I was consciously choosing to leave it, probably for good as a place of residence. Yet I felt alive and free, with a new beginning unfolding before me.

I had temporary lodging with a friend from group, but she was married, so I hoped to secure an apartment in short order upon my return. As much as I wanted to live on my own, financially it would be better if I had a roommate. Who would that be?

This led me to thinking about men and dating. I vowed to myself, while driving across the flat, open landscape of Nebraska (and they say Iowa is flat), that I would not date for one year.

I realized I wanted all of my past relationships behind me. There was much I was not proud of, and I needed to cleanse myself before inviting someone new into my life. Because yes, the next time it would be an invitation to share in my life. I decided on that day, if that person did not, or would not, treat me with the same love and respect with which I treated myself, there would be no invitation. Period.

By early fall, a bookshop colleague and I had secured an apartment together. Anne was great. In fact, all the people I worked with were great. I have never been in an environment with so many down-to-earth people. To this day, many of us are still friends. In fact, both Anne and I married people we met at the bookshop.

During my year-long hiatus from dating, I enjoyed being with friends and spending a lot of time with my new self. I realized my intuition not to date was spot-on. I needed time for this new me to emerge, to fully bloom and take root. All of my dysfunctional seducers were still about, but over the course of that year, their powers weakened.

I had no real nightmares during this time. In fact,

whenever I had lived on my own while in my twenties, I had no nightmares. My tornado dreams had virtually disappeared since my father's shooting, and the gun dreams dissolved once I was no longer sleeping next to a man whom I felt was preying upon me. In other words, the dreams left when I felt safe, and I no longer needed to be guarded.

I'm stunned by the prophetic nature of my tornado dreams, but I believe those dreams were preparing me to walk through this world on my own two feet. Time and again, I had to choose the path of dysfunction (staying upstairs and dying in the tornado) or the path to health (going to the basement and rescuing myself). By the time I entered therapy, my system was conditioned to go into the basement alone. I was conditioned to emerge alone into utter destruction. I was conditioned to turn my back on what I could not change, and walk away into an unknown future.

By the time I was twenty, I had done this so many times in my dreams that I understood it as the only course of action to take past the destruction.

I did not want to live the rest of my life in the debris field.

I did not want to merely survive.

I did not want to spend the rest of my life suffering through one bad decision after another, which would be my burdens to bear once I was an adult, no matter what my parents had placed inside me.

I wanted to do something more than survive.

I wanted to live.

I wanted my heart to dance.

I wanted to rebuild.

Given that dreams have played such a major role in my life, it is no surprise that I first met my husband in a dream, and my daughter in a pre-birth meditation.

The meditation happened first.

I was at a weeklong retreat with Kelly somewhere in the country around the Kettle Moraine in Wisconsin. On a morning when the sun was white-bright and the small pond outside the main building glistened from its reflection, she had us lay back and breathe.

She led us through a pre-birth meditation.

Very quickly, I left the room and her voice, and found myself flying through dark, twinkling space. I felt birdlike, but then I also felt just like me. A small, younger bird, who I called my Little Bird, was flying beside me talking about how odd it was to simply thinkfly.

"Yes," I said. "It is a strange and awesome feeling."

I turned my head to smile at Little Bird and SMACK! I flew into a brick wall. Startled that a brick wall was out in the middle of the Universe, I slid down the wall in a daze. With my cheek still smashed against the wall, I came to rest on a platform.

I saw a young boy and a man walking down a sidewalk that led to a door next to me. The boy looked very sad. The man looked very mad. He rang the doorbell, and another man opened the door. He looked very judgmental.

"Hi, son," the man behind the door said.

"Hi, Dad," the boy was obviously stuck between guilt and relief.

The two men had a rather heated debate about how the boy

would be returned to his mother and stepfather, who now stood behind the boy, with his hand strongly gripping his shoulder.

I kept watching the boy. I couldn't believe neither man would shut up, look at the boy, and see the obvious pain their selfishness caused him. I saw a small boy just wanting to be loved standing in the crosshairs of a loveless fight over him.

"What's happening?" Little Bird asked me.

"Something that must be stopped," I said, and flew off.

I found myself sitting at a desk talking to someone powerful. I won't say God, because he didn't feel like God. He felt more like the person or power put in charge of dealing with people, souls, or energies seeking to help others.

"This has to be stopped. Why are people doing this to each other?"

"It's something they have to learn. That's why they are there and not here right now."

"Yeah, I get it, but that poor little boy," I was beside myself.

"You can go down if you choose. I won't stop you, but I advise against it. You will have to endure a lot in order to be able to help this boy and others like him."

"That's okay. I want to," I said.

The next moment, I emerge into the light from between my mother's legs. I am placed in her arms, which feels like ambivalence given form. And then a dark shadow, tall and looming, comes to the side of the bed. I snuggle into my mother, choosing ambivalence over malice.

When we were brought out of the meditation, I sat up, silenced by my experience. Did my life create this meditation, or did the meditation teach me something about my life? I couldn't deny that I am compelled, beyond reason at times, to be a secure, trustworthy, loving force in the lives of children, and to protect them.

Later, I went out and sat by the pond. I reflected on the whole of the meditation. I began to cry as I realized that perhaps my entire earthly life has been about shaking off that higher vibration in order to live: to be alive here.

I am alive.

I am on Earth.

I said these two things out loud.

And whether or not any of my meditation was real, subconsciously created, or fantasy, I thought, I am here, and I do want to help people recover from suffering. To let them know there is a life to be led past the pain. It's not necessary to just survive. You can live again. I would be lying if I denied this about myself.

I looked up into the blue morning sky. The sun warmed my tears.

"Well," I said to the sky, "I'm here now,"

"I'm here now, and I want to be. I want to experience this life fully," and then I laughed. "As if I my life has been so empty up to this point," I added.

"I'm going to go about living this life, listening closely, and trusting you will take me where I need to go to fulfill the reason I am here," I said to the sky: that giant universal ear.

I looked at the pond, suddenly overwhelmed. I knew that I had just committed myself to being as honest, truthful, and as responsible as possible. I had to walk through this life with integrity. Otherwise, I would have no credibility. How could I look at other people and encourage them to discover their own truth and offer them courage in the face of the unknown? How could I tell them to plumb their deepest abyss? How could I say that walking into their own darkness was the path to freeing their hearts of pain and despair, if I had not done so as well? At that point, I'm just a textbook, pontificating without humanity or credibility.

"Okay," I said. "I'm in. I will do my best to continue growing, and to become more conscious of myself and the world around me. The rest, I trust you will take care of," and as I offered that up to the sky, birds that I didn't even know were nearby flew out of the foot-high grass around the pond. More and more birds. How could there be so many?

I watched with amazement and delight as they took flight.

As I noted earlier, I spent my year-long dating hiatus incorporating all I had learned about myself into my new being. I washed my body and energy clean of my prior relationship. A person's touch can linger on your skin, and in your soul, for a long time. When that memory is mixed with feelings of self-disgust, it is wise to thoroughly purge that sense before moving on with someone new.

Halfway through that year, I had a dream that *I was walking down a beach. The day was waning, the sky was purpleorangepink, and the atmosphere was lazy. I met a man and we started a conversation. It was easy, natural. Oddly, his face was blotted out. He was tall and lean. He was witty and serious. But what color were his eyes? How big was his smile? Did he have a pleasant or a pained countenance?*

We walked until we arrived at his apartment. He invited me in. I accepted. Halfway up the second flight to his apartment, a woman from outside called for him. She was obviously in need of help. We turned and ran down steps that kept going and going and going. We had only gone up a flight and a half, but we ran down no less than twenty.

Once outside, she explained she needed him to go with her. There was an inside nature to their conversation. As I listened to them, an awareness that I can only describe as rightness washed over me. This is the man I will be with, but I won't know him when I see him again. I began to panic when he told me he needed to go.

"Please," I started to say.

"Sh," he said in the most secure, calm, knowing way. "We'll be together again."

"But how will I know you? I can't see your face."

He reached out his hand and placed it on my shoulder. His energy was strange and yet distinct to me at the same time. I knew I would never forget it.

"You will know me by my touch. But now I have to go," and he ran off with the other woman.

The dream ended.

Six months later, I was out with a group of friends listening to a band, when a group of well-dressed men walked into the club.

"Hey," a friend said, "That guy is really good-looking."

I turned and looked.

"That's John Malloy. I know him. That must be his band."

"You know him," she said.

"Yeah, we worked at the bookshop together. I'll be right back."

I went over to John. We hadn't seen each other in quite awhile. I still worked at the bookshop, but he had transferred to another location a couple of years before. We would see each other occasionally, but that was it.

I tapped him on the shoulder. He turned around. He obviously did not expect to see me. Once he realized who I was, he greeted me with a happy, warm smile. We chatted for a few minutes and found that we were both leaving the bookshop at the end of August. We decided to get together and catch up before our last day.

John and I had always gotten along at the shop. We had the same sense of humor, the same beefs about our employer, the same love of books, the same intellectual curiosity, and the same understanding of what it meant to be a working artist. The night we went out, which I can now officially call our first date, given that we've not been apart for the nearly twenty years since, was easy and comfortable. I believe, in part, this was because it was just two friends getting together.

As we sat in a club that night, two young women eyeing John caught my attention.

I heard one of them say, "I know that's Kid Malloy."

Amused by their apparent admiration, I put my hand on John's in order to direct his attention to his fans.

He placed his other hand on top of mine, and asked, "What?"

My world stopped.

His question "Is everything okay?" confirmed that yes, I looked shocked.

Oh, yeah, sure, I thought, *let me tell you about this dream I had, and how just now when you touched my hand it reminded me of an overwhelming sensation from said dream; and how this is the most unlikely place, and you are the most unlikely person, to remind me of said sensation. I could have never guessed it would be you. But according to this feeling…*

"Yeah," I gained my composure, "I was just amused at these two women who were obvious fans of yours. They're gone now."

We started dating, and everything was going really well until about three months in.

Anne (as an employee at the shop she knew John too) came home to find me sitting on the sofa, hands under my legs, with a trash can at the side of the sofa.

"No matter what you have to do, keep me from calling John," I said.

"What?" She looked at the can, "Are you sick?"

"Yeah, but not in the way you probably think I am."

It was very simple. My heart was opening up. I was allowing him in. And it was making me violently ill. I was ready to sabotage the entire thing to make this feeling go away.

To run.

To flee.

To start calling him incessantly to make sure he was there. To question him time and again to make sure that he actually cared. I was very aware that in a week's time I could make him think I was nuts. My IT was fighting to resurface. If I let it take hold I would soon find myself sabotaging this relationship by merging my past with the present. I would fulfill what I had been programmed to do and set John up to abandon me.

John liked me. John was sincerely interested in me. Both of these truths created unfamiliar and uncomfortable feelings inside of me.

My ex-boyfriend, now I knew what he felt like. I knew how to be in the presence of a jerk. I knew how to feel manipulated, abused, and used, but I didn't know how to feel, dare I say it, loved.

Let me repeat that: I did not know how to feel loved.

It scared the living crap out of me.

My insides ran the gamut of self-abandonment and sabotage.

I'm still screaming myself alive, I thought as I sat on that sofa, hands smashed under my legs, stomach ready to heave its contents into the can.

I loved this man, I had to admit it: I honestly did.

But loving him was easy. It was allowing him to love me that sent my world into the whirling twirling spiral of a tornado.

John would never manipulate me.

He respected me.

He believed me, and believed in me.

He let me present myself to him, and he liked the real me.

I was not guarded around him. I didn't need my defenses.

He would not, could not, hurt me. It wasn't within him.

I had been patient with him, and allowed him to present himself to me. I didn't make assumptions about who he was, though I had a good idea of his character from working with him for a year. I liked who he was. I didn't need him to be anyone but who he was, and who he was was someone I could respect, trust, and be vulnerable with. Therein lies the snag. I trusted John, so to accuse him of being insincere was out of the question. It would have been hurtful and mean.

I essentially sat on that sofa for three weeks. At night, when the world quieted down, I could hear the breaking of the ice-like shield around my heart. It was warming and melting and cracking, and I was letting go of its protective cover.

Loving, healthy relationships are extremely difficult for people who have been abused, who have been unloved, and who have had to become narcissistic in their self-preservation for one key reason: receiving love makes them ill.

Sick.

Opening the heart is the worst stomach flu ever.

Another reason to get help young: long-term dysfunction only adds to the thickness of the heart-shield.

The thicker the shield, the more paralyzing the risk becomes.

If a jerk leaves me, I expect that. It feels natural, familiar. If John leaves me, I have lost a real opportunity at love. Under normal conditions of dysfunction and self-preservation, this is when I begin to sabotage the relationship by becoming inexplicably needy; by pushing my partner away and pulling them back in through passive aggressive behaviors; by atoning and atoning and atoning; by bringing the past into the present and holding my partner accountable for all my fears.

Without therapy and Kelly, I turn John into my father and I become my mother. I create a circumstance that makes him leave me. In so doing, I would create the same feelings of disgust, shame, and worthlessness inside of me that being with people like my father create. Sadly, after a lifetime with my father, feeling disgust, shame, and underserving of love was like putting on a well-worn-formed-to-my-feet pair of slippers.

This desire to make John become my expectation was all an attempt to keep me from letting him in, from opening my heart.

From getting what I had worked so hard to have.

And it was all brand new.

It was the first time in my life that I had been with a man whom my healthy, conscious self wanted to be with.

I wanted to share my life with someone like him.

Losing him due to my inability to let him in was not an option.

By the end of the three weeks, my heart was new to the world. I was vulnerable, but I embraced my fragility. I kept my feet on the ground, took deep breaths, and opened myself to him. I, who so comfortably looked deeply and directly into the eyes of others, finally allowed John's eyes to penetrate mine.

My learned ability to separate my reality from my past, and my desire to live and not merely survive, allowed me to let him in and the circle of giving and receiving to flow between us.

For the first time in my adult life, I was thriving in a relationship.

I was fully myself with another person.

Oh, joy!

We were married in the spring of 2001. Later that year, I opened a dance studio, and life was good. Although it handed us our fair share of complications, as it does everyone, we handled them as a team, with grace and compassion, always working together to solve our problems.

At the age of 41, I became pregnant. I had a blissful pregnancy, a quick delivery, and my relationship with John moved to a deeper level.

When our daughter was nearing two, I tucked her in one night and kneeled beside her bed. I began to weave a story for her to take with her into her dreams. She stared at me with her big blue eyes wrapped in the fantasy I spun for her.

Since the day of her birth, I recognized something familiar in her eyes that I could never place. Maybe it was just the intensity in her eyes. She always had an air of knowing that seemed unnatural for a baby to have.

As I finished the story, her eyes opened wide, and a smile filled her chubby-cheeked face.

Immediately, I knew who I was looking at.

"Little Bird," I said. "I recognize you. You are my Little Bird."

"Your Little Bird," she said, her eyes full of the promise of another story.

I told her the story of my meditation. "You were, you are, my Little Bird."

To this day, I still call her Little Bird. She and I have been flying together through space and time for all of space and time.

While married, I have had a new serial dream. *It always starts with me in a different house than the one I live in with John, and then one of the men from my past walks in the room. I immediately panic in the dream. What is he doing here?*

There is always some verbal altercation, and generally my

daughter comes into the room, and the man in my dream, who is her father and my husband in the dream, begins verbally or emotionally abusing her.

I go ballistic.

And then, because these dreams are so lucid, I stop in the dream and orient myself.

"This is not real," I begin to tell myself as I pull my daughter away from her dream father.

"I didn't marry you," I say to the person.

"You're not my husband, and you're not her father."

I wake to find my pulse beating violently and loudly. I'm sweating.

I turn to see that yes, John is the man in the bed beside me.

I had these dreams long before our daughter was born, but the first few times I had them after she was born, I would go to her room to make sure she was there.

That she was real.

That she was safe.

Before going back to sleep, I would repeat, "This is my life. This is my reality. We're all okay."

Very recently, I had my first tornado dream in more than two decades.

The evening is beautiful. I'm returning home after taking a walk with a friend. The sun is breaking through the ash trees in the front of the house, lighting its red bricks and the picture window.

And then it all changes. I'm not quite sure what is taking place.

The air falls deadly still.

A metal scent fills my nostrils.

The sun is muted.

"Oh, God!" I shout. I know this. I've been here many times.

I run. I fall up the small hill in the front yard.

I see, in the reflection of the picture window, the dark funnel cloud. I look behind me.

There it is.

The tornado is already dropped. It's raging towards my home. Not my parents' home.

My home.

I spring up and run to the house yelling, "John!"

The wind whips up. I can hear the tornado. It's getting closer.

I fly in the house overcome with panic.

"John, where are you?" I run through the kitchen.

"We're right here," he says, as he and our daughter come downstairs.

"What's up?" he asks, completely unaware of the change in the weather.

"There's a tornado coming. We have to get to the basement. Now," I'm so afraid he won't go.

"Oh," he says. He doesn't look out the window. He doesn't question me.

He picks up our daughter and says, "C'mon. We need to get down there now."

We run to the basement, huddle together under our steps, and I know no matter what happens we're together. I know we'll pick up any pieces that may happen to fall, and together we'll rebuild our future.

We can hear the wind, but that's really all.

Soon the sky clears, and we crawl out from under the steps.

We walk upstairs. The entire house is intact.

We go outside. The sky is a brilliant blue again. Other than scattered branches, everything is undamaged.

I look into the sky in my dream, and I am reminded of a time in reality when life was testing the strength of John and me. We were in the car on the way home from taking a walk, and our daughter was in the backseat listening to us ponder when things would take a turn for the better.

As if an angel spoke through her to us, she said, "Tomorrow, the moon will melt, the snow will melt, and we'll have a brand new day."

I look at my husband and daughter in my dream, and I believe with my whole being that I have been given a brand new day. I have created a life for myself that is my *life, and it is not a reflection of the one set in motion for me.*

I exhale and dance until twilight with Little Bird.

I awake to a cool, quiet summer morning after this dream. I turn to see John still asleep. His hair is graying now, and his smile lines, like mine, no longer fully fade when his face is relaxed.

He is my husband.

I was able to fight my demons and choose him as my friend, my confidant, and my mate for life.

My daughter, I trust, is still sleeping in a pile of her favorite stuffies with her two favorite blankies tightly embraced in her arms. I'm so grateful for the unencumbered sleep she enjoys.

My life is abundant.

I have found my way home.

Epilogue

I have a picture of my parents. They are twenty, married, and living in Alaska, where my father was stationed during the Korean War. They are at one of the couples' quarters (a one-room, wood-paneled trailer) along with six other people. Some are smoking. They are probably all drinking except my mother. The women, with their hairdos and dresses that easily date the picture, and the men, with their army physiques and regulation buzz cuts, all look to be enjoying themselves. Except for my father.

My parents are the only two not looking at the camera. My father is looking straight ahead, and my mother is looking in the opposite direction of the camera towards the woman next to her, who is looking at the camera instead of my mother. What shocks me most about this picture is that my parents are both in a very familiar posture: my father in one of annoyance, my mother in one of denial.

There is no warmth or affection extended from my father towards my mother. He sits with his arm around her shoulder as if he is biding his time until the worst blind date of his life ends. My mother, smiling with her head turned away from him, will not allow herself to feel the energy he is exuding.

I am saddened to see this dynamic present so early in their young married life. I'm hopeful it wasn't omnipresent at this time, but the fact that it was present at all is disheartening.

One of the unique benefits of my dance career is that I taught many children from the age of 4 or 5 until they graduated from high school. I have stayed in contact with many of them well into their adulthoods. I have counseled, consoled, inspired, and loved so many young people in my life, and I sit here today looking at this picture wondering what I would have told my parents had I been in that role in their young lives.

The strange thing for me is that I know their future. I know where this dynamic leads. I know what their stubbornness, pride, and fears do to them and their children. Right here, in the moment of this picture, my father was already through with my mother (and as she was later told, already cheating on her), and my mother was already resigned to a life of delusion in which she constantly told herself that things weren't what they seemed.

A part of me wants to scream at her, "Run. Run as fast as you can, as far away from him as you can."

And then I think, if she had, where would I be?

Recently, she repeated to me one of her refrains, "I just thought things would turn out differently."

"Based upon what? What in your experiences with dad made you think things would turn out differently?" I asked her.

"I've never thought about it. I just thought things would turn out differently," she said.

Half jokingly, I asked her if she ever thought about the consequences of any actions, his or hers.

She laughed, and said, "No, not really."

"Hmm," I said, "you didn't think about any consequences, and you gave birth to a daughter who thinks about the consequences of everything."

The fact is, I love both of my parents and I have great compassion for them. I know their lives could have been very different. And while I think my father's condition is clinical, he has a story that led him to marrying my mother, against his real desires, and my mother has a story that led her to marrying my father and staying with him.

They are now and forever trapped in the legacy this picture of their young selves foreshadowed.

But I no longer am.

Now, listening to John play "Be Thou My Vision" while our daughter hum-sings along, I am reminded that I have inherited, incorporated, suffered, and freed myself from my parents' legacy so that my daughter can know something different.

My parents have been my vision. I am filled with intense gratitude for that vision.

Thank you Mom and Dad.

Acknowledgements

I am humbled by, and grateful to, the many people who have walked this journey with me.

Thanks to my readers, Amanda McGrew, Mary Piwaron, Andy Tuler, Katie Woody, and Mary Yentz. To Gina Gral, Mary Hickey Zander and Sue Swing, who also contributed to the book summary. To Emily Blaser for her thoughtful questions, and for her time spent editing.

Thanks to Laura Leach. The cover still takes my breath away. To Shannon Ishizaki, the owner of TEN16 Press. We've come a long way since our chance meeting in the park so many years ago.

Thanks to my mother who has braved many difficult conversations with me. Her support and encouragement freed me to write the story that needed to be written.

I offer many kisses to my Little Bird for her enthusiasm in this endeavor. I also appreciate her understanding of the time and quiet writing requires.

And lastly, thank you to my husband John for his patience and understanding, for his trust and support, and for the time and care he dedicated to editing the pages of my life. I am most grateful for the beautiful music he fills our home with. Both he and his music are irreplaceable salves for my soul.

About the Author

Constance, a gemini, has always been split between two passions: dancing and writing. After a long and rewarding career in dance, she retired in 2011 to raise her daughter and to begin a writing career. She lives in Milwaukee, WI with her husband and daughter.

Constance would love the opportunity to be a guest author at your next reading group. To book a date, email her at: CONSTANCEMALLOY@GMAIL.COM

Follow Constance and her blog *The Burning Hearth* at CONSTANCEMALLOY.COM